STAR PERFORMER

STAR PERFORMER

◇

NINE BREAKTHROUGH STRATEGIES TO HELP ORDINARY PEOPLE BECOME EXTRAORDINARY PERFORMERS AT WORK

Robert E. Kelley

ORION BUSINESS
BOOKS

Copyright © 1998 by Consultants to Executives and Organizations, Ltd.

All rights reserved

The right of Robert E. Kelley to be identified as the author
of this work has been asserted by him in accordance with the
Copyright, Designs and Patents Act 1988.

This edition first published in Great Britain in 1998 by
Orion Business
An imprint of The Orion Publishing Group Ltd
Orion House, 5 Upper St Martin's Lane, London WC2H 9EA

First published in the United States in 1998 by Times Books, a division
of Random House Inc., New York, and simultaneously in Canada
by Random House of Canada Limited, Toronto.

A CIP catalogue record for this book
is available from the British Library.

ISBN 0-75281-392-7

Printed in Great Britain by
Butler & Tanner Ltd
Frome and London

To Grandma and Grandpa Kelley and PoPo and
GongGong Chew,
who produced two constellations of stars

To Pat, Lauren, and Luke, who are my universe

SPECIAL THANKS

DR. JANET CAPLAN joined the star performer project in its early stages, and we continue to collaborate in its evolution. During these years, she devoted much time and tremendous energy in the development and organization of the program. She shares the credit for the substance of this work, the impact it has made to the field of productivity improvement, and its overall success with companies and brainpowered workers. I am deeply grateful to her as a valued colleague and friend for her substantial contributions to this work.

DOUGLAS ROOT, a talented Pittsburgh-based writer and editor, helped me immensely in my writing of this book. He adapted my original words into more readable prose, searched out timely "star" examples, and coached me in clearer, more reader-friendly writing. During the numerous revisions, his careful editing contributed to a better book and a more pleasant process. He helped this research come alive for the reader.

ACKNOWLEDGMENTS

In the course of ten years, many people have helped me, personally and professionally, to make this book possible. In that sense, this book is a result of a very large collective enterprise.

First, Pat Chew—my truest colleague, counselor, and partner—encouraged me to undertake the odyssey that began at Bell Labs. All along the way, she has been a constant source of great ideas, a cogent but gentle critic, and a source of comfort when things did not go well. She often reminded me of how important this work is, motivated me to overcome my reluctance about writing this book, and read every page, offering up her keen insights. She always made time in her busy schedule to help me meet the project's many demands.

Next, Lauren and Luke, my children, hung in there with me. They understood this work's importance but never let me fool myself that it was more important than them. As a result, they forced me to incorporate the star performer work strategies into my own life so that I would have more time to spend with our family. I am grateful for their persistence, insight, and hugs.

Janet Nordin and Don Leonard initiated the idea for this project at Bell Labs and guided its development. Their commitment to the power of human productivity and their concern for human dignity inspired us to do our best and set the standard for our work. My admiration for them is only exceeded by my gratitude at being able to work with them.

Many others at Bell Labs contributed to this work, including Howard Seckler, Dave Carney, Judy Lindner, Tom Cruz, Bonnie Prokopowicz, Ron DeLange, Steve Sentoff, Doug Newlin, Marge Hillis, Carol Bidrawn, Steve Miranda, Ann Banovetz, Joe Halter, Marie Todd, Jerry Yingling, Kathy Marsala, Wendy Bohling, Brian Fink, Brian Ostberg, Bonnie Clemens, Brendan Cain, Dick Carline, Jerry W. Johnson, John Janik, Dan Carroll, all the Bell Labs employees who allowed us to study their productivity, and all the star performers who helped design and facilitate the productivity-improvement program. Without their collective participation, the study would never have occurred.

Terry Boczek, Paul Husby, and Charles Kiester of 3M provided the opportunity to validate our research using their brainpowered workers. With their help and the cooperation of many 3M professionals, we were able to demonstrate the robustness of our model across industries and jobs.

Dick Hayes, a colleague at Carnegie Mellon University, participated in the initial phases of the research and made valuable contributions. Joel Greenhouse of CMU's Statistics Department and the late Jerry Salancik of CMU's Graduate School of Industrial Administration provided helpful input during the early stages.

Syed Shariq, a longtime collaborator and friend, constructively critiqued the star performer project over the years, reacted to drafts of this book, and gave me the benefit of his considerable wisdom and insight.

I would also like to thank all my colleagues and students at CMU's Graduate School of Industrial Administration who have listened to and critiqued this work during the last eleven years. Deans Doug Dunn, Bob Sullivan, Ilker Baybars, and Fallaw Sowell have been extremely supportive of my work and its value to the school. My research assistants—Kris Rey, Allis Ghim, Chris Tang, Scott

Olson, Erica Levy, Lisa Leonardo, and Sigmunde Sommers Freed—helped me in innumerable ways on the actual project and during my book writing.

The staff at Development Dimensions International (DDI) have committed themselves to bringing our program to the widest possible audience. In particular, I would like to thank Bill Byham, Rich Wellins, Alice Pescuric, David Binder, Renee Grandchamp Davis, Nancy Fox, Richard Goldberg, Linda Appel, Bill Koch, Pete Weaver, and all the staff who have worked to make the program a success.

John Mahaney, my editor at Times Books, believed in this book and brought it to market with true dedication. Frank Weimann, my literary agent, worked hard to convince me to write this book.

Finally, my large extended family stemming from the Kelley and Chew families deserve credit for my work. Their support of me is strong and endless. I only hope that my work reflects well on them.

Thank you to all of you!

CONTENTS

THREE
SOME PRODUCTIVE LAST WORDS

PREFACE

I want this book to change your life at work—to help you gain more control over your career trajectory and to help you perform in your field as an eye-popping top producer—if that is what you want. In every field and every company, you will find star performers. Whether it be money managers or people managers, Silicon Valley software developers or Hollywood film producers, scientists opening new horizons or salespeople closing deals, about 10 to 15 percent of all people will outperform their peers by a wide margin and rise into the star ranks.

The purpose of this book is to help you understand what it is that separates the stars from the rest and what you can do to become a star at work. It pulls together ten years of "from-the-trenches" research that highlights how people at all levels of organizational life go about succeeding.

If you are holding this book, it is likely you believe you have what it takes to be a star performer and are, perhaps, tired of sitting in the shadow of a coworker's starlight. You are trying to figure out how to maintain or increase your value in a produce-or-perish economy. You are searching for skills that will connect you to the bottom line.

Most workers naturally strive for star status in the workplace, to achieve personal bests, and to use their star performer reputations to gain more personal control in charting their careers. Also, workers want to be more productive in less time so they have more personal control over their lives—more flexibility and less supervision at the office; more leisure time at home.

Workers know they can be more productive and are searching for ways to get there. They are not willing to give up the conviction that they are star producer material. They want to be in the select "ten-for-one" club whose members' productivity output is worth ten average workers'.

As one of those workers, you know well how keen the competition is for top job opportunities. And even if you land a coveted job, you know you must prove yourself repeatedly to keep it.

It is this prove-it-or-lose-it tension, then, that may tear away at you or other workers you know. On the internal track, you are competing with yourself to be the best that you know you can be. This fulfills deep psychological needs of mastery, personal investment in the job, a striving for respect among peers, defining personal identity, and realizing self-image. On the real-world, outside track, though, there is that often heartless competition with others for limited slots and professional opportunities.

But it doesn't have to be that way.

Your productivity fate rests with you, not with your bosses in the workplace, not with some divine force that bestows grace or misery regardless of what you do. This book provides you with powerful tools to achieve your dreams.

For more than a decade, I have been fortunate to be involved in an intensive study of star producers that has resulted in the powerful work skills program that is the heart of this book. We set out to study brainpowered people like you to understand what made the difference between the productivity stars and star wanna-bes. After thousands of hours of painstaking observations and research—in office cubicles, in labs, and in team meetings—we learned that subtle, day-to-day behaviors of these stars make astounding differences in their work.

Developing that productivity improvement program through the years, we have changed the work lives of hundreds of workers—from marketers to engineers to managers—who had been stuck with the dreaded "average performer" label by bosses and colleagues. Those who used our findings to supercharge their productivity were able to make the leap into the star performer ranks, increase their value in the job marketplace, and also feel better about themselves and their lives.

Now those findings are offered here in detail for you to incorporate into your own work life.

WHY THIS BOOK AT THIS TIME?

The powerful benefits reported in the personal reviews of people I knew well convinced me to stay with this project, even during those times when ten years seemed more than enough. But the clinching motivator for writing this book was my distress over the proliferation of misguided approaches to productivity improvement—whether they are unfounded productivity theories spouted by self-proclaimed experts or the orgy of downsizing and restructuring that swept through much of American business in the late 1980s and early 1990s.

Everyone, it seems, believes they know how to make other people more productive. Books, magazine articles, and media stories bleat that they have the answers. Some are harmless (for example, if you take time each day to let your workers tell fables and stories to one another, they will be more productive). Others are just flat out wrong (for example, some racial groups have higher intelligence and are therefore destined to be more productive). With its solid research base, this book sets the record straight on what leads to higher productivity and what does not.

What caused more harm was a decade-long quick-fix obsession—downsizing—where short-term gains were cheered by many on Wall Street but where long-term damage went unrecognized. Its legacy is: 1) fear and loathing in the ranks of blue-collar, professional, and managerial workers; 2) unremarkable long-term performance for their companies; and 3) a critical shortage of loyal, trusting workers that employers now need to spur growth into the next decade.

The downsizing fad ran counter to a basic discovery from our research: that getting superior work out of all your employees instead of relying on just one or two is the best way to lasting profits. The key to economic growth is higher productivity, not downsizing. There are no short-cut solutions to long-term growth problems, not in Fortune 500 businesses, not in the global marketplace. You don't make people more productive in the long run by threatening layoffs or by saddling downsizing survivors with the work of terminated coworkers. As we discovered, you raise collective productivity by teaching the productivity secrets of the star performers; you equip people with the personal tools that lead to stellar performance; you invest in them because the returns are enormous and long-lived.

So it is from these two motivations—encouragement from workers who had benefited from our work and the need to offer a counterbalance to the wrongheaded approaches to productivity—that this book has been produced. It is with the absolute conviction that most workers have only skimmed the surface of their true potential that I offer the powerful results of our research clearly laid out and prioritized in this book.

How to Use This Book

This book is separated into three sections. The first introduces the star performer model and the benefits that it can yield to you, the reader. The second section is the heart of the book, containing the nine work strategies that the star performers use to achieve so much. Each work strategy has its own chapter which lays out through real-life examples how the star performers do it. The third section provides the economic context and research methodology for readers who want that level of detail.

I would urge you to resist skipping around to chapters that seem most interesting. The first section lays the conceptual and practical foundation for the work strategies that follow. Likewise, the nine work strategies are highly interdependent and build on one another. For that reason, I recommend you start at the beginning with the model and read through the work strategy chapters in the order presented.

A word about the examples in this book. They are the stories of real people and real companies. But executives are very protective of the identities of their star performers because they *are* the company's intellectual capital, responsible for much of their competitive advantage—today's and tomorrow's. They don't want headhunters or competitors trying to steal them away. As a result, my colleagues and I had to sign confidentiality and nondisclosure agreements in order to have access to the stars. This included not identifying the participants in our research.

For this reason, I have left out company names and used only first names of star employees in most examples. In some cases, I have shaded details considerably to avoid the possibility that the individuals could be identified in any way. For those examples already reported in news stories or made public in other ways, I have used the person's and the company's full names.

ONE

THE PRODUCTIVITY SECRETS OF THE STAR PERFORMERS

1

What Leads to Star Performance?

Whenever people hear about my star performer work—whether sitting next to me on an airplane or at a professional conference—they invariably want the thirty-second sound-bite answer to years of research: "So what's the Big Secret, Kelley? What is 'it' that separates star producers from average performers?"

"I'll be glad to share the answer," I tell them. "But before I do, would you mind sharing with me what you think accounts for the difference? Think of someone who is a star performer. Get that person vividly in your mind. Now think of an average performer. Compare these two and tell me what separates them."

I ask these questions because I have found that most people have preconceived notions about the underlying causes of star productivity that leads to success. And most of those notions are as wrong as can be.

I can empathize with them because I was once in their shoes.

. . .

Ten years ago, I was living a consultant's worst nightmare. For twenty-four months, my investigative team—originally consisting of Janet Caplan from the New School for Social Research, Dick Hayes from Carnegie Mellon University, and me—had been working with executives at one of the world's high-tech giants, Bell Labs, all of us convinced we could crack one of the great mysteries of the modern workplace: what separates the star performers from their average coworkers. When they hire the world's best and brightest, why do only a few become "ten- or twenty-for-oners"—those who outshine and outproduce their peers by factors of ten or twenty?

We had set out to answer the question gnawing at Bell Labs' top management and recruiters: How is it that a company with access to cream-of-the-crop graduates from the world's most prestigious schools ended up with only a sprinkling of star producers in an otherwise solid but mostly average workforce?

For executives at Bell Labs, these were not questions of idle curiosity. As the world's premier R&D organization, Bell Labs' reputation and its future depended on the productivity of star performers. The mid-1980s were a critical time for Bell Labs. Top management was beginning to preach about the need for thinking ahead of the curve, for coming up with ideas for improved productivity.

There was good reason for the new attitude. The monolith known as Ma Bell was no more. In its place after the dust settled from the court-ordered breakup of AT&T were seven Baby Bell companies. Hundreds of sheltered scientists and engineers at the big Bell Labs think tank in New Jersey, and at the satellite centers outside Chicago and Columbus, Ohio, were being thrown into the competitive arena for the first time in their working lives. Forward-thinking managers were concerned about finding ways to prepare them for this sea change by boosting productivity.

The way Bell Labs managers figured it, if they didn't find a way to better measure their workers' productivity and develop a plan to improve it, someone else was going to do it for them—perhaps competitive pressure would force a restructuring, Wall Street would force layoffs, or a new owner would force them all out of the company.

Bell Labs was investing in technical tools to improve productivity, but Janet Nordin, the director of a 250-member lab, and her boss, Don Leonard, Bell's vice president for switching systems, recognized the human side of the equation—much more complex but just as vital. They believed human brainpower, not technological wonders, would provide the longest-lasting productivity advantage.

At the beginning, my investigative team had what I thought was a rare opportunity to do the most definitive research yet on productivity. We had a company with enormous patience and real-world problems, and we had access to a remarkable group of study subjects—workers in the top ranks of the global professional elite, workers who were turning communications products fantasies like pocket-sized cellular telephones into reality.

Bell Labs and I came together because of a mutual belief in the power of brainpowered workers to drive the success of business organizations. Productivity had been my field of research for much of my career. Janet Nordin had read some of my earlier writings in which I first introduced the notion of an emerging, professionally proficient, brainpowered segment of the American workforce. I call them "gold-collar workers," because they are the company's most valuable asset.

Janet and Don wanted a better understanding of the people who did Bell's most important work, and they wanted us to bring it to them. What I didn't realize then was how elusive the answers would be, how many dead-end roads would be traveled following others' research before we finally decided to roll up our sleeves and blaze our own trail.

NAÏVE ASSUMPTIONS ABOUT HIGH PRODUCTIVITY

One of the first things we discovered is that most workers and their bosses don't agree on who the star performers are. We first asked managers to list their star performers. We then suggested that they narrow the list to those individuals they would turn to if they had to staff an important new project, if they had a crisis that needed a SWAT team, or if they were going to hire for their own business.

When we showed the list to a group of star performers, they took issue with the managers' picks. "How did Joe get on the list?"

they asked incredulously. "Joe hasn't done much for years. And why isn't Maria on the list? She's the one everyone turns to when they hit a brick wall or need new ideas." These reactions gave us pause: managers and their brainpowered workers had different views on who deserved the mantle of "star performer."

We took a step back and asked both groups to nominate those people who greatly outperformed their peers—the cream of the crop—especially those who achieved with methods they admired. We wanted to weed out the high producers whose tactics are to slash and burn their way to greater productivity but whose wake of destruction negates any positive contribution that they make.

The result of this exercise was a 50 percent overlap between the two groups. *Brainpowered workers and their managers disagree half the time on who the stars are.* In Appendix I, I explain why this disagreement occurs and why it can have devastating productivity effects on individual workers and the entire organization. A goal of this book is to eliminate the definition gap and the productivity deficit that can result.

For our original research at Bell Labs, we chose as star performers only those people who made it to both *managers' and coworkers' star lists.* In our later work with 3M, we added the requirement that the stars also had to receive a similar approval from customers. At both companies, we also took into account the number of awards, honors, and performance bonuses won, as well as patent or publication credits where applicable. These undisputed stars were the group we studied and the ones whose performance provided the research basis for this book.

Our research team asked top executives, middle managers, brainpowered workers, and other researchers what makes the difference between star performers and middle performers. Our goal was to find out what made the stars so much more productive and valuable. We received these typical responses:

- Stars are smarter; they have higher IQs.
- Stars are better problem solvers and more creative.
- Stars are more driven and ambitious; they have a "will to succeed."
- Stars are more outgoing; they get along well with people.
- Stars are risk takers and mavericks.

When the list was final, we had accumulated forty-five factors that managers and star performers close to the action believed led to star performance. They grouped nicely into three main categories: (1) cognitive factors, such as higher IQ, logic, reasoning, and creativity, (2) personality factors, such as self-confidence, ambition, risk taking, and a feeling of personal control over one's destiny, and (3) social factors, such as interpersonal skills and leadership.

It became clear that most people—managers and brainpowered workers alike—believe that the stars among them are better in a fundamental sense. Average performers, they assume, lack the traits necessary to leap above solid, steady, work—a leap that is the hallmark of stars.

So we put two hundred star and average performers in meeting rooms across the country to administer a two-day battery of tests to figure out which of the forty-five factors on our list separated the stars from the average performers. We even added a few measures that weren't mentioned but that we thought were important, such as the worker's relationship with the boss, job satisfaction, and attitudes toward rewards. We did surveys and developed detailed individual case histories. We interviewed employees and the managers who hired them. Engineers and managers also supplied us with personal biographical information and personnel file material. We became such fixtures in the Bell Labs workplace that employees began to include us in the office gossip mill.

Then came the day when we fed all the scraps of information into a computer, analyzed it for four months in dozens of different ways, and expected to come up with the breakthrough data that would show what Bell's star producers had that separated them from their average coworkers.

AND THE ANSWER IS . . .

The project meeting to discuss our landing of the Big Kahuna of productivity took place around a large mahogany table in a dimly lit conference room on Bell's sprawling campus outside Chicago. I was surrounded by company executives who had lent reputations and considerable resources to the project. Even though I was flanked by two members of my research team, it had fallen to me to break the news that all our careful gathering of data, our testing, our analyzing had resulted in only one significant finding: We had made a lot of money for the paper industry.

In terms of unlocking productivity secrets, *our data showed no appreciable cognitive, personal-psychological, social, or environmental differences between stars and average performers.*

"Could this be possible?" we asked ourselves. No IQ difference! No logic or reasoning differences! No creativity differences! No self-confidence, risk-taking, or controlling-your-own-destiny differences! No leadership or motivational differences! No attitudinal differences in views on management, work environment, or company rewards!

For each traditional measure—whether alone or in combination—we had come up empty.

We compared the numbers a dozen different ways, stretching computer analyses to their limits, and with each run the computer spat back what I thought at the time was some kind of terrible methodological mistake: There were no quantifiable differences.

These results also highlighted that no one—not the stars, not their bosses, and not the average workers—knew what actually leads to high productivity or star performance.

Although my gut feeling and experience told me there were differences between stars and their average coworkers, I had no data to back up this intuition. Researchers are trained to let their gut feeling help determine what they should investigate but not, of course, what the outcome should be.

Despite my utter conviction that there were differences to be found out, would it be unfair to continue to spend Bell Labs' money to prove my professional instincts were superior to the reams of data piled up on the conference table? Was I locked into my own tunnel vision, unable to face the hard truth?

I remember thinking, rather bitterly at the time, about the story of Thomas Edison's early attempts to come up with the right material for a lightbulb. He had tried a thousand different elements and all had failed. A colleague asked him if he felt his time had been wasted, since he had discovered nothing. "Hardly," Edison is said to have retorted briskly. "I have discovered a thousand things that don't work."

Lofty anecdotes about the trials of creative geniuses were small comfort to a researcher who went into a meeting to tell the people who hired him that he and his team had found nothing.

"How can this be?" asked Janet Nordin, who had been, and still was, one of the most supportive of the project among Bell Labs executives.

The beginning of that meeting was depressing for the damper it put on Bell managers' hopes for productivity leaps, but it also rubbed salt in the wound I was carrying into the session. No one was more disappointed than I. "Stunned" would be the more accurate description of my reaction to the testing evidence. Our research team had staked our reputations on uncovering a secret—shedding light with insightful reading of clues and leads, uncovering the key differences we were seeking. We would present it on a platter to management and help them find a way to identify those traits in applicants. Productivity problem solved. Publish results. Applause.

No one in our fields of work, in business or academia, makes a long-lived career out of publishing negative findings—"Big news! No news!" doesn't cut it with clients or research journals. But from the depths of that feeling of absolute failure, in the midst of the meeting with justifiably disappointed Bell Labs executives and my depressed colleagues, came glorious revelation. As people were trying to explain why the data didn't uncover differences they knew existed, we flashed on a question that would have made Edison proud:

By recognizing that there were no differences from the factors we collected, had we not discovered something critically important—that the factors we thought were so basic to star performance—cognitive, psychological, and social characteristics—were not the real drivers at all?

And that was followed by perhaps the most significant question of all:

If the differences weren't fundamental, would it be possible for average-performing brainpowered workers to be turned into stars?

While managers and project team members were buzzing among themselves about the possibilities, I quickly pulled out of my briefcase a list of the individuals who scored highest on the cognitive tests. I taped it on a wall.

"What do all these people have in common?" I searched the faces of my colleagues and the management team, all the people who had lived the project for two years, who knew detailed information about these workers. "Very smart engineers but not all of them are stars" is the way one described these individuals. Others in the room nodded, offering reasons why many of these engineers didn't warrant star rank. Then I put up other lists; each list contained only the names of those who scored high on a particular factor that we had previously thought led to star performance—risk taking, reward seeking, company loyalty. Similar assessments were shouted back.

The process started to reveal that other factors were at play. The productivity mystery lay not in the test scores but in patterns of behavior on the job. Day-to-day work strategies and results led to the assessments of the people around the room. *It wasn't what these stars had in their heads that made them standouts from the pack, it was how they used what they had.*

The meeting eventually turned into the kind of frenzied brainstorming session that happens when people are exploring something completely new. From the threads of Bell Labs executives' work experiences with engineers, the boost of our own intuition, and a willingness to see "no differences" as a path instead of a dead end, we had moved onto a new track.

Thomas Edison was right. The real value of our twenty-four months of selective searching was in everything we eliminated. We had tested and found wanting just about every plausible theory about what leads to high productivity in brainpowered workers. In the process, we eliminated all the pet theories that people hold. We came to call them "naïve notions," not because their proponents were naïve but because their theories had not undergone rigorous, large-scale testing. With the results of our empirical work, we could silence all the armchair psychologists who thought the answer lay in brain capacity or personality.

The hunt would take off again, this time with the goal of unlocking the work-behavior secrets of the stars and sharing them with managers and with the professionals: the engineers, marketing whizzes, lawyers, software writers, accountants, teachers, science researchers, journalists—people I refer to as "gold-collar workers"—just like you.

2

STARS ARE MADE, NOT BORN

WHY PRODUCTIVITY NOW?:
THE BRAINPOWERED ECONOMY

Bell Labs is simply a microcosm of the larger economy. Where once labor was primarily viewed as a low-level input by which goods were produced and shipped to market, the worker role has shifted in an economy now better understood to be defined by information, services, and intellectual capital.

In the 1990s and beyond, knowledge professionals are at the heart of this new economy. I prefer the broader terms "gold-collar workers" or "brainpowered workers" to encompass the hundreds of professionals whose chief asset is mind, not muscle. The new ideas generated from the technical smarts and creative talent of these workers feed the productivity engine on which a company rises or falls in a ferociously competitive global marketplace.

In today's brainpower-driven global economy, all companies are looking for higher productivity to fuel growth. The problem is they don't know where to begin. Managers have finally realized that downsizing has left gaping productivity holes in their workforce. The glittering short-term profit gains have not held, while creating long-term revenue and profit growth is proving much more difficult than the quick fix of downsizing.

So there is good reason why so many are so interested in understanding the mysteries of star productivity. The futures of individual workers, the companies they work for, even entire lines of businesses depend on the answers.

Whether a company succeeds in this supercompetitive global economy depends more than ever on the productivity of its brainpowered employees—on having a high proportion of star producers to average workers.

In the 1980s, company profit margins were enhanced or diminished by how well the intellectual capital of their best brainpowered workers—the stars—was translated into consumer products and services. Traditionally, companies adopted the same staffing tactics as professional sports teams that have set their sights on national championships. Team strategy and performance were often centered on a star "franchise player" who carried everyone else.

In the late 1990s and into the next century, how well companies do in getting maximum brainpower from all their employees, not just the stars, will determine their very survival. The wider and deeper the pool of these star players—as in the case of the five-time national basketball champions, the Chicago Bulls, for instance, where there are at least four players who would warrant star producer status—the better the chances that the team will reach the top. These players take direction from coaches and managers, but it is the quality of their individual talents and teamwork on the court that makes the team's fortunes.

Boosting the productivity of the entire brainpowered workforce, not just depending on one or two stars to carry the team, is the key to success. If you can boost the productivity of many of your workers into the world-class category, instead of just the few, then you become unbeatable.

WHAT'S IN IT FOR YOU TO BE MORE PRODUCTIVE?

Solving the productivity puzzle became a personal mission for me, because I realized the new direction of our research paralleled the direction of the economy. Our research team was in a position to offer so much more to those already in the workforce. Not only would the recruiting staffs at companies like Bell Labs benefit from our research, it would now be possible for brainpowered workers themselves to adopt the behaviors of the star producers we had studied so exhaustively.

Now, after the years of research, the superproductive behaviors have been identified and have been approved by the star workers and their bosses, as well as validated through a popular workplace productivity improvement program based on the star performer work strategies. (An in-depth description of the productivity improvement program and its results is in Appendix I.) The core of our research and experience is detailed in the pages of this book and offers enormous rewards to any brainpowered professional willing to work hard to incorporate the star producer skills into a daily work routine.

Just by virtue of your position as a brainpowered professional, you already have a deep-seated motivation to be respected by your peers and supervisors. You have the requisite intelligence and technical ability or you wouldn't have the career track you've managed thus far. But although these helped you get in the door, they are not enough. This book provides the critical third resource—the work strategies blueprint—to help you boost your productivity to levels you (and probably those around you) never dreamed possible.

Brainpowered workers have plenty of personal incentive to enhance productivity, and there are some powerful outside forces that are demanding it from workers.

In the work world, there will always be a place for solid though less stellar performers, but the richest rewards go to the star producers, who carry the team. Aside from the obvious financial benefits, star producers write their own tickets. They have more employment options—they're always actively recruited by others—and they are virtually assured of challenging and satisfying work assignments.

Another force that argues for boosting your personal productivity may prove to be the most compelling. If you're a brainpowered worker in the prime of your career in the 1990s, you know how much more time is being demanded from you on the job and how little time is left over for other important aspects of your life. You want to be more productive, you want to maintain a high level of performance, but you want to be able to do it in less time. You want more personal control—more flexibility and less supervision at the office; more leisure time at home.

By adopting the star performer work skills detailed in this book, you will be able to "get a life" beyond work, "keep a life" at work, and set goals you never dreamed would be possible.

I'm confident in promising all this because the material in this book is written for you, derived from people whose lives are just like yours. The productivity principles you will learn come from hundreds of star performers in jobs ranging from marketing to engineering at highly admired companies like high-tech Bell Labs to the industrial giant 3M, maker of Post-it notes and Scotch tape. By supercharging your productivity with these concrete, day-to-day work strategies, you can make yourself a value creator, not just value to the company's bottom line but value to your community of coworkers as well. That's where the star producer reputations are formed that make you employable and mobile.

DEBUNKING THE STAR PERFORMER MYTH: STARS ARE MADE, NOT BORN

Through our ten years of research and productivity improvement work, we have been able to debunk the productivity myths about fundamental superiority. Being a brain may land you on *Jeopardy;* being a social schmoozer may get you invited to the parties of the rich and powerful; being a workaholic may get you a few words of admiration from the overnight security guard. But none of these, even when they're all combined into one human dynamo, necessarily creates a star producer.

So if you are a brainpowered worker searching for a productivity boost, what do you have to do to become a star performer?

You need to change the ways in which you do your work and the ways in which you work with others. **Star performers *do* their work very differently than the solid, average-performing pack.** At the heart of this book is a program that instills star performer strategies into a consistent pattern of day-to-day behavior. The power to be more productive can be learned by every brainpowered worker with the smarts and motivation to make it happen.

There is no such thing as a "Big Bang" revelation in studying this kind of productivity, however. There is no magic pill or silver bullet that will blast you to the top. Nor does our research lend itself to the format of a twelve-step program.

Instead, stellar performance is based on how well the star performer work strategies are incorporated into the many interlocking activities done in the workplace each day. Practiced consistently, the work habits offered in our program will put you in the ranks of hundreds of workers who have been shocked to see their productivity soar.

The star secrets so elusive to workers who have labored for years under labels like "average," "competent," and "mediocre" are revealed here in detail—nine key work strategies that will help you become the master of your own productivity. They are ranked in order of importance and synthesized into an expert model:

- INITIATIVE: Blazing Trails in the Organization's White Spaces
- NETWORKING: Knowing Who Knows by Plugging into the Knowledge Network
- SELF-MANAGEMENT: Managing Your Whole Life at Work
- PERSPECTIVE: Getting the Big Picture
- FOLLOWERSHIP: Checking Your Ego at the Door to Lead in Assists
- LEADERSHIP: Doing Small-L Leadership in a Big-L World
- TEAMWORK: Getting Real About Teams
- ORGANIZATIONAL SAVVY: Using Street Smarts in the Corporate Power Zone
- SHOW-AND-TELL: Persuading the Right Audience with the Right Message

There are hundreds of progressing, achieving brainpowered workers who can offer testimony about how ordinary people can learn to do extraordinary work.

One of the best examples I know is Peter, a star at Bell Labs who, without benefit of college degrees, learned to work productivity circles around Harvard MBAs and MIT PhDs. Peter began his career as an hourly worker climbing telephone poles to do line repairs. When confronted with an unusual or recurring problem, he didn't just do a quick fix. Instead, he would trace the problem back to its root cause, searching for one global solution rather than repeated local solutions by the repair staff throughout the country. His initiative and diagnostic skills were noticed by field engineers, who began consulting him on difficult field problems. Before long, he was offered a job at Bell Labs to help troubleshoot system-wide problems.

Today, Peter is one of the most highly respected professionals at Bell Labs, where he leads teams loaded with PhD and master's-degree-level coworkers. But his IQ, problem-solving skills, and personality are no better or worse than theirs. His secret is in how he uses his talents—his initiative, his being plugged into the "guru" network, and his ability to bring multiple perspectives to bear on his work projects.

For example, Peter was working on a cellular phone project when a telephone switch went down, knocking out phone service for a portion of Chicago's suburbs. Although this crisis was far removed from his work assignment, he called some colleagues in that group to understand the problem better and to determine whether he could be of any help. What he heard convinced him that he could play an instrumental role in getting telephone service back to the customers. He explained the situation to his boss, got his boss's consent, and then volunteered himself.

His first step was to plug into his knowledge network, which stretched from gurus in Bell Labs' headquarters in New Jersey all the way back to his fellow pole climbers. Within a few hours, he had tapped their collective experiences with similar outage problems, generating a list of potential causes and solutions. By further working his contacts, he was able to whittle the potential causes down to seven. He drew on his own considerable work experience to further narrow the list down to three possibilities.

Armed with this information, he went to the ongoing crisis team meeting. Several solutions had already been tried and had failed. Tension was high and tempers were thin, since all present knew some harsh spotlights—both internally and from the news media—were trained on them. As an outsider not originally assigned to the crisis, Peter knew he had to tread softly. But when it came time to decide on another course of action, he volunteered his information.

From his point of view, they were going off on wild goose chases. Rather than dump the results from his legwork on the group, Peter sized them up, especially the team leader, Jeff, who seemed to be floundering. He didn't want to usurp Jeff's position, but he wanted to help get the team on track. Looking around the table, he knew that Su Li had worked on an outage in Omaha, but she had not spoken up during the meeting. He asked her to describe what the Omaha team had learned. Then he turned to Sidhar, who had worked on the development of the downed switch, quizzing him about possible software faults. Their remarks provided the lead-in for his findings and plan of action.

He went to the blackboard and drew a diagram of the problem as he understood it. He then identified the twenty potential culprits that he had gleaned from his knowledge network. Zeroing in on the seven top contenders, he asked, "Who would we turn to if this was the problem?" When the group offered up the name of a guru he had networked with, he said, "I just got off the phone with her and this is what she said."

In this way, Peter led the group to his action plan. Although a vigorous debate ensued over the three root causes that Peter wanted to pursue, the group finally decided to hone in on four—two of Peter's and two others. They then split up to tackle the work.

After twenty-four grueling hours, the team discovered the problem and had telephone service up and running. Not surprisingly, Peter's recommendation had been right. Everyone on the team recognized that without Peter the solution could have escaped them for days as they used trial and error. Jeff, the team leader, thanked him profusely and sent a glowing reference to Peter's bosses. The shine of Peter's star extended even further within the company.

Once again, Peter outperformed his more educated counterparts, both on and off the crisis team. It was his initiative to find out more about the problem and to volunteer his help; his organizational savvy to get his boss's buy-in; his early use of his knowledge network; his building of his perspective on the problem; his awareness of team dynamics; his followership, so as not to alienate Jeff; and his low-key leadership of the team that achieved success. Add to that the time savings and customer satisfaction that resulted from his involvement. No one item made the difference, but put them together in one person and you have the makings of a star.

After reading this book, workers and managers will realize that the highly admired experts who share their productivity secrets with us—the first picks on any team and those who manage to be highly productive on a daily basis—aren't that much different in basic makeup from their more average coworkers. The stars we studied are not geniuses or demigods; they are more like us than we care to realize.

Almost everyone can be a star at something, and you can find the star within you. A group of elderly, mostly retired women in a backwater Illinois town bested 90 percent of the highly paid Wall Street money managers. Who would have ever thought that the "Beardstown Ladies" could become investment stars, especially without access to all the inside information and technology available to the Wall Streeters?

You Can Improve the Rate of Your Productivity by 100 Percent

Our hard-won discovery—that the stars are no more fundamentally smarter or ambitiously driven than their average coworkers—has led to some surprising breakthroughs in the nature of productivity and how it can be measured in the brainpowered worker. As you will learn in Appendix I, we conducted a long-term evaluation study where we asked managers to rate the productivity of their workers before and eight months after going through our productivity improvement program to learn the work strategies of the star performers. Based on these managerial evaluations, we have documented productivity improvement rates of 100 percent on average in various groups of brainpowered workers. Like Peter, the telephone-pole-climbing star performer, these workers solve problems faster and produce higher-quality work than their peers and consistently impress their customers.

The program based on this model is the first program we know of directed toward improving the productivity and management of brainpowered workers like you. Moreover, it is the first ever to be put to extensive front-line testing, evaluating long-term effectiveness, and documenting productivity boosts far beyond workers' expectations.

The star-strategies program is not a remedial course for poor performers, however. About 30 percent of the participants in our productivity improvement programs already were wearing the star producer label. Their productivity gains have been similarly impressive. In fact, they're the first to recognize why: *No one star has all the answers or holds all the secrets to superior productivity.*

Superior producers are interested in the program for the same reason their average coworkers are involved: No one wants to be left behind. It isn't just the entertainment world that's filled with flamed-out former stars.

Born and tested at Bell Labs and revalidated at 3M, the star-strategies model has been adopted at other successful companies employing a variety of brainpowered workers—sales representatives, product managers, engineers, administrators, research-and-development scientists, and marketing staff.

WOMEN, MINORITIES, AND NEWER WORKERS IMPROVE 400 PERCENT

It was in the ranks of brainpowered women and minorities that our program showed the most dramatic improvements, according to their bosses' pre-program and post-program evaluations, with productivity shooting up 400 percent on average. Members of these groups often have to work longer and harder to achieve recognition equal to white, male coworkers. Minority group members also are more likely to be kept out of hearing range when secrets of the star performers are being whispered to the favorite few. When these excluded groups are clued into the same secrets, their productivity soars.

Leon, a soft-spoken thirty-seven-year-old African American

with a master's degree in computer science, had enrolled in our training program at the behest of his supervisor in the work-products unit. He believed Leon wasn't working to his potential, and Leon believed his boss was out to get him. He came into the program with a bad attitude, convinced he was being sent to a remedial camp because of poor performance.

"Because I'm quiet, I tended to keep to myself and just do my job," Leon told us. "I never went outside my job description or tried to help out others. Rather than proactively look for and seize opportunities, I waited till my boss assigned me to projects. I gave priority to those things that interested me rather than paying attention to the critical path and to those work products where others depended on me. To be honest, I never talked to a customer to see what they expected from me.

"But I've learned that you can't do that. So now I'm taking initiative to look for ways to help out the department. I'm taking the lead more often on the challenging projects. Now, rather than just look at my work from my perspective, I seek out the customers' point of view and I'm more open to suggestions from other departments. As a result, I'm churning out a lot more high-priority work. And it has moved me up to the top rating on my performance review."

The success of these groups underscores a key finding in our work. Becoming highly productive doesn't require magic. When women and minorities do have lower productivity, it is *not* because they are less capable. It is because they were never told or did not learn the work strategies that lead to high productivity.

Mastering the star performer skills is a matter of learning and practice. Once these groups are given access to the strategies that turn ho-hum work into sizzling performance, they can hold their own with the established stars. Since our productivity-improvement program helps level the playing field, women and minorities have a greater chance of entering the star performer ranks.

THE PRODUCTIVITY RETURN TO THE ORGANIZATION IS 600 PERCENT

When you improve your productivity, it has a payback not only to you but also to your organization. We've traced all these individual boosts to the company's bottom line, establishing an average 600 percent return on the company's productivity investment in the first year.

If you can demonstrate a 10 percent productivity increase, you return 10 percent of your total compensation costs to the company's bottom line. Let's assume your annual salary, including fringe benefits, is $75,000. The investment return comes to $750 each year for every 1 percent increase in productivity. A 10 percent productivity gain, then, reflects a $7,500 gain for the organization in the first year alone. Such productivity gains increase your value to the company and help you advance your career or justify a raise.

Our program graduates report that their productivity continues to rise each year as they get better at incorporating the stars' secrets into their work lives. The result is a faster-growing, higher-yielding, compounding payoff for you and the company long after the initial investment is made. We might expect that given those potential rewards, managers would realize that investing in human-productivity improvement is the major source of sustainable competitive advantage, since technology improvements are so easily copied.

LEARN WHAT DOES *NOT* IMPROVE YOUR PRODUCTIVITY

Another key discovery in our research is that just as stars have work strategies that spur productivity, average performers have a long list of habits that drag it down. Just as we were able to eliminate IQ and personality from the starmaker machinery, we also were able to identify work habits that have the cachet of productivity enhancers but don't measure up.

There are dozens of business-oriented self-improvement books on the market offering one-size-fits-all programs that will make you a better time manager, a sharper dresser, a Machiavellian power wielder. Not only do they fail to bring productivity gains, they can be counterproductive. At their worst, they create a false sense of being on the road to success.

Messy-desk types who are forced to keep clean tabletops, multi-colored files, and day-runner schedule books will be miserable and less productive. The night owl expected to hit the ground running at 7:30 A.M. will be unproductive and cranky. Generic formulas almost never work.

Our research shows that the biological and personality quirks that make us individuals don't make the difference between the stars and their average coworkers. If you are a messy-desk person, you are better served by learning the strategies of messy-desk stars than by trying to continue as an average worker with a clean desk.

The point is that you need to remain true to who you are and retain your basic nature in the workplace. Disrupting that basic pattern will guarantee failure; the star strategies will only be dabbled in, not internalized.

Brainpowered workers who have used our program to launch their productivity have accomplished this by changing how they do their jobs, not by changing who they are. The program doesn't make ridiculous demands on the order of personality cloning. You take the secrets of the stars that our research found to raise productivity and tailor them to your own personality and your distinct workplace routine.

This book gives you what you need to start enhancing productivity today. No longer do you have to depend on admittance to the old-boy network or jockey for a mentor in order to gain access to the insider secrets of productivity. If you get these, sure, it will probably help your career. But for the vast majority who never will, this book gives you a powerful compensating tool.

Each star skill has a chapter all its own, but we will begin with a brief introduction telling how the model for those skills was developed. Finally, as you read through the case histories of people who have mastered a particular skill in our model, keep in mind that many of them have backgrounds just like yours—the same allotment of talents, the same insecurities, the same dreams of being able to achieve more. The first step toward unlocking the star power inside you is to visualize yourself doing the work of the brainpowered workers in our examples who have mastered one skill at a time. Eventually, what you'll discover is that their most productive strategies have become part of your daily routine. Your star power will be unleashed and you will be astounded by your new capabilities.

This book is about offering brainpowered workers like you and your managers a source of hope—a way to find peace of mind in a business culture that is wallowing in insecurity and could use a much-needed growth boost. Doubling your productivity can make the difference between a promotion and/or being stuck in a dead-end job. Being labeled as a person who contributes value directly to the bottom line provides you leverage and options, especially when the work skills introduced here are so portable.

Finally, this book also strives to meet a much more intangible need—to help you realize the star potential you know is inside you.

3

◙

CREATING THE STAR PERFORMER MODEL

It is morning on the third day of October 1996. John Jacobs, a marketing manager for Westinghouse Electric Corporation, is up at 6 A.M. for a routine that begins with a three-mile jog through his suburban Pittsburgh neighborhood.

This day marks a milestone for John—ten years as a member of the "corporate family." It is an anniversary that, by cruel coincidence, the company will mark in a different way. As John goes through his warm-up stretch, he marvels at how quickly the years have slipped by. There are the usual regrets: He wishes he had climbed higher, accomplished more.

The stretch routine ends with a hunt through the shrubs for the daily paper, and before tossing it inside the door, a quick scan of the front page to make sure the country wasn't invaded by UFOs during the night. But the big story this day reports a threat far more dire for John Jacobs and his wife and three children than any hovering spaceships:

WESTINGHOUSE TO SPLIT-UP COMPANY TO PROPEL GROWTH; RESTRUCTURING LIKELY

He pores over the story while standing in his front yard, numb, but not from the October chill.

When he is finished, there is an uncomfortable fluttering in his stomach. There will be no run this morning. On the day he should be celebrating a decade of hard work and loyalty, John Jacobs is facing something that he has only known vicariously since job hunting after college—uncertainty.

How will he fit into a split-up Westinghouse? Will he be considered worth keeping? If he does survive the restructuring crunch, what will his workload be like? Will he have the same job satisfaction?

If he had been sure the answers to these critical questions would be based on his credentials and seniority, John Jacobs would have been able to toss the newspaper aside and run without worry. Standing in his front yard, he stifles the urge to shout to the neighborhood, "Hey! Listen up! I have an MBA in marketing! Excuse me! I have credits toward a doctorate!" He has been in Westinghouse's industrial systems since he graduated from college, back in that time before "downsizing" was a word, back when layoffs only happened to blue-collar workers.

In those first few years, John was considered a potential star, a sharp, enthusiastic up-and-comer. Now, at his ten-year mark, the glitter has rubbed off.

After several years of average evaluations, the general impression is that he is an okay producer, a second-tier performer in a unit sprinkled with high achievers. After the morning paper headline, John's occasional bouts of insecurity have been turned into full-blown career angst.

John retreats inside, sitting at the kitchen table in his running clothes, taking stock of his job situation as he stares at the headline.

He has never felt so vulnerable.

John sees himself as a stifled high achiever, but he realizes his reputation in the office is "average." There is a hard reckoning on this anniversary day; John realizes that merely okay might no longer cut it in a company where new owners and new management will size him up on the estimated worth of his future contributions, not on his years of service.

He begins to make mental notes on how much longer and harder he will have to work if he's going to improve his performance. His in basket is swamped, a dozen e-mail messages are waiting for responses, and he already brings a lot of work home. John has read the horror stories on downsizing in the professional workforce. Few of those who get the boot end up finding jobs with pay and benefits equal to what was lost.

He thinks of the stars in his division and knows the company will do everything possible to keep them. And if the company foolishly lets them go, they'll be snapped up by others as soon as they walk out the door.

"The sad part is," John tells his wife later, after showing her the newspaper, "I always felt like I could be a star. I know I've got as much talent as some of these others, but I just can't seem to make it click."

He thinks of Pat Lee, in the office across the hall, who seems to know exactly what to do and when to do it. He knows Pat is one of the undisputed stars of the division—it wasn't just hype—but he is at a loss to figure out how she manages to produce so much high-quality work yet still keep regular hours.

She gets choice assignments like being part of the strategy team that identified the opportunity to buy CBS. High-visibility projects like that can rocket a career. She overcomes obstacles—technical and organizational—that trip up a lot of her coworkers, and still finds time to push her ideas for new products. Top managers were buzzing about her latest hot idea that went far beyond her marketing assignment: the leasing out of Westinghouse computer professionals as "SWAT teams" when nuclear power plant customers run into trouble. If a crisis arises or if someone is stuck on a problem, Pat's name comes up first as the rescuer.

John Jacobs is the poster boy for a growing segment of the American workforce caught up in the most significant economic restructuring since industrialization shifted Americans from family farms to the factories in the 1800s.

As we approach the twenty-first century, knowledge professionals are driving this new economy, and the productivity spotlight is being focused on them. In previous generations, blue-collar and clerical workers bore the brunt of productivity improvement efforts, because their efforts drove the economy. For the most part, brainpowered workers were left alone. This is no longer the case. (See Chapter 14 for a fuller description of the brainpowered economy.)

John Jacobs has to "get with the program," but he doesn't know what the program is—he only knows the consequences of failing. If he asked Pat, his star colleague, it's likely she wouldn't be much help either. Most stars are like virtuoso musicians. They are able to perform at superior levels but can't distill the factors that make their stellar performances possible. They find it even more difficult to transfer them to others. Consequently, advice they give is well intentioned but often ineffectual.

Since our research shows that top executives, middle managers, and brainpowered workers themselves are not good judges of concrete differences between star and average performers, we have filled the void with our own years of studying the star performers themselves.

This chapter reveals the subtleties and nuances of the star orchestration of day-to-day brainpowered work in jobs like yours.

MOLDING THE MODEL

Early on in our direct observational work, we settled on the approach of developing an expert model. We invested scores of hours into detailed interviews, focus groups, and observations of high-performing Bell Labs professionals—a critical step after the breakthrough meeting that established how much patterns of behavior define stellar performance. While the field interviews and observations were mind-numbing at times, they eventually yielded rich behavioral information.

Our original plan had these workers keep detailed diaries, but that method eventually asked too much from them, in terms of both time and judgment about what was important enough to write down. Our direct observational approach—from morning greetings of office mates to flipping the lights off at the end of the day—was invaluable to the study.

We were, in effect, turning the usual approach on its head. Expert models were invented by artificial-intelligence researchers in an effort to get computers to mimic the skills of human beings. Researchers have created such models by interviewing expert welders, for example, and asking them to explain in concrete detail how they go about their job. Researchers then used the interview data to construct a computer program that translated the experts' skills into behavioral commands for a robotic welder. But based on our interviews with Bell Labs (and later 3M) experts—in this case, star performers in research, software development, and engineering—the expert model was one that could be used by people, not computers.

Not only did we want to cover the range of workers with our model of star behaviors, we also wanted to make sure it was based on their own experiences, not developed from a computer program with no grounding in human experience.

That was the basis for meeting with stars, middle performers, and managers in as many as four groups for two sessions each week. We refined our models and behavior checklists into two categories—cognitive/technical skills and work strategies—that influence high productivity (see Figure 1).

While I keep stressing our finding that cognitive abilities neither guarantee success nor differentiate stars from the pack of average producers, that shouldn't imply they are unimportant. Every job and every work environment requires a certain level of cognitive ability. Without it, you won't get in the door; if you do slip in by chance, you probably won't last long. But once you have passed the cognitive hurdle, having more cognitive ability than the requisite amount does not seem to yield star performer benefits.

But the work behaviors identified in the second round of research were very intriguing. The groups identified nine work strategies that do make a difference in performance.

The model depicted in Figure 1 is a quasi-developmental model in two ways. First, it ranks these strategies in order of importance based on the experiences of brainpowered workers from all levels of performance. For example, initiative is the core strategy in this expert model, while organizational savvy and show-and-tell, although necessary for star performance, are less important on a relative scale.

Professionals who develop these last two work strategies may

Figure 1
The Star Performance Model

Developed by Robert Kelley and Janet Caplan

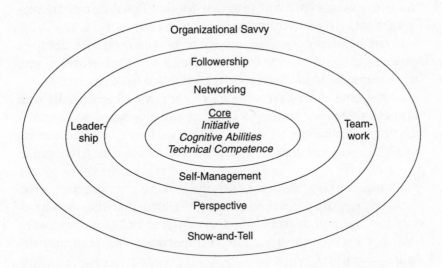

have a leg up on garnering attention and promotions, but giving riveting presentations and being an adept player in office politics are less essential to being known as a valued star worker. Without initiative, a high-quality knowledge network, top self-management skills, and good perspective, it is almost impossible to earn a star reputation with managers and coworkers, no matter how good your show-and-tell and organizational savvy skills are. Star performers and managers considered them as terrific "icing on the cake," but the cake is more important and must come first.

The second developmental aspect of the model is that the work strategies closer to the center must be demonstrated earlier than those in the outer rings. A brainpowered worker must be able to take initiative or develop the ability to do so in the first six months to one year on the job. Proving to your manager and colleagues that you are an initiative taker is generally expected before you wow them with your presentation skills. In a competitive environment, it's unlikely that you can survive otherwise.

Each strategy, then, is detailed in later chapters, and the examples included in each chapter borrow from some aspects of the productivity-improvement program we developed using star performers themselves as instructors, not hired outsiders.

In the Bell Labs program, the model proved itself with dramatic increases in productivity from middle-of-the-pack workers who began using the work strategies that we culled from the stars.

At the same time that we were refining the expert model with star performers, we were also creating a model based on the work behaviors of middle performers. When we first compared our research, it appeared that stars and middle performers gave similar answers.

Both groups, for instance, identified taking initiative as a useful work strategy. But closer inspection revealed that the answers of stars and those of average engineers differed in two critical ways: how they ranked the strategies in importance and how they described them.

To begin with, middle performers inverted the expert model's ranking of the nine work strategies. According to these average workers, show-and-tell and organizational savvy were the core strategies and, they wrongly believed, were largely responsible for high performance ratings from managers. It's easy to understand why these nonexperts came to this conclusion: One of the few times senior managers see knowledge professionals in action is when they give presentations.

Some executives do use such public presentations to infer skills and strategies that produce good work. And in a few cases, mediocre professionals with a flair for show-and-tell are rewarded by top management, even though they don't deserve it based on their total performance. Picking up on only the superficial aspect of these occasional cases, the middle performers fell into the trap of overly focusing on impression management rather than adopting work strategies, like initiative and perspective, which achieve results that get much more notice from management and your colleagues.

Average performers often do not understand the difference between real stars—as judged by managers, colleagues, and customers—and those few who squeak by on impression management alone. They find it hard to distinguish between form and substance, between those who are living examples of the Peter Principle—those people who get promoted to their level of incompetence—and the many who have earned their star reputations because they embody the entire star performer model. Remember, to qualify for star status, you need to prove your worth to managers, colleagues, and customers. It is highly unlikely that you can do so without both the cake and the icing.

Finally, the nine strategies work together, not in isolation. Like Peter, the telephone-pole-climber-turned-star-troubleshooter, you must draw on all the star work strategies to achieve great results. Being good at just one or two is not good enough.

TARGETING BEHAVIORS THAT BUILD PRODUCTIVITY MUSCLE—THE NINE WORK STRATEGIES

Now that you have a better idea how the star performance model works, we can explore the content of the model—the work strategies that separate stars in your workplace, the Pat Lees, from the John Jacobses. Although each work strategy is covered in detail in its own chapter, with specific job-related examples, it is helpful to see how the stars and average performers differ in their basic understanding of the concepts.

1. Initiative: Blazing Trails in the Organization's White Spaces

What an average performer like John Jacobs thinks it is: Coming up with ideas that help me do my job better and get me noticed by upper management. Or: Volunteering to do the little extras in the workplace, like planning the annual picnic or recruiting for the blood drive.

What a star producer like Pat Lee knows it to be: Going above and beyond the accepted job description or busting out of everyday work routines to offer new, often bold, value-adding ideas, such as Pat's "SWAT team" leasing idea; doing so for the benefit of coworkers or the entire organization and following through diligently to ensure the implementation of those ideas. Initiative involves some risk taking and is not just window dressing.

2. Networking: Knowing Who Knows by Plugging into the Knowledge Network

What average performers think it is: Building a communications grapevine so that I am "in the loop" on the latest office gossip. Socializing with people in my field and with executive head hunters who can help me in future job hunting.

What star producers know it to be: Proactively developing dependable pathways to knowledge experts who can help me complete critical path tasks. When called upon, I share my knowledge with those who need it. The goal is to minimize the knowledge deficit that is inherent in every brainpowered job.

3. Self-Management: Managing Your Whole Life at Work

What average performers think it is: A skill that helps me manage my time and projects better.

What star producers know it to be: Much more than time or project management, this work strategy helps me proactively create opportunities, direct my work choices, ensure high job performance, and carve out my career path. It allows me to develop a portfolio of talents and work experiences so that my value to the company increases.

4. Perspective: Getting the Big Picture

What average performers think it is: A one-dimensional skill of seeing the world deeply from my point of view and making sure my point of view on a project or assignment is the one that gets the most attention, protection, and connection.

What star producers know it to be: A multidimensional skill that allows me to see a project or problem in a larger context and through the eyes of the critical others—customers, competitors, coworkers, and bosses. Having broad perspective enables me to evaluate the relative importance of various viewpoints, so that I can improve on the product or develop better solutions to problems.

5. Followership: Checking Your Ego at the Door to Lead in Assists

What average performers think it is: A work behavior that shows managers and coworkers that I know how to toe the line and not threaten the leader, take orders without question, and stick to the boundaries of my job description.

What star producers know it to be: A work strategy that involves being actively engaged in helping the organization succeed while exercising independent, critical judgment of goals, tasks, and methods. As a star follower, I have the ability to work cooperatively with a leader to accomplish the organization's goals even when there are personality or workplace differences.

6. Teamwork: Getting Real About Teams

What average performers think it is: A skill that allows you to be on a team, to do your part, and to work cooperatively with others on a project or problem.

What star producers know it to be: A complex series of skills that involve taking joint "ownership" of goal setting, group commitments, work activities, schedules, and group accomplishments. It also means being a positive contributor to the group's dynamics: helping everyone feel part of the team, dealing with conflict, and assisting others in solving problems.

7. Leadership: Doing Small-L Leadership in a Big-L World

What average performers think it is: An inborn trait that allows me to flaunt my ego by being in charge, to have the power to make most key decisions, and to delegate whatever does not interest me.

What star producers know it to be: A work strategy that employs my expertise and influence to convince a group of people to come together and to accomplish a substantial task. This can involve a range of efforts—helping the group create a clear vision of where they want to go along with the high commitment and trust necessary to get there; finding the resources to accomplish the task; and shepherding the project to successful completion.

8. Organizational Savvy: Using Street Smarts in the Corporate Power Zone

What average performers think it is: The talent for brown-nosing and schmoozing in the workplace to help me get noticed by the right people. It also requires obsessive devotion to office politics.

What star producers know it to be: A work strategy that enables me to navigate the competing interests in an organization, to promote cooperation, address conflicts, and get things done. This can involve expertise in managing individual or group dynamics; knowing when to avoid conflicts and when to meet them head on; knowing how to make allies out of potential enemies.

9. Show-and-Tell: Persuading Your Audience with the Right Message

What average performers think it is: The ability to get noticed by upper management through slick presentations, long-winded memos, and public displays of affection over my own work. My focus is primarily on my image and my message, not on the audience.

What star producers know it to be: A series of skills involving selecting information to pass on to others and developing the most effective, user-friendly format for reaching and persuading a specific audience. At its highest level, show-and-tell involves selecting the right message for a particular audience or the right audience for the particular message.

MAKING A COMMITMENT TO STAR PERFORMANCE

If you are the type of worker who is open to productivity improvement, then the work-strategies chapters in this book will be especially valuable.

These skills, however, may be ranked differently in your profession. A marketing department, for instance, may find show-and-tell much more critical to star performance than leadership.

In the following chapters, you will notice the human factors that stand out in each of these skill areas. In the new knowledge economy, it is your mastery of these interactive, behavioral work strategies that will determine your value to the company, more so than your mastery of the latest complex technology.

A pertinent motto from the business world is: There Is No Such Thing as a Free Lunch. To boost your productivity, you have to commit to the hard work of practice and discipline in adopting the skills introduced in the following chapters.

Unfortunately, it is too often the case in the 1990s that productivity improvement studies have involved many other elements of the workplace, like new technology or cost-reduction systems, rather than the worker. In fact, employees judged less than productive are usually tagged for "outplacement" in productivity calculations, rather than viewed as assets that, if invested in, would reap long-term rewards.

What we offer in the next nine chapters is a proven guidebook to a set of essential work strategies—for managers who distrust quick fixes and want to improve productivity by investing in the staff they have and for brainpowered workers like you who are ready to use the starmaking tools placed in your hands.

TWO

THE NINE WORK STRATEGIES OF THE STAR PERFORMERS

4

INITIATIVE

Blazing Trails in the Organization's White Spaces

For ten years, Kathleen Betts was a dependable cog in the massive wheel of Massachusetts state government. Across her desk in the Department of Public Welfare came the bills from hospitals for their treatment of the state's poorest and sickest.

While most of her workday was spent processing the bills, she was well aware of the human faces behind the numbers. State governments were struggling more and more each year to meet their share of health care costs for Medicaid patients. Among these patients were children from poor families, the elderly, and those dealing with life-threatening illnesses who had used up their own resources.

At thirty-eight, Betts was a brainpowered worker with a master's degree in public health, but she also was the mother of two young children and chose to split her job with another mom. In January 1991, Massachusetts government was in dire budgetary straits, and she knew important programs for the poor were in jeopardy.

Not only that, but the state's newly elected Republican governor, William Weld, had vowed to lay off hundreds of state employees and furlough others before raising taxes to close a $460 million gap in a $13.5 billion budget.

Betts realized her part-time job in the pack of bureaucrats could be on the hit list and that others in the public welfare department were on the governor's mind when he talked during the campaign of a bloated state bureaucracy and described many state workers as "walruses."

If Kathy Betts had just minded her own business and continued to process bills, hospitals in the state would have been forced to cut services to the poor and many of her coworkers would have been cleaning out their desks. But instead, Betts decided to take some personal initiative to deal with this problem that was not part of her job assignment and that no one expected her to work on or solve. The budget deficit had already stumped the best brains state government could muster.

While continuing to do her own job during the day, Betts, at night and on her own time, began bringing home the weighty Medicaid manuals and federal Department of Human Services guidelines, scouring them for ways to squeeze a bit more money into the system.

Slogging through pages of reimbursement regulations one night, Betts found what she thought was a roundabout path to a vein of gold buried beneath the leaden prose. It was an accounting wrinkle, a difference in the way the state and federal agencies calculated hospital operating costs and income. The result was that the state program was getting less reimbursement than it was entitled to—lots and lots less.

As it turned out, Betts's quiet little initiative made national headlines when it resulted in a windfall of a whopping $489 million from Washington. That check closed the budget gap in one fell swoop, saving the day for the poor and causing a red-faced but grateful governor to rethink the productivity value of the average walrus.

"I've said that I think that state government should be downsized, but maybe we need to give more thought about how we do that without losing people like Kathy Betts," Weld told reporters after receiving assurances from federal officials that the check was in the mail.

Weld was so delighted with Betts that he pushed a bill through the state legislature setting a $10,000 cash award each year to a state government employee whose initiatives make government more productive.

Accepting the first award later that summer, Betts, a registered Democrat who had voted for Weld, said she hoped the contact she'd had with the governor might help change his opinion of state workers. "I think very few are hacks. Most are very dedicated, very valuable employees."

Throw a requisite love interest, a few car chase scenes, and a bit more cloak-and-dagger plot into Kathy Betts's story and Hollywood movie moguls would be tripping over one another to do her story.

That may still come to pass, but for a few weeks that summer, it was the national media doing the tripping. Betts was featured as the ABC News Person of the Week, landed on the front page of *The New York Times*, and was invited to be on David Letterman (she politely declined, worrying about "serious issues" being sandwiched between Stupid Pet Tricks and a roving camera stunt).

So why was she the nation's darling in the summer of 1991? Why was America in love with a state government bureaucrat in, of all places, the public welfare office?

Because Kathy Betts had shown initiative. She had taken a step forward above and beyond her job assignment and accomplished what all the Boston Brahmin budget experts at the highest levels of state government could not. She had eliminated the $460 million budget deficit, balanced the budget, and thrown in an extra $29 million surplus as a bonus.

Americans may love the underdog best, the one who finds courage and skill at the last minute to "win one for the Gipper." But just behind that are the ordinary types who draw upon some mysterious reservoir of confidence and commitment, assume some personal risk, and take some initiatives that go well beyond what is expected. While few contributions may be as spectacular as Kathy Betts's, the brainpowered initiators' day-to-day efforts end up resulting in something quite extraordinary—boosting productivity. Some days, the boost may be more like a nudge; other days, it packs real power, doubling or tripling productivity.

Betts's daughter may have framed it best when, in the midst of the media flurry, she crayoned a cardboard sign for Mom to wear around her neck: "Congratulations. You are smart. But you are also a star. I love you."

In her simple sign, nine-year-old Brooks Betts had a better understanding of the difference between smart workers and star workers than many brainpowered professionals and department managers.

Of the nine work strategies we developed in our research, demonstrating initiative proved to be the most powerful work skills tool for bridging the chasm between the intelligent, average worker and the superproductive, star worker. Stars proactively look for and seize opportunities to go the extra mile for the good of the department or company.

Initiative earns its place at the center of our model for another critical reason. It is the first work strategy that coworkers and managers look for in new hires.

If you are starting out in a new workplace, you will quickly be judged on whether you go beyond your specific responsibilities and take initiative. While no one expects you to set the world on fire in the first six months, the work group will be determining whether you can be counted on to go beyond pulling your weight, to chip in on work that falls outside your job description.

When Lai and Henry were hired at Bell Labs, they had very similar credentials: 3.8 GPAs from top-ranked electrical engineering programs, summer internships at computer companies, and glowing recommendations from professors. Yet each took a very different approach to the assignment they were given for their first six months. In the morning, they took classes in telephone technology and in the methods Bell Labs uses to conduct its work. Afternoons were spent on break-in projects—work that needed to be done but would not jeopardize crucial projects if done badly.

Henry holed himself up in his office as if he were writing his dissertation or studying for a bar exam. He collected volumes of technical documents to acquaint himself with the latest ideas. He began learning how to use exotic software programs he thought might be helpful in his work. He would surface only for a bathroom break or a mandatory staff meeting. "What's going to count," he remembers thinking at the time, "is whether I can prove to my coworkers how technically smart I am."

Lai set aside three hours each afternoon to work on her assignment. In whatever time was left of her workday, she introduced herself to coworkers and asked questions about their projects. If one of them needed a hand or was facing schedule pressures, she volunteered to help. And even though Lai was new to the workplace culture, her colleagues appreciated her willingness to help them out, especially given that their problems were not hers.

One afternoon, a colleague couldn't get a program to work in a software project that was due the next week. Lai thought that a new programming tool that she had picked up in an advanced course could handle the problem. She offered to work on a solution while her colleague focused on the larger project. Her coworker was grateful to have help fixing the program so that he could keep to his schedule, and he also appreciated the information on the new tool.

When some sophisticated software tools needed to be installed in everyone's office PCs, the traditional but very unproductive company process forced each person to install it by trial and error. Lai had experienced the same cumbersome installation process during an internship and thought it made more sense for one person to do it for all the machines. Since no one was specifically responsible for the work, she stepped forward to take on the job. When it turned out to be tougher than she realized, requiring two weeks rather than the four days she had planned, Lai could have backed off, but she saw it through.

"Once I got up the learning curve, it seemed silly to make everyone else go through the pain I did," she says. Volunteering for the project forced her to come in early and stay late for several days so that neither her work assignment nor her class work would suffer.

On another occasion, a colleague who had been scheduled for a dreaded all-night lab testing session had to attend an out-of-town funeral, and another staffer had to fill in. More physically than technically demanding, these sessions take place from midnight to 7:00 A.M., the only period when the computers can be freed up to accommodate large-scale testing. At a hastily called staff meeting, the veterans kidded one another about grabbing the "plum assignment." At the point where the staff expected the supervisor to assign someone arbitrarily, Lai volunteered.

"I figured that it was most important to get accepted into the team, and what better way than to help them out?" she said.

Even the drudge work of a midnight shift, she said, was like a mini-apprenticeship. "I got a quick peek into the work they were doing and what kind of things I would need to know. Sure, some of the work I did for them was grunt and gopher stuff, but . . . to meet the schedules, they needed a hand. Since my schedule was more flexible than others', it made sense for me to help out. Plus, they got to know me and my capabilities."

After six months, both Henry and Lai had finished their technical classes and their first assignments. Both of their projects were successful and judged to be technically competent. Indeed, Henry's work may have been slightly more technically proficient than Lai's.

But when it came to workplace reputation, Henry came up short. While he was known as a nice guy, he also was pegged as a loner. Henry was seen as technically adept, but there were question marks about his ability to share his skills with coworkers. He carried on as if he were still in school, where individual performance is the rule.

Lai was seen as an initiative taker, someone who saw a problem that was not her responsibility and stepped forward to solve it. Lai had been able to create the impression of being in the lab group for much longer than six months. Managers noticed this, of course, and already were looking at her as a candidate for fast-track assignments.

Our observations of Henry, Lai, and dozens of other Bell Labs engineers show that any newcomer in a unit of professionally skilled, competitive workers must demonstrate the initiative skill within the first six to twelve months. Otherwise, the new hire will be relegated to the pack—labeled, perhaps, like Henry, as competent but not productive in ways that benefit the group. In the late 1980s, when managers across the country were forced to cut staffs, the workers who hadn't shown initiative, like Henry, were often vulnerable.

Yet learning how to take initiative effectively is not taught in school or even in the workplaces that now demand it. Even where it is taught, learning on the job is not easy. Stars have the initiative moves down, but most can't teach them to others.

One engineer who was languishing in his unit for six years before adopting the skill in our productivity improvement program likens the learning process to diving off a ten-meter board. It takes more than a willingness to step onto the platform, he says. You have to master the moves.

Initiative is the most widely misunderstood of all the star performer work strategies. In fact, some people see initiative one-dimensionally as common sense. But our research shows it is hardly common even in a brainpowered economy. Average performers—who constitute 60 to 80 percent of the workforce—don't get it. That group is most likely to view initiative taking as activity for activity's sake, getting stuck doing someone else's work, or taking on work that is not part of their job description. Cynical average performers see it as kissing up to the boss or colleagues.

It might surprise readers to know that Henry, the loner Bell Labs hire, believed he was taking initiative. "I gathered up the latest technical information and learned about the latest software tools so that I could do a bang-up job on my assignment. Nobody told me to do any of that," he told us.

What Lai understood and Henry did not is that only certain actions earn the initiative label.

Masters of star-quality initiative:

- Seek out responsibility above and beyond the expected job description, as when Lai did the late-night testing session and state worker Kathleen Betts buried herself in Medicaid manuals.
- Undertake extra efforts for the benefit of coworkers or the larger group, as was the case when Lai offered to help fix the software program on her coworkers' project. Similarly, Betts took her initiative in the name of coworkers and Massachusetts taxpayers.
- Stick tenaciously to an idea or project and follow it through to successful implementation, as Lai did when she committed herself to installing new office software. And Betts made sure her Medicaid loophole discovery didn't get lost in the day-to-day business of state government. Instead, she shepherded it up through the layers to the governor's office.
- Willingly assume some personal risk in taking on new respon-

sibilities. In Lai's case, the risk was that she might flub the software installation or neglect her own work in favor of helping her colleagues. For Betts, the risks involved tangling with political agendas and wandering into areas that weren't connected to her job.

Many average performers mistakenly believe that the only worthwhile initiatives are the big-bang variety, on the order of Betts's wiping out a $460 million state budget deficit. If it doesn't make the front page of the *Wall Street Journal* with a headline proclaiming a dramatic increase in bottom-line profits, then it isn't worth the effort.

Star performers in our studies were adamant that while they are always looking for roof-raising initiatives, the small, day-to-day efforts had the same impact over time. In fact, they noted that the whopper initiatives seldom happen without a long string of smaller efforts preceding them. If you don't create a work climate that values small initiatives, they will dry up and the big ones will never get a chance to happen. Lai's helping-hand initiative, for instance, may have given a coworker the breathing space needed to make a significant breakthrough.

The stars also believe that expectations for the type of initiative you take will be shaped by your experience level. As a new employee, Lai was not expected to take big initiatives, but her record for taking smaller initiatives pleasantly surprised her coworkers and helped establish a quick reputation as a productive engineer. As she gains more experience, Lai will be expected to take on higher-level initiatives with greater difficulty and risks. But expectations also include continuing with the smaller initiatives that contribute to the group's performance.

Workers who take initiatives are apt to get noticed as standouts—perhaps not on the order of being invited, like Kathleen Betts, to chat with David Letterman, but noticed where it counts, in the workplace, for reasons of merit, not grandstanding.

INITIATIVE OR INITIATIVE LITE?: A WORK SKILLS SESSION

A key finding of our research showed striking differences in the way average performers and star performers defined initiative and ranked it in importance on our expert model. Put yourself in the following scene, taken from an interview with a star producer and his average coworker.

Caren, a production specialist for the past four years in an advanced-materials ceramics company supplying the auto industry, emerged from her annual performance review confused and angry. In her mid-thirties she had gone back to school to get a combined master of science/MBA degree and expected a higher evaluation than the previous year's. Yet she once again was rated "strong and consistent," the euphemism for average in the company's ratings. Yes, Caren's work was technically competent, even outstanding at times, her supervisor acknowledged. Yes, her work was completed on time and met the objectives. Yes, she had a good record for attendance and as a team player.

Frustrated, Caren asked her boss what more she could do to earn a higher rating.

"Technical competence can only take you so far, Caren. You need to show more initiative—that's key to being more than average around here."

But when Caren asked what kinds of initiatives were expected, her boss wouldn't offer specifics.

"You should try to be more like Gary," was all she offered.

Gary! Well, why not? Everyone in the office would like to have Gary's reputation, Caren fumed to herself. He was one of the department's stars, known for taking on the tough projects. In his late forties, Gary had most recently spearheaded the department's difficult but necessary transition into computer-assisted manufacturing technology. He had turned down promotions to the management track, he told surprised coworkers, because he preferred his product-related work to paper pushing.

Caren knew Gary outside the office through the company volleyball team. It was after one of the matches, as team members from the department settled around their usual table at their favorite pizza shop and pitchers of beer were set down, that the talk turned to work and to the performance reviews. There was the customary dumping on the system—what a farce the reviews were and how much reviewers and reviewees hated the ordeal.

"What I really don't like," Caren said, "is how unhelpful my supervisor is in telling me what to do differently." Heads nodded around the table.

Caren then recounted her boss's comments about taking initiatives. "The worst part is that I take lots of initiatives. I know it's important, but my boss acts like I'm clueless and she's Moses giving me the Ten Commandments." There was another round of sympathetic nods.

Then Gary spoke. "Tell us about one."

Caren didn't even have to think about it. She had done one recently that she was particularly proud of, she told the group. She had been assigned by her boss to attend a series of long, technically challenging meetings with another team and their managers, she told the group. After each meeting, she was to send a detailed summary to her boss and brief the rest of her team. Caren was worried that detailed note taking would get in the way of her participating and representing her team in discussions, so she decided to tape-record the meetings and take notes from the tapes later in the day. "After listening to the tapes, I was able to give a complete blow-by-blow report to my group. Taking the tape recorder was an important initiative."

Some around the table nodded in agreement, but Elena, another star performer, shook her head. "I'm not so sure."

"It most certainly was," Caren said defensively. "Taping the meeting allowed me to add important points without losing track of the information. I was much more productive for having done that," she said.

"It was a good idea, maybe, but it seems you were just doing your job," said Elena. "How you do your job is up to you. If you want to take notes, that's up to you. If you want to take a tape recorder or to rely on memory, it's all up to you. But doing your job is not initiative."

Elena's comments led to a spirited discussion about what constitutes initiative and what kind of initiatives count at their company.

"When I think of a great initiative," said Gary, "I remember the time Elena went to the productivity-and-quality conference even though her boss didn't see the point, since it was not directly related to her work. There were no travel funds in the budget, so Elena took vacation time and paid her own way. While she was there, she learned about Europe's new upcoming quality standard ISO 9000. These bidding requirements were to ensure higher-quality raw materials, products, and processes—all designed to help improve European companies' competitive advantage in world markets. If supplier companies, like ours, couldn't meet it, they wouldn't be allowed to bid on European projects.

"Elena came back all jazzed up," Gary told the group. "So on her own time, she got up to speed on ISO 9000 requirements and introduced us to them in one of those brown-bag lunches. If this had been another top-down directive, we would have avoided it like the plague. But Elena has a good rep."

Elena said that getting her boss to sign on was another matter. She wasn't thrilled that Elena had gone to the conference without her support, and Elena knew the risk in doing that. But Elena said she was careful to follow up, sitting down with her to go over the benefits of getting ahead of the learning curve on Europe's ISO 9000 bidding specs. "She also volunteered to lead the effort in addition to her regular work assignment," said Gary. "Her boss had a hard time refusing that kind of commitment."

Upper managers were a harder sell, Elena told the group. They didn't believe the Europeans would ever agree on these new standards, let alone enforce them. After all, the United States had not set up national quality standards based on the Malcolm Baldridge Award criteria. But she kept working on the decision makers, sending relevant articles and writing memos to her boss about the benefits of being first. Finally, the company's top executives saw some concrete advantages and got behind it.

"Well, you all know the rest of the story," said Gary, filling his mug from the pitcher. "Europe is now our biggest customer, and our improved quality is attracting U.S. business as well."

Elena's initiative had all the critical ingredients—a willingness to move beyond her narrow job description, even the boss, to reach a goal that benefited everyone. Plus, she wouldn't give up.

Elena was dead-on correct about why Caren's boss would not see the tape recorder as a workplace initiative, and Gary's understanding of why Elena's initiative merits the label reinforces his star performer rating. Taking initiative involves more expansive thinking than going after ideas that make you more productive at your own job. If the ideas Elena picked up at the conference had only made her more productive, she still would not have reached the level of star initiative.

NOT MY JOB: LIVING IN THE WHITE SPACE

One of the foundations of American business in the twentieth century has been the job description, a document that proposes to detail the tasks and responsibilities of the person collecting a regular paycheck. But in the brainpowered workplace, job descriptions are becoming more of an anachronism each year.

Fewer and fewer positions are defined by what one person can accomplish in isolation. The increasingly complex, technically based products produced in our workplaces are beyond one person's knowledge capacity. Knowledge sharing and team interaction are essential.

Consider the telephone switches that connect your phone call to whomever you are calling. Every worker on that marvelous machine has a job description buried in a desk drawer somewhere, but the nature of the beast—so many gizmos, so many complex functions, so much sensitivity—requires a completely different orientation to the workplace. No engineer would be able to meet individual job description responsibilities without cooperation from colleagues.

Job descriptions are giving way to job spheres that can permeate other job spheres—think of them as soap bubbles—gently merging ideas, experience, and specific technical knowledge.

Taking initiative involves moving out of your own protective job description to bridge the spaces between job spheres. This bridging of spaces is more conventionally referred to as "managing the white space"—the areas poorly covered or not covered at all by job designations or the organizational chart (sometimes they're huge chasms). These white spaces exist in abundance in every organization, but the downsizing trend has caused them to expand. Brainpowered organizations are defined by white spaces, since so much is unknown—rapidly changing knowledge and technology, new competitors, and the impossibility of fully knowing what any job will eventually entail. To succeed, brainpowered businesses demand a workforce flexible enough to float from one job sphere to another.

When Kimby was hired as a human resources professional after completing her doctorate, her boss and colleagues had high expectations. They assumed she would fill in some of the white spaces created in a recent restructuring. But within the first few months, it became clear that Kimby took a very narrow view of her role. As a team in the department rushed to meet a tight deadline in developing a new training program, they asked her to take over the registration end of the program. Kimby balked at the request. It was clerical work, she said, not befitting the job description of an employee with a PhD. That didn't sit well with other team members, some of whom also had graduate degrees and job descriptions similar to hers.

In fact, coworkers noticed that Kimby only responded to assignments that came directly from her boss. Rather than becoming the sorely needed extra bridge across responsibilities, she was viewed as a stumbling block.

Those who willingly move out of their job description spheres to fill gaps are showing initiative. Yet our research offers an important qualifier: Stars don't let the job responsibilities that are specifically assigned to them slide in the pursuit of outside initiatives.

If the emergency room of a large metropolitan hospital has reported an alarming increase in the number of drug-addicted pregnant women brought in for treatment, the charge nurse does not put aside regular shift duties to take an initiative on the problem. His efforts to start a program to station drug counselors out in the waiting room close to the patients' families is done above and beyond the regular job sphere.

HELPING OTHERS OUT

A true initiative as practiced by the stars always ends up benefiting someone else—a group of coworkers, the department, or the entire company. It is true that by reflection, stars often end up benefiting themselves, but the primary emphasis is always on someone other than themselves.

Shannon, a mechanical engineer, was visiting a plant to solve a production problem on a new $8 million stamping machine. Over coffee in the lunchroom, she heard the plant engineer worrying aloud about a just-announced government safety inspection. That was a big problem, Shannon thought. She knew an internal company safety review was required every five years. But the plant engineer revealed that this facility hadn't done one in that time period. Worse yet, managers couldn't locate the report from the outdated last review. Managers were wringing their hands, the engineer told her, because there wasn't enough time to go through the normal inspection scheduling process at the company's headquarters.

"So I'm thinking to myself," Shannon reports, "this plant is up a creek without a paddle and so is the company. When the CEO finds out, this plant manager will be in a world of hurt. Even though he's only been here two years, he shouldn't have missed this. And the plant engineer shouldn't have missed it either."

What plant officials didn't know was that Shannon is a certified safety inspector, experienced in doing safety reviews. "They didn't know it, but I did. Even if they did know it, they couldn't expect me to do a review on the spot. It wasn't my job, and I had no responsibility for this plant. I was already doing them a favor by flying there to work on their downed machine. I could've just let them hang out to dry."

That might have been Kimby's view, but not Shannon's. She quickly called her boss to explain the problem and was given permission to stay on the extra week required to do the review. Then she made arrangements to have safety review materials delivered overnight.

"Before I knew it, the plant manager was down talking to me, saying whatever I needed, I'd get it. We did the review and, thank God, there were no big problems."

Shannon's initiative saved the plant considerable regulatory trouble, which would have included a record of violation and a hefty fine. The plant manager and engineer were off the hook, but perhaps most important, the workers were assured of a safe workplace. Everybody won. Problems were avoided and performance was enhanced across the board because of one visiting mechanical engineer's decision to initiate.

Clearly, Shannon had little to gain in the short term from her initiative, especially compared with everyone else involved. Sure, a glowing letter was placed in her personnel file. But in the long term, initiatives like these are what create the star aura.

Follow-Through: From Good Idea to Reality

A good idea is the best starting place for an initiative. Yet writing your boss a memo that merely spits out the good idea is not enough. Too often, average performers assume their responsibility ends with presenting the idea. It's now the boss's responsibility to do something about it.

Stars champion their initiatives by demonstrating their own personal commitment, their ownership. But they disagree on whether the initiator has to be responsible for the entire implementation. One star may opt for getting the ball rolling and then let another interested colleague take it over. Another may ask someone more persuasive to champion it from the very start. But they all agree that the initiator must be committed to seeing that it gets completed, rallying resources behind the idea, and getting people involved.

Implementation is the acid test of any initiative. But that doesn't mean that every initiative you undertake will be successful. No one expects that. It simply means that no one, including you, will know unless you try. The trying is what people expect, and the trying is the hard part.

Art Fry, a company veteran in engineering, had a new product idea for 3M, a company that made $15 billion in 1997, with over 50,000 items on the market. The 3M company prides itself on innovation, expecting 50 percent of revenues each year to come from products that didn't exist five years before. As a result, thousands of new product ideas are generated each year by 3M's workers. In 1974, Art Fry's was one in the pack, but no one wanted Art Fry's new idea. The marketing division told him customers didn't want it. Manufacturing told him that the product was impossible to make.

Although Bob Molenda, Fry's boss, liked the idea, he had been told to assign Fry to another project. But Fry and Molenda didn't cave in, follow orders, and forget about this idea. They didn't let it drop just because others wouldn't pick up on it. So on his own time, Fry, with Molenda's help, set about turning his idea into reality.

Fry had friends in a lab who let him experiment with different materials to build a prototype. Again through friends, he found a plant that would let him use an idle machine to do a short production run. With the prototype product in hand, he went back to marketing and manufacturing, but still ran into a brick wall.

Rather than give up, Fry started handing out his product within the company, asking people to try it out and to see if they could find uses for it. Within weeks, he was getting calls with glowing comments and requests for more. Fry and Molenda then took user comments and other research to the naysayers, gradually convincing them that the product could be one of the biggest sellers in the company's history. The birthing process of Post-it notepads was long and tortuous but the rewards are evident, as any household refrigerator, computer monitor, or wall phone will confirm.

After the fact, we tend to see successful initiatives as obvious, a sure bet. In the reaping of rewards, we often forget the struggles. Stars know all too well that just as much effort can go into failures. Overall, it is the effort that builds the worker's initiative reputation, as much as success or failure.

Risk Taking: Choosing the Right Initiatives

While much of this chapter has focused on the necessity of taking initiative in order to achieve star productivity, learning how to choose the right initiatives is another important mark of the stars.

The risks of taking initiative are twofold. First, there is the worry of making enemies, because you often upset the status quo when you initiate. For example, our Medicaid reimbursement hero, Kathleen Betts, had enough cognitive ability and technical experience to assume she was on the right track when she wrote a memo to her boss detailing the path to a possible windfall.

But closer analyses might have found a flaw. Worse, she might have been called on the carpet by a misanthropic manager who would rather bury a four-star initiative than see an underling get credit.

Sometimes, taking an initiative involves reaching out to correct what a coworker may be doing poorly, which carries its own set of risks in this regard.

Consider the touchy situation created by an initiative undertaken by Fernando, a star computer software programmer and a member of a three-person team employed to develop a new word-processing program.

Each member of the team is responsible for one aspect of the program, and down the road, merging his or her work into another facet of the program being developed by a second team.

After several sessions between the two teams, Fernando and his coworkers on Team I realize that a member of Team II, Ralph, the loner down the hall, the one with the black belt in karate who is prone to abrupt mood swings, has written a bunch of bugs into his program.

Two of the three programmers believe Ralph's work is Ralph's work. He should find the bugs and exterminate them himself. After all, they get enough grief in their own jobs, and all things considered, it would be very uncomfortable to go picking on the work of a different team member.

But Fernando is thinking way out of his job sphere to the point down the line when all the individual efforts are supposed to come together and harmonize. Instead, there are going to be some nasty bugs running amok in the system. Going back in to fix the problems at that point will be very expensive, and production will be delayed.

Fernando takes the initiative to go see Ralph in his cubicle. He begins his visit by complimenting Ralph on the fourteen karate tournament trophies displayed on a nearby table.

"Wow, all first place, huh? Very impressive," he says, swallowing hard. "Look, Ralph. I couldn't help but notice at that session the other day that there were a few minor bugs in your end of the program, and I thought I might point them out to you. Maybe you could handle it. Or we could go through it together and I could show you how I'd fix it."

At this point, Ralph could become defensive and angry, even running to management to force Team I to adapt its software code to his bugged-up program. Or Ralph could be relieved and grateful, all part of Fernando's risk in taking the initiative.

Star performers in our research who involved themselves in similarly uncomfortable initiatives were resolute about making sure the gap was bridged, even in the face of anger and wounded egos.

The second element of risk is that you put your personal reputation on the line both in the initiatives that you choose and in whether you succeed or fail.

Risk management, then, is an important element of initiative. To minimize these risks, you need to call upon the other star performer work strategies described in the following chapters. For example, organizational savvy, in Chapter 11, comes into play when you are trying to determine who might be opposed to your new idea. Likewise, having good perspective, from Chapter 7, can reduce the second risk of choosing the wrong initiative.

When the stars choose their initiatives, they take the following steps.

1. Do Your Current Assignment Well

As mentioned earlier, the stars always remember that their first obligation is to their assigned job. Like Kathleen Betts or Lai in our earlier examples, they never let new initiatives get in the way of basic chores. In the current economic climate, where most companies have been downsized or restructured, most workers are expected to do more with less. When considering a new initiative, the stars review their current commitments, which may already include some previous initiatives that are not yet complete. They avoid overcommitting.

2. Follow the Initiative Value Trail: Who Benefits?

As mentioned earlier, your initiative needs to have some payoff for someone other than you. For Art Fry at 3M, it was the larger company and customers. For Shannon, who did the impromptu safety review, it was her colleagues. For Fernando, the software programmer who confronted Ralph, it was the larger project. If there is nothing in it for someone besides you, don't call it an initiative.

3. Stay Close to the Critical Path

Most companies evaluate an initiative by how well it improves the flow on what I refer to as the critical path—the line that moves all the efforts of workers and managers toward a delighted customer, where, in turn, profitability and increased shareholder value are sent back down the path. For example, sales and manufacturing are closer to the critical path than the company's cafeteria or facilities management. Initiatives that are closer to the critical path are generally better.

Profitability, in its most fundamental sense, results from efforts either to reduce costs or to increase revenues. No matter which department you are in, these are good places to enter the critical path. Determine how your initiative will affect costs, revenues, or overall profitability and package it under that banner.

Let's start with costs.

Patrick Sinner, a twenty-eight-year-old real estate credit supervisor in the Corporate Banking Program at PNC Bank, described his initiative as "just being a careful observer of problems that were falling through the cracks" and then stepping in to fix them.

For Sinner, the problem was sitting on the desk of nearly every brainpowered worker at PNC's corporate headquarters in Pittsburgh, and the solution was as simple as turning off a light. For months, he had been among the last people to leave his department each night, and the routine would be the same: He would pass row after row of personal computers, all left switched on, all sucking up electricity long after their human operators had gone home.

His back-of-the-envelope calculations factored in the number of personal computers throughout the bank, the amount of electricity each uses, the cost of that electricity for sixteen hours of non-use time, and the estimated total electric bill for the bank over a year's time. In researching his initiative, upper managers waved him away at first under the assumption that he didn't realize shutting down computers slightly decreases the life of some components. But Sinner, then a recent MBA graduate, discovered that most large business computer systems were retired as obsolete long before they showed the effects of nightly shutdowns.

The bottom line was an annual savings to the bank of $268,000.

Sinner's effort is the crown jewel in a two-year-old effort, the Open Line Process Improvement Program, designed to institutionalize initiative in the bank's culture.

Sinner's $268,000 savings might not seem like much for a major money bank. But remember the big-bang trap referred to earlier: Small, successful initiatives undertaken over time can mean as much in productivity gain as one large flash-in-the-pan effort. Moreover, any effort on the cost side gets leveraged when put in the context of revenues needed to have the same impact on profits. For example, IBM estimated that if every one of its 400,000 employees had one idea each year that saved the company only $1,000, the total savings would be $4 million. It would take over $2.4 billion in new revenues to match that amount. In that context, Sinner's cost-saving efforts are enormous indeed, requiring almost $2 million in new revenues to have the same impact on the bank's profitability.

Some initiatives require intuitive leaps. Yumi, a new engineer at Hitachi, was on a plant orientation program. Although plant rotation is not common in large Japanese companies, she worked for short periods—six months to eighteen months—in different factories as an entry-level worker, even though she had an engineering degree from Purdue. One of Yumi's assignments landed her in a small industrial town as a line worker in a silicon-wafer fabrication plant that made computer chips.

This plant had a big problem. Its rate of defective products was 20 percent higher than that of any other plant. Hitachi had sent their best quality-control team to study the situation, but they had come up empty-handed. The stakes were high. Since there is no secondary market for defective chips, Hitachi was considering shuttering their $30 million investment rather than risk losing customers dissatisfied with the plant's output.

On most mornings, Yumi, like most of her coworkers, pedaled her way to work. One morning, she got stopped by a speeding train that ran in front of the plant. As she waited next to her bike for the train to pass, she noticed the vibration from the train travel up the handle bars into her hands. She quickly pedaled to the train station and grabbed a train schedule.

At her workstation on the production line, she watched the clock as the 10:00 A.M. train was due. Then she felt the equipment for signs of vibration as the train arrived and departed—9:45, 9:50, 9:55, 9:58, 9:59, 10:00, 10:05. She couldn't feel anything. Yumi repeated her experiment several times over the next three days. Sometimes she thought she felt something but wasn't sure.

Yumi worried about her less-than-solid research and her position as a guest worker, but she still summoned the courage to pass her hunch on to the plant manager. He was skeptical, but he saw no harm in passing it on to the corporate quality engineers, and they attacked the problem with sensitive vibration-detection equipment. Still nothing.

Undeterred, Yumi researched vibration problems on her own time. She discovered that some low-level vibrations cannot be distinguished from the earth's natural movements, yet they can have very profound effects. When this kind of vibration is suspected, Yumi learned, the cheapest and most efficient way to solve the problem is to use water as a buffer. If the company would build a moat between the railroad tracks and the plant, the water would absorb the shock—if, that is, the train vibrations were the problem and if she could convince management. Big ifs indeed.

Yumi first set out to convince her coworkers. Yes, she was new, she told them, but she had this hunch. Were there any better ideas to keep the plant from being closed and disrupting the entire community both within the plant walls and in the town, which depended on the plant?

Work-group members decided they had nothing to lose and brought it up to the supervisor over beers during one of their frequent night staff outings. They badgered him with questions: What would become of the plant and their jobs if they didn't find a solution to the defect problem? Building a moat wouldn't cost that much, especially if they chipped in to help—would it? It could be done on the weekend so it wouldn't interfere with their work schedules—couldn't it?

Finally the supervisor agreed to approach upper management. They bought the cost/benefit argument and agreed to build the moat—on the weekend and with the plant chipping in the manual labor.

The defect problem disappeared almost overnight. The plant was saved, all because Yumi took a critical path initiative well beyond her job as a production worker and saw it through.

This is not an isolated example that could happen only in Japan. After hearing the story of Yumi's initiative in one of my speeches, several Intel executives said one of their chip plants had nearly an identical problem—it was located too near a freeway. It was a line worker who bested Intel's quality-control experts and played the same hunch as Yumi. His initiative also saved the plant and hundreds of Intel jobs.

Cost reduction, then, is one important lane on the critical path. Increasing revenues is the other, exemplified by the initiatives taken by Art Fry at 3M, Kathleen Betts in Massachusetts state government, and Elena with the auto ceramics supplier. All three increased revenues and had a significant impact on the bottom line. These critical path efforts led to star performance reputations.

4. Choose Higher-Level Initiatives

When you start taking initiatives as a new employee, like Lai, you generally start out small, doing local initiatives that benefit your coworkers. Seldom do these efforts transfer immediately to the bottom line.

As you gain more experience, you need to consider moving from "horizontal" to "vertical" initiatives. Horizontal initiatives involve taking on a number of initiatives in the same category. If Lai offered to install the next new software or to do more of the graveyard-shift testing sessions, she would be practicing horizontal initiative taking. But within two years on the job, our research shows, star performers' initiatives begin to move vertically. Rather than solving a local problem, star performers begin to look for systemic problems. This higher-level systems perspective enables them to solve a whole set of similar problems throughout the entire system.

Ryan worked in the back-office accounting department of a large grocery chain in the Pacific Northwest. Short and bespectacled, Ryan looked the part of a bean counter. But his star actions were far from the stereotype of a rule-bound, inside-the-box accountant.

One of his department's primary responsibilities was to record and prepare for the bank the thousands of checks that came from stores in his region. Because the work was done by hand, it was boring and time-consuming. "There's got to be a better way," Ryan thought.

Ryan went to the local bank to study their end of the store's check-processing operation and discovered that the grocery store cashed and processed almost as many checks as the bank itself. His grocery chain was effectively running a limited financial institution within its stores.

Armed with this information, Ryan proposed several initiatives. First, he recommended installing state-of-the-art check-processing technology throughout the grocery chain. This solved the problem not just for his area but for every region in the chain. It also saved the grocery chain money, because it increased accuracy, got the checks cashed faster, which improved cash flow back into the business, and reduced labor costs.

But Ryan also proposed that the grocery chain open up a savings-and-loan business in each store. His rationale was that the stores had already captured a market of customers in the habit of cashing their weekly checks in the store. Why not capitalize on the convenience they already offered shoppers by letting them deposit those checks?

Ryan's other rationale for the S&L was rooted in check cashing. Since they already had a back-office operation similar to a bank, they shouldn't pay the bank an additional processing fee for handling their checks a second time. They could handle it all in house, eliminating bank costs.

Ryan did all the necessary research to sell his S&L idea. As part of the team assigned to develop a proposed implementation plan, he was able to influence how it came on line. The S&L quickly became one of the largest in the state by focusing on the financial needs of grocery shoppers from a wide area. Its check-processing operation became so efficient that a number of small local banks and S&Ls contracted out their back-office operations to the grocery chain, creating another profit center.

Ryan's initiatives captured the higher-level systems perspective by going from local to corporate-wide optimization. He solved a check-cashing problem pervasive in the chain, he tied it to the critical path, and he turned his local problem into global profit-making opportunities for the grocery company.

5. Determine the Probability of Success and the Cost of Failure

Before taking an initiative, star performers calculate the odds. Can they afford the time and energy to take it on? Can they deliver? What will happen to others—customers, colleagues, the company—if they do not take the initiative? What are the consequences to them and to others of success or failure? How can they stack the odds in their favor?

Every organization has its own tolerance level for failure. Some organizations forgive small misses but react harshly over major initiatives that fall through. So you can fail on low-level initiatives as long as you hit on all cylinders on the high-profile ones. For other organizations, their failure tolerance is close to zero, which substantially chills initiative and risk taking. So before you take an initiative, you need to know the lay of your organization's land.

The stars often use the critical path as their divining rod. When Art Fry realized that his new product could be worth billions of dollars in revenue for 3M, he determined it was worth the risk even though the odds weren't in his favor. Given a much smaller potential impact, he might have determined that it wasn't worth risking his time or reputation.

Our research has found that people who are known to take and follow through on lots of initiatives are allowed more failures than people who rarely take initiative. If you have a reputation for always going the extra mile, then your colleagues tend to be more forgiving.

Next, the stars often start out their bigger, higher-level initiatives in smaller, more private settings. They want to nurture the idea before it hits the harsh public spotlight. If it turns out to be a clunker, they can abort with minimum notice.

Once they do go public with an initiative, stars seek support from others. This commitment often means the difference between success and failure.

Finally, the stars know when to cut their losses. Sometimes a good idea on its face turns out to be a bad idea when explored more fully. Occasionally, even a good idea can't find an audience and has to be put on the back burner for another day. When, despite their best efforts, they realize an initiative is no longer worth pursuing, they pull the plug as gracefully as possible. Rather than throw more resources at a losing proposition, they move on to the next idea that has a high probability of payoff. "Control your ego and get back on the critical path," a star engineer at 3M told me. "It's all about adding value, not crying over spilled milk."

A Final Word About Initiative

In our early productivity improvement programs, we would marvel at the number of superintelligent, motivated, experienced engineers who would ask depressingly classic average-performer questions, such as "Do you need to come up with initiatives yourself or does your supervisor assign them to you? Why isn't what I did an initiative? Is taking initiative more important than doing your job?"

Every brainpowered workplace has its own variation on the initiative theme, and it is crucial that workers be familiar with their employer's version. Star performers have a keen sense of how initiative is defined in the workplace, not only by managers but also by their peers. But given the complicated tasks that need to be performed each day in the brainpowered workplace, there are dozens of opportunities to take on initiatives. The stars in this area don't just point and run wherever they see a need, they choose wisely. They also learn quickly to work more efficiently in their own jobs to have time to pursue initiatives.

The professional who becomes adept at taking initiatives learns quickly that efforts don't need to be brilliant to have impact. In receiving her award from state officials, Kathy Betts humbly referred to her personal initiatives as "just taking the first step and then . . . finding a solution."

5

KNOWING WHO KNOWS
Plugging into the Knowledge Network

Before Bill Backer ran one of the most successful advertising companies in the world, he was a brainpowered worker in someone else's firm.

He was a star producer early on and his creative talent is legendary. One of the most successful ad campaigns in history came about when the young copywriter-lyricist, flying to London for client meetings, was pinned down in Ireland's Shannon Airport by the country's infamous fog.

Backer noticed early in the day's stranding that his fellow passengers, a veritable United Nations of cultures and races, were foul-tempered and distant. But as the hours wore on, passengers began gathering at tiny tables in the airport cafeteria. Cups of coffee and tea were poured; bottles of Coke were passed around. The sour moods began to soften.

Soon, those who had had little interest in mixing with one another were sharing wallet photos and exchanging business cards.

Warm conversation took over, and by the time the flight left at dusk for Heathrow, many of the passengers had become friends.

Backer, who just happened to have been assigned to write some commercial song lyrics for one of his firm's top clients, the Coca Cola Company, turned that business-trip disaster into a creative spark. Out came a pad of note paper, and he began scribbling lyrics.

The scene in the tiny airport cafeteria became the inspiration for the world-famous "I'd Like to Teach the World to Sing" commercial.

But Backer, experienced in moving a basic creative idea to full-throttle advertising campaign, knew the "Buy the World a Coke" lyrics were only the beginning. Even with a powerful creative spark, much of his productivity was tied to a slew of coworkers and colleagues who had little to do with the creative concept. Each one, however, had a specialty Backer needed in order to move his Coke song from notebook scrawl to prime-time TV commercial.

In his book, *The Care and Feeding of Ideas*, Backer devotes an entire chapter to what he calls the "idea family," which is another name for a well-defined resource network, a relationship tree of "many different kinds of people representing many different skills and interests." Backer's network members were attached to one another by choice, through mutual admiration of one another's talents and a willingness to share skills inside the group.

Back in 1971, when the "Buy the World a Coke" campaign was created, Backer's sense of networking as crucial to productive work was ahead of its time. Indeed, writing about that period from the perspective of a retired ad agency owner in the 1990s, he wondered if the campaign would have survived in today's global, information-churning economy without a much larger network.

The stakes certainly are higher. The move from regionally based to national and international manufacturing has made the work of pitching products massive, more complex, and multidimensional. Where companies routinely spend as much money on a one-year soft drink campaign as state governments spend to educate children, the pressure is intense. New, high-technology communications media offer more choices but also make the work more interdisciplinary. The big clients demand more services and greater expertise for the fortunes they're laying out, and only the giants of the industry can provide the varied employee talents to meet that demand.

In the 1990s, the critical path in most businesses—taking a concept from creative inspiration to client approval to successful production to bottom-line profitability—is more demanding than ever. No one individual, nor even a ten-member team, has all the expertise needed to do the job.

The insight that put Backer ahead of the curve in the 1970s—that creative sparks fizzle without the kindling of a rich network to light the production fire—is necessary just to keep pace in the 1990s.

Networking, more than any other skill in the star performer model, can have dramatic impact on the speed, quality, and quantity of your output. Without a high-quality network, you are unlikely to become a star performer. With one securely in place, you can leverage your knowledge base and give it a tremendous boost.

None know the value of this more than those shut out of the process. A recent survey of 461 of the country's top women executives by Catalyst, a nonprofit women's research organization, found that "exclusion from informal networks of communication" came in second—picked by 49 percent of those surveyed—just behind "male stereotyping and preconceptions of women" as the chief barrier in advancement to the very highest corporate officer positions. Significantly, only 15 percent of 325 male chief executives surveyed rated lack of entry to networks as something women should be concerned about. Why would women rate network access so highly and CEOs give it low concern? Often, the wiring is so intricate, so basic to the work lives of the top executives that they don't realize what networks accomplish for them and their employees each day.

THE KNOWLEDGE DEFICIT: KNOWING WHAT YOU DON'T KNOW

It's an uncomfortable question, but I've been posing it anyway to audiences of brainpowered workers in our training program for years:

What percentage of the knowledge you need to do your job is stored in your own mind? Or put another way: What percentage of your time do you spend reaching out to someone or something else for knowledge that is essential for you to get your job done? Do you know how much you don't know?

In 1986, the average answer from responses to surveys or hands in the air at group seminars was that most people had about 75 percent in their heads. In recent years, the percentage has dropped 15 to 20 points, and in the case of one company I worked with recently, it had fallen as low as 10 percent!

Managers seeing these responses presented in such stark terms worry that their workforce will be judged deficient or ill trained, or that blunt questions will be asked about the hiring process.

The stark reality is that individual brainpowered workers and individual companies suffer from a "knowledge-deficit problem." There is much they need to know to get their jobs done well. Knowledge networks are one crucial way that star performers overcome their knowledge deficits. *Networks are the high-speed infrastructure upon which knowledge is sent and received by those who need it. Without these networks, professionals cannot do their jobs, and companies might just as well shutter their doors.*

But it's not the workforce that's causing the brain drain. To paraphrase a well-worn line from the 1992 presidential election campaign, *It's the knowledge economy, stupid!*

Many observers blame the flow of new technology—from a trickle in the 1970s to a gusher in the current economy—as responsible for much of the workforce knowledge deficit.

In fact, the overflow goes beyond technology. Other contributing causes include the elevated rate of new knowledge production and distribution media for this knowledge, the knowledge loss due to downsizing, and the rise of more complex and interdisciplinary projects.

For starters, important information is spilling out from an ever-increasing number of sources. Experts estimate that more knowledge has been produced in the twentieth century than in all preceding history. While brainpowered workers need much of that information to be more productive in their jobs, not even the best of them can absorb it all on their own.

For millennia, new knowledge only spread through people-to-people contact. Then came books, letters, and newspapers. These were followed by telegraph, telephones, and radio. Today we have twenty-four-hour bombardment via 500-channel satellite and cable TV, millions of Internet websites, video conferencing, thousands of special-interest magazines and journals, and countless fee-based information-retrieval services. Combine all these vehicles for knowledge distribution with the faster pace of new knowledge creation and you have the perfect recipe for information overload.

Networking channels the flood of information into manageable streams and allows participants to pick and choose what they need as the demands of the moment require.

Much of the work done in a brainpowered, global economy is interdisciplinary. Where before an accountant only worked with other accountants, today she will be on teams with people from marketing, production, and research. To become a value-added contributor, she needs a much broader base of knowledge outside her own specialty.

Similarly, an advertising agency that might have done just fine in the 1970s with TV, radio, and print staffs can't survive in the 1990s without experts on the Internet or specialists in foreign cultures. The computer memory chip builders who were able to do well with a staff limited to computer scientists, programmers, and marketers now are adding biologists and chemists, on the premise that a future generation of chip may have more than an electronic base.

Networks, then, act as a kind of informal, highly customized, personal "knowledge business yellow pages," providing a handy expert to fill in the brainpowered worker's knowledge gap.

Another facet of the brainpowered economy contributing to the knowledge deficit is downsizing. Those who survive in companies that have undergone significant cuts in the workforce are expected to do more with less. They assimilate jobs that were once the full-time responsibility of others. Or the increased workload is juggled by teams of workers who are assigned to massive projects. Even those cut out of one workplace by the downsizing ax expect to be working longer hours with a heavier workload in their next job.

The final knowledge deficit creator has to do with the nature of work in a brainpowered economy. The smart observers know that brainpowered work is more ambiguous, more complex, and more problem-plagued. Meanwhile, the projects at which it is directed are larger and more interdisciplinary.

A safety engineer for a major airline, for instance, realizes that most of the easily identifiable flaws in plane parts that could cause a crash have already been detected. With the "low-hanging fruit" already picked, future progress is going to require more painstaking work and a broader base of skills. Instead of the huge leaps of twenty-five years ago, strides in safety improvement will be measured in smaller incremental steps requiring exponential knowledge from a range of disciplines. Long-term goals will not be so easily identified.

In order to be more productive, you need to be aware of the changes that have produced knowledge deficits. But just as important, you need to become adept at knowing what you don't know. Only then can you begin the beneficial work of closing the knowledge gap.

NETWORKING: THE CRITICAL PATH GOES FROM MULE TRAIL TO AUTOBAHN

This Arabic proverb of centuries ago must have been written in prophetic anticipation of the plight of today's brainpowered workers:

> The best possible situation in life, the saying goes, is to know that you know. The second-best is to know what you don't know. The third-best: to not know that you know. The worst situation is to not know that you don't know.

It's an excellent model for the types of knowledge-intensive jobs we're focused on here, and it's form-fitted to the behaviors of the star producers we studied. Invariably, it was the stars who had a better grasp of the pieces of information they needed to do their jobs, and it was the average performers who spent varying amounts of precious work time wallowing in the bottom category—not knowing what they didn't know.

So once brainpowered workers recognize where the gaps are, how do they go about closing them?

Katy is a senior associate attorney tapped by the partners in her large law firm to set up a new unit specializing in issues of copyright law on the Internet. There are good reasons why management chose her. She's bright and well grounded in the basics of copyright law; she's self-directed and disciplined and she knows what it takes to meet a challenge.

But Katy has a problem: she has no experience with the Internet. What are her options?

From our research, we know a professional like Katy would consider one of two paths:

- *Do-It-Herself* Katy delays setting up the unit by six months while she takes computer science classes at a local university. Or she may do a quickie self-study, where she crams just enough information on Internet workings and culture to enable her to set up the special unit and get the door open for clients.
- *Work a Network* Katy identifies law school professors teaching or writing about the Internet, she digs up in-house attorneys at companies providing Internet services, or she locates computer law experts at noncompeting law firms in other cities. She gathers the best ideas from this network, combines it with her own expertise on copyright law, and develops a plan to build the new unit.

This first option is frequently the path of choice for average performers. While it's the worst option for maximizing productivity, it does follow the educational and societal patterns of behavior pumped into most of us in our formative years.

The earliest school experiences demand self-reliance in completing projects and in problem solving. That's a worthy concept, but the educational system historically has failed to recognize the value of sharing knowledge and leaning on others. In fact, many education systems have failed to keep up with the fundamental changes in how work is done.

Instead of valuing networks, the education process shuns them. If you have to ask someone else for help, you're being lazy and not developing your own skills. If you adopt and build on the ideas of others, you're cheating.

Extended into the working world, the do-it-yourself syndrome is just as pervasive. Some company cultures foster the "Not Invented Here" (NIH) syndrome, which leads to a "If-it-wasn't-done-here-then-it's-full-of-holes" attitude that discourages employees from building on what already has been done.

If Katy, our under-the-gun attorney, is a star performer, she's long since recognized these schoolhouse dicta as nonsense, and she's pulled onto the networking highway. She has an extended list of sources to help close her Internet knowledge deficit quickly, beating out the other options in both effectiveness and efficiency.

But even when average performers finally come around to understand the effectiveness of networking, there are sharp differences between their methods and those of their superproductive coworkers.

NETWORKS OF THE STARS: THREE DEGREES OF SEPARATION

Decades before the 1990 hit Broadway play *Six Degrees of Separation*, there was the Small World Theory, which posited that on average, only three intermediaries would be required to connect any two people in the world. But how quickly two people could be connected would depend on how carefully the connectors were chosen.

Star performers have recognized a version of this in the networking infrastructure they create to deal with the inevitable knowledge deficits and traffic knots that slow progress on the critical path.

They're asking the question, "What is the fastest route to get the information I need, and who are the people I need to go through to connect with the person who has the best information?"

Claudio, a management consultant working for Andersen Consulting, was assigned to write a proposal to land a $500,000 contract to provide information-technology support for bio-assaying processes used in biotech firms. Under a tight deadline, Claudio had to gather as much information as he could on bio-assaying processes in a short amount of time.

He remembered an undergraduate classmate who had gone to work for Genentech, the industry leader, and called her. She, in turn, put him in touch with the scientist who pioneered the assaying process. In just two afternoon phone calls, he was able to get the critical information for his report.

Compare Claudio's experience with that of his Andersen colleague Newt, who needed the same information. Instead of thinking through his network, Newt used a typical Andersen procedure to post his question on the in-house electronic bulletin board. When Newt logged into his computer the next work day, forty different leads were waiting. Then came the time-consuming chore of plowing through the messages to find the best prospects. Many of the offered answers contradicted one another. Since he didn't know any of the people who responded, Newt couldn't judge the quality of their answers. He was essentially still at square one, with forty potential leads to track down.

While Newt was still struggling with his information overload, Claudio had used his star network to move faster and farther down the critical path.

The current rage in many upper-management circles is to embrace computer "intranetting" as the high-tech solution to knowledge deficits. Managers spend millions of dollars on additional computer hardware and software, believing brainpowered workers like Newt can e-mail their way out of their knowledge deficit quandaries.

But successful networking is most often accomplished in one-to-one interactions, not in the one-to-many impersonal format of computer technology. Star networking requires learning how to build, maintain, and operate within a group of experts who share knowledge for mutual benefit. It has little to do with technology. Although star networkers will use computers, it is the human touch that makes or breaks your network. Many still operate face-to-face and by phone.

The human interactive quality of star networks often separates successful firms, like Bill Backer's ad agency, from their middle-of-the-road counterparts. Hicks Muse, an extremely successful Dallas investment firm, credits its competitive edge to the knowledge networks its stars have put in place. They often get the inside track on potential deals through outside accountants, lawyers, and insurance people from past projects. It was Hicks Muse's insurance broker who tipped them off that San Francisco's Ghirardelli Chocolate Company was for sale. Hicks Muse quickly put together a $65 million buyout package before others in the industry were even aware the firm was on the block. By getting in the door before other investment firms, Hicks Muse brokers shaped the deal at a better price and for better payoff down the road. "Ghirardelli could have turned into a bidding war or an opportunity we didn't even get to see at all," said John Muse. The outside professionals who tipped them off benefited by getting to be part of the deal.

A venture capitalist attributed her firm's shrewd evaluations of emerging technologies to crack networking teams. This star deal-maker calls upon her network of scientists—world-class researchers who sit on the board of directors of other companies that the venture capitalist has a major stake in. With a few well-placed phone calls, she can determine whether the new technology is worth an investment.

Networking Fundamentals

Star performer networks differ from average versions of networks in two fundamental ways. First, they are better, meaning that the quality of knowledge providers in their networks is much higher than in those maintained by average performers.

Most college students using computers for the first time in one of our required class projects will often get stuck on a machine problem and search for help. Early on in the course, they have no basis to discriminate when seeking help from classmates. Often, they turn to the person sitting closest to them—a risky strategy, since physical proximity is no guarantee of expertise. Invariably, they end up wasting time with a well-meaning but computer-clueless neighbor, dragging down the productivity of both.

The more productive students learn from that experience, and when faced with another computer glitch, spend more time searching out the students in class who have computer skills. They create a network of computer wizards who can give them the right answer the first time.

Second, star networks operate much faster, meaning that the response time from their high-quality experts is dramatically less than that from the sources for the average coworkers. Anecdotal time estimates collected during my work indicate that for every hour it takes a star performer to get an answer through her network, the average performer will wait three to five hours.

Let's return to our law firm star producer, Katy, and introduce her counterpart at another law firm across town, Rob. He is given the same assignment as Katy: Start a unit dealing with copyright law on the Internet. Let's assume that both attorneys are the same in all respects except the quality and turn-around time of their networks.

As they begin the assignment, they move down the critical path at exactly the same speed and get stuck at exactly the same spot, and they turn to a source network at exactly the same time. Thus far, it has been an even competition, but now the networking engines take over.

Katy has gone out and developed excellent sources of Internet-savvy academics at top law schools to help her with the technical issues. With a few phone calls, she has broken through her critical path barrier in about an hour.

Rob, however, is stuck on an 800-line call tree at the Internet service provider used by the law firm. He waits fifty minutes to connect with a service technician but gets none of the legal-tech expertise needed to solve his problem. He pulls out of that blind alley and heads in another direction while Katy is cruising down the critical path. Chances are that Rob will lose from three to five precious hours before he gets back on track.

Katy and Rob are an even match for the 60 percent of knowledge from their own brainpower, but Rob's network is no match for Katy's when it comes to closing the 40 percent knowledge deficit they face on their new assignment.

While Rob's thin, time-draining network may not significantly affect his productivity over the course of one work week, its debilitating effects will be striking over a month's time and will probably cost him success on the project over the course of a year.

What results between Katy and Rob is a variation on financial compound-interest problems. Katy's lead just keeps growing bigger and bigger as time goes on. A well-placed network source will yield many times the original investment. The results are all too clear when Katy is billing enough hours to bring on an associate, while the managing partner at Rob's firm is beginning to ask a lot of questions.

The critical component of a star performer's network is the package of personal skills used to build valuable sources. In addition to the skills detailed in this chapter, there are supporting factors that are often evident in a first-rate network:

- *The knowledge itself*—high-quality information retained by experts and dispensed to members of the network. Both donor and recipient are making judgments in the context of the network: what is important and what is not.
- *Organizational support*—a top-down recognition that networking is valued. There will be skills-training programs, time allowed in the workday for employees to cultivate their individual networks, opportunities for employees to attend conferences and seminars to build on existing sources, and rewards for those whose networking contributes to the firm's success. At the same time, there is restraint in attempting to institutionalize private networks.
- *Technical/physical environment*—Workers who are most apt to share information and be players in a network are often in close physical or psychological proximity to one another in the workplace. Communications systems like e-mail are employed to help cultivate networks, but again, the network members determine the conduits, not managers. When companies strive to take control of employee networks, members often burrow underground. They go through the motions of using a company-mandated network, but they rely on an informal one operating beyond management's scope.

SKILLS OF THE STARS: THE EIGHT NETWORK NODES

So how does our average attorney, Rob, beef up his emaciated network? And what does he do once he gets access to real experts, the people who can deliver high-quality information?

There is a series of skills that top producers employ in their networks. I refer to them here as nodes, in the sense of important points of concentration. While some of these may seem simple or "commonsense" on the surface, it is the *expert manner* in which they are used that spells the difference between productivity and lackluster performance.

Node I: Mental Models of Networking

Star producers recognize a critical point about their network at the outset: Different members have different ideas about how the network is supposed to work for them. We refer to these as individual mental models of the network. While the star makes an effort to understand these models, the average performer doesn't bother. When the performance of the network is measured, the differences are astounding.

For example, many average performers see knowledge as a free public resource. Taking a telemarketing approach, they call anyone in the company phone book and expect to be accommodated (usually with unproductive results, however). Stars seldom assume that fellow employees in the same company are required to make themselves available to coworkers to impart valuable information. In the star's mental model, knowledge is not a public resource and access to it is not a basic right; it's a privilege that must be earned.

Claude, a middle manager for a very large insurance company, learned about mental models the hard way. He was in a new position, assigned to a nine-month project analyzing the company's future liabilities. Claude needed up-to-date actuarial information to prepare his report, so he asked his secretary to track down the person in charge of the section where this information was collected. When the secretary finally located the person, Claude picked up the phone only to get the source's VoiceMail. He left a message explaining who he was and that he needed the actuarial information. In closing, he added, "I'm in a hurry, so can you get it to me by lunch?" Then he hung up.

It was well after lunch when Faye, the actuary Claude was trying to reach, heard his message. It was sandwiched in with the fifteen other callers trying to reach her that morning while she was making a presentation to top managers. Since Faye had no idea who Claude was and she was *not* the one responsible for the numbers he needed, she turned to more pressing requests on her phone list.

For Claude, the afternoon came and went with no data forthcoming. He was back on the phone to Faye at 5:15 P.M. and managed to get through. "I left you a message that I needed the data in a hurry," Claude said fuming. "Now, where is it? Do I have to go to your boss?"

"Who is this jerk?" Faye thought. But on the phone, she was

cool and professional. "I'm sorry, but I don't have the information you're looking for," she said. "That's not in my area."

"Why didn't you call and tell me that?" Claude sputtered.

"Because I've got a job that needs to be done too, and I don't know you from Adam."

Calming slightly, Claude asked who Faye would recommend he call to get the information he needed.

Faye knew that Len, a coworker in a nearby office, could supply the statistics he needed, but she also knew it would take a lot of time and effort on Len's part. She decided to protect him from this turkey named Claude. "Gee, I'm not really sure who would be able to deliver on that," Faye said. "If there is anything you need from my area, just call back and I'll try to help."

Claude had just been thrown on the slippery slope to networking hell.

As soon as she finished talking to Claude, Faye was out of her office and heading down the hall to warn Len. She found him with three other stars of the actuarial department, and she replayed her phone conversation for the group, recounting how Claude broke several networking rules: his general rudeness, how he tried to force his way into the network, how he demanded when he should have asked, and how he made huge demands without even so much as an introduction.

With a shake of their heads in disbelief, these star actuaries each decided on their own to have as few dealings as possible with this character. With two clumsy phone calls, Claude was effectively locked out of an extremely valuable network.

The next morning, Len picked up the phone to call a friend who works in Claude's department. Claude, it turns out, is known as a willing taker of coworkers' time and talents but tends to be slow returning such favors.

Later, Len urged Faye to call Claude back and pass along his name, just to cover herself. But if Claude followed through, Len planned to beg off for a week or two, complaining about his heavy workload. If pushed, he planned to force Claude through the section's chain of command. Claude had been effectively frozen out. His report would either be delayed or would lack the critical analysis.

These star actuaries are guilty of indulging in some petty and unprofessional behavior that may hurt the company's overall effectiveness. But they are also true to form in the way most technical networks operate. They are justifiably suspicious of someone like Claude and are trying to avoid him without making a scene. Although Claude may think his report is more important than nourishing the network, the star performers understand the network is a critical personal and community infrastructure that must be carefully maintained.

Claude has a mistaken mental model of the network—how it operates and what constitutes acceptable behavior. As a consequence, his productivity will suffer.

A more accepted mental model of the stars is to visualize their networks operating as an economic barter system. In a brainpowered economy, knowledge is the currency of choice, and it is traded around just as goods and services are exchanged in the world economy. To be part of such a network, you have to have something worth trading in order to attract trading partners.

The first skill star performers demonstrate early on is the ability to establish some kind of expertise—a specialty area that will be of value to others by reducing their knowledge deficits. They will look around to see what important knowledge deficits exist in the department and which ones they can help fill.

When Dariko joined a pharmaceutical firm researching the genetic structure of diseases like AIDS and diabetes, she was just another young biology PhD graduate. Few of the experienced researchers would give her the time of day, and those who did treated her like an apprentice. Dariko realized the importance of establishing a niche for herself—getting a reputation in one area and being accepted by the group. She searched for ways to contribute that would give her access to the company's stars. The area that seemed most promising was the department's skill base. She did a careful survey and discovered that the company wasn't using the latest statistical tools in its research.

When she first suggested applying her computational-mathematics background to the project, no one paid much attention. But when she successfully used it to ferret out different contributing genes that had eluded her more experienced colleagues, heads started to turn. Soon, Dariko's day was filled with coworkers asking for help in applying her mathematical models to their projects.

Through computational mathematics, Dariko had created her initial networking currency. Now other researchers had a self-interested reason to share information when she called.

Many stars trade with a shrewd sense of cost and benefit. They choose their network "trade partners" by comparing the time and quality of information imparted with what they receive. Those who are seeking entry to the network for the first time may get generous consideration at the outset, but if they don't prove themselves quickly in terms of their own value, they'll be screened out.

Node II: Weed and Seed

The second skill area where stars excel is in a shrewd ability to choose their trading partners—identifying qualified knowledge givers and making them part of their network.

Tim, a star producer in the computer-engineering section of a large software company, is taking copious notes at weekly staff meetings and occasional product seminars. His colleagues can't imagine why he needs to pay attention to such mundane subject matter, but Tim's focus isn't on the agenda. He's evaluating the participants—those who handle issues well in discussions, those who seem to have special expertise in a given area, those who come across with less flash and more substance.

While his average coworkers are watching the clock and wishing the meeting over, Tim is making up his dream-team list—identifying the favored few whose networks he will make a point to join, or who he will invite into his.

Another tool Tim uses to identify worthwhile network sources is the seeking out of other stars: "When you need quick information on digital signal processor semiconductors, whom do you talk to?" he will ask coworkers. As Tim's interests and assignments change, so do members of his network of sources.

Experts, by virtue of their high value in networks, are sought after by many more colleagues than they can possibly accommodate. Average performers are more likely to be weeded out or given short shrift because they haven't laid the personal groundwork necessary to establish connection and value.

Node III: Proactive One-Way Trading

The worst time to be building your network is when you need it to work for you now. Star performers try to get their networks in place well before they might ever need them. Star performers who have identified a sought-after expert and want to assimilate that person into their network have mastered the skill of proactive, one-way giving long before they need to be on the receiving end. They build bridges to these experts by being helpful to them.

This critical relationship-cultivation skill is usually scaled down from work-related issues to the personal.

Let's assume our two cyber-law attorneys, Katy and Rob, are both still desperately searching to close their knowledge gaps on cyberspace law issues. Both have left a phone message with an esteemed law professor at a local university, but Katy had made a point two months before to attend his lecture at a state bar association conference. She had introduced herself at the reception afterward, asked questions about his lecture, and as the conversation expanded, learned that he had a passion for science fiction novels. A week after the conference, she had sent him a note with a copy of a soon-to-be-published legal brief written by a software trade association that she had uncovered during her research, along with a newspaper article about a local lecture series featuring a famous science fiction writer.

Rob, on the other hand, has never met the professor, and his phone message doesn't even include the name of a mutual contact as a referral.

So as the professor rushes into his office from teaching class, with several students waiting in the hallway for conferences, he hurriedly checks his watch and flips through the dozen phone messages on his desk. He's puzzled over Rob's name and sticks it at the bottom of the stack. But when he sees Katy's name, he smiles and picks up the phone.

By laying the connection groundwork, Katy is able to recruit solid experts into her network and have them poised to respond quickly in those crunch periods when the knowledge gap has to be closed quickly.

Node IV: Networking Etiquette on the Critical Path

One of the revelations from the years we spent on the front lines observing and analyzing the work habits of brainpowered professionals was the critical importance of small courtesies and considerations in the networking process.

The star performers may not be polite in all their work interactions, but in dealing with their network sources, they are the very model of Victorian manners.

It is just as revealing to discover how little consideration many average performers, like our insurance manager Claude, give to etiquette in their attempts to network and how miserably they fail as a result.

Stars are acutely aware that the people they find most valuable for their networks are also in demand by others. Unlike the artless attorney Rob, who cold-called his source, expecting a prompt reply, the stars seldom go network recruiting without an old-fashioned reference or introduction.

Think about yourself. When you get requests for help, whom do you respond to first: the cold caller whom you have no relationship with or the caller who tells you that your close colleague suggested the call? Are you more responsive if your close colleague also drops you a message telling you to expect the call and would appreciate your responding? Few people would put the cold caller on an equal footing.

The Victorian-era handwritten letter of introduction may have been "teched-up" to include e-mail and VoiceMail messages, but the basic premise is the same—vouching.

In fact, the formality of vouching may be even more appropriate in today's high-technology, need-it-yesterday business environment, where experts in networks are inundated with requests for information and forced to choose carefully in order to salvage time for their own work.

Those without vouchers seldom get access. Even if they do get in to see an expert, it will probably be much later than they had planned. When they do finally make contact, they are usually disappointed in the amount of time the expert is willing to spend.

Many star producers out in the workforce earn their places in valuable networks not by being phenomenal experts but by acting as solid vouchers and reference pointers. Many Washington insiders point to no less a star than former Joint Chiefs of Staff Chair Colin Powell as a midcareer officer who was valued not so much for his expertise in any one area but for being a well-established reference pointer in government networks.

Some average performers confuse vouching with the seeking or repayment of favors. In the latter case, the requestor is pulling out a favor, knowing that the other party will be too embarrassed to say no. Certainly, this happens during networking. Vouching, on the other hand, is the enthusiastic passing along of a contact that could help all parties involved.

In essence, stars become screeners for one another. They save one another time and effort by reducing the noise of random requests and by focusing one another on the high-value contacts.

Nowhere is this vouching more apparent than in Silicon Valley. Every day, hundreds of wannabe entrepreneurs try to get the attention of venture capitalists like Arthur Rock or high-powered executives like John Young, the former CEO of Hewlett-Packard, or Regis McKenna, the PR whiz who helped make Apple Computer a household name. You can forget about getting an audience with any of them unless you can break into their tight network. But if McKenna calls Rock and says it might be worthwhile for him to meet with someone who has an intriguing product idea, Rock will make time. Why? Rock knows from his personal experience working on projects with McKenna that if the idea attracted his attention, it must be worth a look.

Star performers in any brainpowered field, from software code writing to screenplay writing, network in much the same way as these Silicon Valley power brokers.

Node V: Do Your Homework

So let's assume you've followed all the etiquette steps and you've made it into the good graces of an expert who is willing to help. How do you make a good impression and set the stage for a long-term networking relationship?

Stars producers value their own time and therefore work very hard to make sure they don't waste the time of the experts they're trying to court. Albert Einstein was famous for carefully screening new networkers who were stumped with physics or math problems. But even when the novice got to the point of sitting down with him to explain the problem, Einstein had to feel his time was being well spent; he had to be convinced that finding a solution was beyond the person's abilities. He would tell the person to put his or her equations on the board so that he could understand where they were in the solution process. Then, if he wasn't convinced the problem required his talents, he would send them away saying, "You can solve this one yourself," or "I can refer you to other people who will help you solve this one."

Once granted time with an expert, stars do their homework in preparing for the session. Our research found that:

- Stars do a quick self-study on as much of the general subject area as possible to save the expert's having to run through basics before tackling the specific problem.
- Stars summarize their attempts to solve the problem or find elusive information. Experts can size the person up and understand the direction for a solution much quicker if they are familiar with the blind alleys the new networker has already visited.
- Stars spend time forming the right questions. There is such a thing as a dumb question, but it only occurs when people haven't done their homework. Experts would rather have a new networker ask a lot of questions, showing an understanding of the subject, than to ask very few questions and return for another round.
- Stars link their problem to a discipline or an area of interest that intrigues the expert. The more you can entice an expert to share by offering something in which he or she has an active interest, the better your results will be. If the expert can deepen his or her own knowledge by helping you, the exchange is viewed more as an enriching collaboration than a donation.

Node VI: Credit Lavishly

Perhaps the worst sin that can be committed by those seeking access to experts in a network is failing to recognize both privately and publicly their contributions to your work.

Star producers cement their new contacts by following up a

meeting or phone session with a note of thanks. More important, they make sure public credit is given for contributions leading to completion of a project or product, even if the assistance was minimal in the scope of the entire effort.

In an economy where knowledge is the stock-in-trade of so many businesses, there are no reputations worse than being pegged as an idea thief, as a pseudo-star who stands on stage and acts as if there were no supporting players, or as a taker who doesn't reciprocate. These behaviors relegate workers far beyond the average ranks to the small minority that no one wants to work with.

While a dozen or more networking contacts may turn out to be unimportant in the just-finished undertaking, several of them could be critical to the success of future work. Star performers bank on this by opting to share the limelight with those who helped in supporting roles.

Pete, a broker in the real estate department of a large Chicago investment firm, was ecstatic and desperate at the same time. He had just received a call from an old business school classmate who managed a large shopping center in Seattle. The current owners were on the edge of bankruptcy and wanted to unload the property. They would give Pete's firm one week to put together a bid before they made it an open competitive-bidding process.

Pete knew that his firm wanted to get into the Seattle market and that this deal could boost the firm's regional reputation and his own career. But in order to pull it off, he had to complete a month's worth of work in one week.

The biggest stumbling block would be the due diligence report to verify the seller's claims. The firm normally subcontracted out this procedure, but he didn't know how to find a competent firm in the Seattle area capable of completing the job on such short notice.

So Pete turned to his network. He called Sherrey in the legal department, who promised to have an answer within the hour. By calling some of her legal contacts on the West Coast, she located two firms qualified and able to do the work. Pete was relieved to have that major worry taken off his mind.

Pete repeated this process on many aspects of the deal. As a result, he was able to put together a successful deal at well below the price of an open bid. Without his network, he could never have gotten the work done in such a time crunch.

After each network contact, he sent a quick note of thanks to the person who helped him. He also sent a note to that person's supervisor, relaying how the help had made a difference. After the deal was successfully completed, he wrote a group note to everyone who helped, their supervisors, and the top managers of the Real Estate Department informing them of the positive outcome and thanking them once again.

These acts of recognition increased Pete's standing with his network colleagues and solidified them for use in the next crisis.

Node VII: The Benefit of Newness

Our research shows that new employees trying to break into an established network for the first time are given much consideration. A lot of one-way trades are made in their direction; established stars will go out of their way to make newcomers feel comfortable. But it is not without an eventual price. The establishment is going to expect some future return on their investment.

Newcomers to a network or those out recruiting a recognized expert should keep in mind that there is an informal probation that winds its way through the process. Access seekers need to offer something of value back as quickly as possible. On the other side, failing to abide by the homework rules or breaching network etiquette will earn a freeze-out from the offended source. What average performers fail to understand is that bad assessments travel faster than good. The negative impression quickly extends beyond that source to the rest of the network, even beyond that network into others. The word is put out that it is counterproductive to deal with the newcomer. Newcomers can be smart, experienced, and well connected, but they will be shunned quickly if their antinetworking behaviors outweigh their potential contributions.

Node VIII: Be a Good Network Citizen

The network is not just about taking; it is also about giving. The traffic has to flow both ways for the network to thrive and run smoothly. Some star performers refer to this as replenishing the well.

As we have seen, most stars will begin the traffic by giving, in order to have the network ready when they need to take. They want credits built up in their account. This makes other members of the network amenable to trading.

When someone in the network does call upon you for help, you have to hold up your end. It is important to find out what deadline the person is operating under and how important the information is to the critical path. Also try to ascertain whether she or he needs a general one-minute answer or a full-blown tutorial on the subject. The point is to make sure you give as efficiently as possible.

Once you find out the requirements, then you have to deliver. If you can't answer on the spot, inform your contact when you can get back to her or him. Be realistic. If it turns out that you cannot deliver as expected, then let the person know as soon as possible.

The point is that you need to develop a reputation as someone who gives as well as takes and who is dependable. If not, you will devalue yourself in the network.

UPSIZING NETWORKS IN A DOWNSIZING CULTURE

The specific networking behaviors identified in our research and laid out here make the difference between the stars, who connect with valuable networks, and the average performers, who sit waiting for the phone to ring or the e-mail message to pop up.

But there are some institutional behaviors that brainpowered workers need to adopt, especially in the current environment, where jobs, even an entire career track, can change abruptly. The networks developed during an employment period should be portable. When star performers leave, a lot of key information sources go with them. Portable networks also effectively blunt another high-pressure reality of the late 1990s: doing more with less.

As brainpowered workers are expected to carry heavier workloads and greater responsibilities with less management help, networks step in to fill the breach. Instead of losing a week's progress slogging through a problem on their own, they have had to develop a list of experts who will get them through it in half the time.

Stars also excel in recognizing the stark differences between social and professional knowledge networking. The workplace social grapevine is a different structure that can support lighter-weight issues like office gossip. Some of it may even overlap into sections of the professional network.

But there are dramatic differences in the productivity value of each network. The workers who are most wired into the company's social networks, who have the scoop on who is dating whom, for instance, or which executive is the big loser in a power struggle, benefit in the star performer work strategy of organizational savvy, which will be covered in depth in Chapter 11. But as discussed earlier, when I introduced the star performer model, the skill of knowledge networking is more central and critical to your success. Workers who focus primarily on the social network aren't nearly as productive as those who excel in information sharing and networking to reduce knowledge deficits.

In fact, the stars are choosier, not just in the types of networks they enter into but in the extent to which they will be involved. They settle into networks and recruit experts not with an eye toward some hypothetical perfect solution or the most complete briefing but with an eye toward getting the best job done on the critical path. Stars don't create high-powered networks in order to be able to drop important names at cocktail parties. They view networks as dependable, high-quality car-pooling teams that will get them down the critical path as effectively as possible.

Without networks, the stars know, they are on their own. And to be on your own in this mind-boggling knowledge economy is to be lost.

6

Managing Your Whole Life at Work
Self-Management

Jerry Meyer is CEO of Pinnacle Brands, a company that makes sports trading cards. When he took over four years ago, the business was big—bigger than a lot of the products hawked by the athletes pictured on Pinnacle's cards.

But Meyer's timing was unfortunate. A few months after he took over, storm clouds began gathering over professional baseball. Fans were incensed over the greed and gall displayed in contract talks between baseball players and owners. As each side dug in its heels and the weeks went on, card sales went down and down and . . . then baseball went on strike and the season was lost.

That left only hockey and football as the sellable cards for Pinnacle, but as winter came around, the other athletic shoe fell—this time an ice skate instead of a baseball cleat. Hockey followed baseball's lead off the cliff, and poor Jerry Meyer was left with a warehouse full of pictures of smiling athletes. What's more, the football season wasn't coming around fast enough to pay the bills.

Meanwhile, Pinnacle's two chief competitors were already moving on damage control. Topps, a producer of trading cards for several other professional sports in addition to baseball and hockey, quickly turned to downsizing, laying off two hundred workers. The other competitor, Fleer, whose trading-card division was one among several business lines, was even more brutal. The day after Thanksgiving weekend, Fleer's workers showed up at the plant to find security guards blocking the gate and trucks loaded up with their machines leaving the lot.

Fleer had opted not just to downsize its card business, it amputated it; several hundred longtime workers were out on the street. But less than a month after management's cut-and-run decision, the company was handsomely rewarded on Wall Street. Fleer's "restructuring" greatly increased the probability of higher profits, crowed an analyst for Bear Stearns in recommending the stock as a buy.

Pinnacle, however, was a privately held company, and Jerry Meyer was left with no stock-enhancement choices. He could preside over a heartless gutting of the workforce and try to squeak through until professional sports luminaries came to their senses, or he could shutter the plant and move on to a product line less dependent on their whims.

Meyer didn't much care for either option. Alone in his office late one night after reviewing the latest depressing reports on the strikes, he began to fashion a third choice to deal with the crisis, one that would forgo automatic layoffs in favor of a new policy: self-management.

Days later, he called all his employees together. To their surprise, he had no announcement of cutbacks, no wage whacking. Instead, Meyer announced, each member of the workforce would take on the burden of finding new markets to replace those lost to the strikes, new ideas for marketing the products, new ways to boost productivity. Henceforth, all Pinnacle employees would manage themselves to prove their productivity or move on.

Lest employees think Meyer was a CEO on a white horse protecting them from the Downsizing Dragon, he added a warning in the no-nonsense style for which he is known: "From this day on, I want you to know that this company owes you no loyalty. The only way you're going to keep your job, the only way, is for you to produce. And if you don't drive results, I'm sorry, I'll bet you don't end up staying here."

From then on, each member of the workforce, but especially the company's brainpowered workers—creative staff, managers, sales agents, and others—would have more self-management responsibility and a heavier workload and would be held accountable for doing better work. If employees made the transition successfully, said Meyer, "we will all survive. Otherwise, we won't."

Recounting the events of that day for journalists who covered the company's transition as a novel alternative to downsizing, Meyer remembers the reaction of uncertainty that swept through the ranks: "Does this guy really know what he's talking about?"

But in the months after the meeting, employees began to respond to the self-manage-or-perish directive, spurred partly by a huge turnover in the workforce: Many who resisted the change were shown the door. Others simply left on their own.

Out of a workforce of three hundred in place before Meyer arrived, only about forty remain today. But Meyer has hired hundreds of replacements who know the rules and thrive on managing their own productivity.

And profit-generating ideas came through.

A graphics person developed the idea of creating splashier trading-card versions of universally adored Baltimore Orioles shortstop Cal Ripken—the hologrammed Cal and the Golden Cal sold especially well.

A longtime business secretary, who had been Pinnacle's contact person for years with a firm that did trademark searches, decided she could learn to do the work on her own, saving the company $100,000 a year.

While Jerry Meyer's version of the much-written-about art of self-management may strike dedicated brainpowered workers as harsh, the switch in emphasis brought bottom-line results. Those employees who survived the transition reported enormous boosts in self-confidence, in their personal productivity, and in their esteem for coworkers.

The story of Pinnacle Brands is merely a more dramatic example of a change in business philosophy that I first began writing about in the early 1980s. Back then, many managers thought the self-management ideas I introduced in *The Gold-Collar Worker* were radical and threatening, especially when I argued that giving employees the power to manage themselves was "an ideal solution to several of the most serious problems—low productivity, employee discontent, and managerial ineffectiveness—currently besetting U.S. businesses across the board. . . . Self-managed employees are . . . free to unleash their creativity and increase their productivity on behalf of both the organization and themselves." Since the publication, in 1985, of *The Gold-Collar Worker*, these same self-management ideas have taken root and are now growing as quickly in American workplaces as companies are growing into the global economy.

The long-standing pyramid-style management structure has undergone a number of mutations, all in the direction of putting greater productivity responsibility on the backs of brainpowered workers. Technology leaps that allow workers to be more mobile, lifestyle changes that demand more flexible work schedules, and the changing nature of the work itself have blurred the traditional lines of management and supervision.

In knowledge-based companies, self-management becomes essential from the company's standpoint. As W. Brian Arthur, a dean and professor at Stanford University, explains,

> Knowledge-based companies are competing in winner-take-most markets. . . . Managing becomes redefined as a series of quests for . . . the Next Big Thing. In this milieu, management becomes not production-oriented but mission-oriented. Hierarchies flatten not because democracy is suddenly bestowed on the workforce or because computers can cut out much of the work of middle management. They flatten because, to be effective, the deliverers of the next-thing-for-the-company need to be organized . . . in small teams that report directly to the CEO or the board. Such people need free rein. The company's future survival depends upon them. So they . . . will be treated not as employees but as equals in the business of the company's success. Hierarchy dissipates and dissolves.

Self-management, whatever the self-serving form in which it is dressed, is here to stay.

But the behavior did not earn a prominent place in our work

skills model merely because of its trendiness on the corporate land-scape. The star producers we studied adopted a much more open version of the skill and had developed more day-to-day uses for it in their jobs than the narrower versions practiced by average coworkers.

The stars do not consider self-management to be a matter pri-marily of better organizing one's daily schedule or keeping an eye on time, as so many companies have interpreted it. I have seen the stunted version of this skill in practice so often I worry that it has become a brainpowered-workforce productivity hazard. I've even given the condition a name, Day-Timer syndrome, a take-off on the time-management craze of a decade ago, in which managers turned brainpowered employees into time-logging robots who wouldn't have so much as a hallway conversation without noting it in their Velcro-tabbed schedule books. Today's version is the palm-sized electronic organizer.

Even at Bell Labs, the professionals we studied didn't escape the time-management fad. In an attempt to justify the time expended in meetings, for instance, no gathering was allowed to end until "Ac-tion Steps" had been taken—things that would be done as a result of the meeting. And each Action Step had to be assigned to some-one who would have the responsibility to get it done.

The stars, however, look at catch-phrase schemes like time man-agement as commonsense scheduling of the workday, not the secret of productivity-boosting self-management.

In their day-to-day behaviors, star self-managers aren't just watching how much time is spent on each activity, they're evaluat-ing what the activities are and working to make good choices. Be-fore high-priced consultants and authors started pushing "first things first," we documented that star performers were operating at a much higher level, skillfully labeling tasks according to their im-portance—"important vs. unimportant"—then balancing that re-sulting list against what is merely "urgent vs. not urgent." That final, honed list—about 60 percent important/urgent and 40 per-cent important/not urgent activities—is where they concentrate their energies.

That's the first step to star-quality self-management—managing to work only on those activities directly tied to the critical path. Their success in doing this depends on a deep understanding of what the critical path is in their organization and where they should be positioned on it to contribute in the most productive way.

As we introduced it earlier, the critical path is the most direct, essential, value-added route that can be plotted from the work of a brainpowered employee to the delighted consumer of the product or service affected by that work. Critical path work ensures the organization's profitability and sustained success in the marketplace.

The stars know they can't depend on traditional management structure to put them on the critical path. Dan, a star performer at Bell Labs who created the initial designs for new telephone switches, learned the hard way. Now in his forties, he recounted his personal struggle with getting on the critical path. "I first thought I was productive because I got through all the items on my to-do list each day. Then one day I realized that I wasn't sure how things ended up on my list. What I discovered was that many of my activities were reactive responses to things my manager or coworkers wanted. I was okay with that for a while, until I realized that just because they wanted me to do something, it didn't mean it was on the critical path. I had to be responsible for getting myself on the critical path. So finally I took control of my to-do list."

Why are the stars so intent on self-managing within the lane markers on the critical path? They want the many benefits that come with having their work recognized for adding value to the bottom line, including a sense of personal accomplishment, an enhanced reputation, and a powerful layer of protection from downsizing campaigns.

"Hey, wait a minute, I'm a second-level speech writer in public relations," said one worker in a recent meeting. "We're the first to get staff cuts because the CEO doesn't see us on that critical path. What do the stars do that I can do to make my job valued?"

PROACTIVELY GETTING ON THE CRITICAL PATH

The first task is to take stock without the rose-colored glasses. It is incumbent on all brainpowered workers to evaluate where they are in an organization and make evaluations and decisions that used to be made by managers. If you don't see any critical path connections in the work you're putting out, you should make the decision to transfer your skills to a more value-directed job before the CEO does.

If, however, you do identify areas in which the present job can be reconfigured onto the path, then the star's vision of self-management will help you get there. Witness, for example, the critical path role that public relations workers have come to play in companies that face public scrutiny—airline companies after a disaster, environmentally sensitive industries such as logging and mining, and tobacco companies facing lawsuits and restrictive legislation. In many cases, individual brain-powered workers carved out the critical path role.

In the pharmaceutical industry, some public relations workers involved in lobbying Congress and federal regulatory agencies recognized the huge competitive advantage that would occur if they could shorten the time it takes for new drugs to pass government review. For every year a product is in the marketplace without competition, the profits and market-share benefits skyrocket.

Several star self-managers at Pfizer realized this back in the 1980s, directing their efforts away from reactive problem solving to proactive strategies that would result in whittling the lead time for new drugs from the standard ten-year cycle to seven years by speeding up the time spent in FDA review. They also were successful in getting their products excluded from legislation allowing companies to produce less expensive, generic versions of brand name drugs, a move that their competitors didn't make and quickly came to wish they had. These two self-managed, critical path initiatives contributed almost as much to the bottom line as new drug development. Within a few years, government and regulatory-agency relations has become one of the hottest critical path units in nearly every pharmaceutical company.

So to the corporate external-communications writer who asked how to get on the critical path, the answer is to tie your efforts, as the Pfizer PR department did, to the firm's bottom line. If you can't, then you have two choices: Stay in your current job and live each day in fear of downsizing, or sign up with a firm where your work has critical path status. Our in-house corporate writer, for example, should consider working for a PR firm or a political-campaign consultant where his efforts would drive the business's bottom line.

Similarly, accounting professionals often get short shrift in many firms because others don't see a direct link between accounting work and the critical path. Indeed, some coworkers and managers see them as speed bumps on the path, fulfilling record-keeping tasks imposed by government regulators, or justifying their own existence in company policies.

How do company accountants stop being treated as third-class citizens and self-manage their way onto the critical path? First, they have to understand the company's goals and bottom line and then connect to them. They might start by providing critical path personnel with just-in-time cost figures rather than historical financial reports that are not as timely. This data might include production-cost data on competitors so that production people know how they compare; up-to-date, activity-based internal figures to pinpoint where costs are too high and to propose solutions; and reducing overhead costs in the accounting department while increasing the value-added services provided.

SELF-KNOWLEDGE IN SELF-MANAGEMENT

Stars who develop good self-management techniques have incorporated them into the mix of traits and quirks that define them as individuals in the workplace.

Personality, work style, and motivation factors are all in play here. Many managers and training programs attempt to form all workers into the same self-management mold. "Clean desk" people want to believe that being organized their way leads to higher productivity. The same is true for early-morning risers and people with the Day-Timer syndrome. As I indicated in earlier chapters, however, the stars we have studied argue for the opposite approach.

What we discovered was that there is no single personality trait that will make you a star performer, no particular brand of self-organizing skills, no evidence that clean-desk workers are better self-managers than the coworkers buried under paper.

What we did learn was that stars know themselves well and are known by others for being comfortable with who they are and with how they are perceived by others in the workplace. They seek to learn self-management techniques from others, but they work to integrate those tips into their own individual style. Productivity stars vehemently reject the one-size-fits-all approach taken in so many self-management programs.

In our training programs, we help professionals discover the strengths and weaknesses of their individual approaches to self-management. Little is gained, for instance, in foisting a generic time-management system, complete with scheduling book and to-do priority tabs, on those who have a reliable system for keeping such information in their heads. It is much more effective for our trainers to work with these employees to develop more effective techniques for storing information mentally.

Every star producer we studied had developed a self-organizing plan that took their individual makeup into account. Some of the star performers we studied, for instance, had a basically worried approach to their work—that it wasn't good enough, that there would be problems, or that they might fail—just as they did in other aspects of their lives. To minimize the negatives that come from an overly pessimistic outlook, they became overachievers—more than the necessary preparation for meetings, leaving nothing to chance, weekends in the office, work brought home—all to virtually eliminate the possibility of a problem.

A manager might look at that situation and decide the employee is trying too hard and needs to conform more to the way others are doing the work. But as long as the worker isn't in danger of burning out or interfering in the work of others, that self-management technique is the result of careful introspection on the part of the worker: "I can't change this basic pessimism about myself, so some overcompensation will help me balance that in order to do excellent work."

Josiah, a midcareer housing-mortgage specialist at a Fortune 500 bank, just wasn't an early-morning person. In his late thirties, Josiah knew his natural rhythm, and early-morning-hit-the-ground-running just wasn't him. Still, for years, he had been forced to abide by his department's idiosyncratic 7 A.M. starting time, even though the bottom-line work of the department didn't begin until 10 A.M. and ended at 5 P.M., to fit in with schedules of home buyers, sellers, and their attorneys. This critical work period is known as core time in the jargon of many time-management programs.

But Josiah wasn't just concerned about time schedules. He was a slightly above-average performer who knew his productivity would soar if his workday was more in keeping with his own personal productivity cycle, starting at 10 A.M. and going until early evening. He was convinced several others in the department would see the same improvement.

When a new CEO embarked on a justify-or-die evaluation of each department, Josiah saw his chance to introduce a flex-time program to managers who were desperate for productivity-improvement ideas.

Within weeks, half the department had switched over to a 10 A.M. starting time, and within months, personal productivity among those working the new hours had soared. Rather than continue to spin his wheels trying to adapt to an arbitrary work cycle, Josiah self-managed his way into one that fit his routine.

SELF-MANAGING AND JOB SATISFACTION

Have you noticed how the star producers in your workplace seem to be into their jobs and to like them?

In a business environment where many aspects of top-down management are no longer effective, where employer-employee loyalty is virtually nonexistent, and where morale in many down-sized companies has plunged off the charts, the stars manage to stay focused on their jobs, minimizing the negatives.

How? The stars have used self-management skills to put them into work that they like and that complements their own personality patterns. The result is work that is more satisfying—not always enjoyable and thrilling, though, because work is often, well, just plain work. But in the long term, star self-managers reported a sense of meaning, accomplishment, and contribution.

Our stars knew intuitively what turned them on. They used their self-management skills to ensure they stayed with the type of work they enjoyed, or in developing a plan to move into the work they wanted to do. This is where self-management is especially powerful, allowing full use of an employee's creative and intellectual capabilities and providing a feeling of ownership in career decisions.

The career story of Wilbert L. Gore is a classic example of the power of self-management among brainpowered workers.

Gore was a young chemist, just a few years out of the University of Utah, in 1945 when he landed a job at E. I. DuPont. His talents were quickly recognized, and Gore was coaxed into several management jobs. But Gore knew himself well and believed his best contributions could be made in research. He declined several promotion offers in order to stay close to the lab.

Even as head of operations research, Gore still worked on a team to develop applications for a chemical known as PTFE in scientific abbreviation and Teflon to the rest of us.

Gore was smart as a whip, but he was a team star—he was simply known as Bill to his coworkers, and he was unassuming, always willing to lend a hand, and well liked by others. He was genuinely excited about working with PTFE, believing it could be developed as an excellent insulator for electronics parts, especially in the manufacturing of computers.

Gore had worked hundreds of hours in the lab, attempting to develop a Teflon-coated cable, but it was at home, after dinner one night in the makeshift lab he had built in the basement, that the breakthrough came.

He had explained the problem to his eighteen-year-old son, Bob, who remembered seeing some PTFE-coated sealing tape made by 3M. Why couldn't the tape be bonded to the PTFE-coated cable, Bob wondered. In the gentle tone of an esteemed chemistry professor speaking to a new student, Gore said he would be laughed out of the lab if he suggested that PTFE could be bonded to itself.

Bob went on to bed but Gore stayed in the basement, deciding to tinker with the ridiculous idea and get it out of his system.

At about 4 A.M., Bill flicked the light on in his son's room. Bob awoke startled to see his father standing over him, a huge grin on his face as he waved a tiny piece of cable. "It works! It works!" he shouted.

For months, Gore tried to convince DuPont managers of the significance of the development—that PTFE-coated ribbon cable could become the standard insulator for every piece of sophisticated electronic equipment or transistor on the market. But to turn the research- and supply-centered DuPont into a fabricator of insulating cable would have required a massive shift of resources, a risk that top company officers were not willing to take.

So Gore was left with a dilemma: go on to other research projects at DuPont or continue with the project he loved, which meant a self-management decision that took him out of the company and into his own insulated wire-and-cable business.

On January 1, 1958, the night of his twenty-third wedding anniversary, Gore and his wife, Genevieve, founded W. L. Gore & Associates. With five children to support, the couple had to pull out most of their savings and take out a second mortgage on their home to finance the first two years of the business.

Instead of a regular salary, the first employees accepted room and board in the Gore home. Before the couple won their first big contract, there were eleven workers bedding down and eating meals in the brick and white-trimmed house in Newark, Delaware.

W. L. Gore & Associates has grown steadily and smartly ever since. Now under the direction of son Bob—the senior Gore died in a hiking accident in Wyoming in 1986—the company has five thousand associates (the company term for employees) and sales approaching $1 billion. Its four lines of business—electronic, medical, fabrics, and industrial products—have earned the company worldwide respect as a leading innovator among applied-technology firms. No wonder, given that the company now manufactures one of the few products with a household name to rival Teflon—Gore-Tex.

The company stresses self-management to new associates from their first day on the job. People are not necessarily hired into specific jobs; they are hired because the other associates believe that the new person can make a critical path contribution. Bill Gore's dictum is "All our lives most of us have been told what to do. . . . It's the new associate's responsibility to find out what he or she can do for the good of the operation."

The self-management lessons we can learn from this brainpowered chemist-turned-entrepreneur in the 1950s are mirrored by the star producers of the 1990s:

1. Know yourself well.
2. Know the kind of work you do best and that you want to do.
3. Take control of your own career path by developing a plan to connect yourself to the work you enjoy most and to connect that work to the company's critical path.

MANAGING FLOW: THE PRODUCTIVE STATE OF MIND

Think of Bill Gore tinkering away in his basement lab as his family sleeps and the hours tick on. There is only the problem, the idea, the piece of work. He is oblivious to the passage of time and other aspects of reality.

Think of the advertising guru Bill Backer stranded in the tiny airport lounge at Shannon Airport in Ireland, seizing on the spark of an idea—dozens of strangers from all corners of the earth who become friends because of a fogged-in airport and bottles of Coke. Then, consumed with the process of transferring the idea to writing, he drifts off, unaware of his surroundings.

This is what Mihaly Csikszentmihalyi, a University of Chicago psychology professor, calls the state of *flow*, the condition that brainpowered workers strive for in the quest for greatest productivity. In his book by the same name, he describes flow as when all cylinders are humming, all energies are directed at the work, other aspects of reality are blocked out, and your best work gets turned out. There is an innate sense of progress, a feeling of moving forward. The stars who recount their experiences in a state of flow also evaluate their workday as satisfying and enormously productive, centered on important contributions.

One key to star productivity, though, is that the flow occurs on work connected to the critical path, not just on tangents and diversions that fascinate the worker but are far removed from the path.

So how do you as a star self-manager kick into the flow state? First, you have to find meaning and enjoyment in the work. Next, you need to create a work environment that gives you the mental space to get into your work. In today's open-door, no-walls, be-available-on-demand work environment, this is often easier said than done.

In one study of daily productivity, we found that a major cause of low personal performance was frequent interruptions. Most managers or line workers would not dream of going into a factory and stopping the production line every thirty minutes to discuss something, yet these same people think nothing of interrupting their coworkers on the brainpowered production line.

Brainpowered work can be compared to launching a spaceship. The greatest amount of fuel is used and the greatest stress is incurred from takeoff to breaking out of the earth's atmosphere and from reentry to landing. The same is true for brainpowered work. The hard part is getting into flow. Once you are there, it is like floating in space. When flow is interrupted, then you waste all that time and energy taking off again.

So when brainpowered workers' concentration is broken, productivity suffers as they lose their train of thought and waste time starting over again.

Stars take varied approaches to both getting into flow and avoiding interruptions. One engineer took to wearing headphones when hunkered down at his computer keyboard. Coworkers thought he was engrossed in classical music to stimulate his transition into flow, but there was nothing playing. The headphones were in place to ward off his chatty colleagues.

Pulitzer-prize-winning writer Annie Dillard insists on the most lackluster office environment possible to induce her writing flow—a cinderblock cell overlooking a tar-and-gravel roof. "Appealing workplaces are to be avoided," she tells aspiring writers. "One wants a room with no view, so imagination can meet memory in the dark."

There were more than a dozen professionals at Bell Labs who had a variation on that technique. When their regular work environment became too cluttered with distractions, they would slip away to the adult version of a tree house—a quiet place where they could find their state of flow and maintain it without interruption.

Joann, a star self-manager and busy grant reviewer for a large philanthropic foundation, is easygoing and approachable. No wonder, then, that she was coming under siege in her regular office cubicle—phone, fax, e-mail, and unscheduled visits from coworkers in need of help. So she found her tree house—a vacant office in the foundation's legal department. But Joann didn't just disappear. In keeping with good self-management, she told her boss about the switch. She also made arrangements to catch up with the world after her flow session by posting a sign-up sheet outside the office and leaving a message on her VoiceMail.

Notice that Joann balanced her need to reduce interruptions with her colleagues' need to have access to her. Coworkers often have to consider one another's needs. When I'm stuck on the critical path and need to network with Joann to get some knowledge that will get me back on track, I may need to interrupt her. Her loss of flow enables me to get back into it. But as the requester, I owe Joann the courtesy of finding a time that works for her. Similarly, she needs to let me know her pressures and when she will be available.

Many average performers we have observed over the years fall into one of two traps in trying to minimize interruptions and maximize flow time. The first trap is to become a just-say-noer in a business environment that demands can-do, cooperative attitudes. These average performers refuse to make any commitments to others, and they turn down requests brusquely, without explanation.

The second trap claims workers who can't bring themselves to say no to any request that comes down the pike. They become so involved in commitments outside their critical path responsibilities that they eventually become overwhelmed and their own work suffers.

Compare these scenarios to our star self-manager grant reviewer, Joann. When she is approached by Matt, a coworker in another section of the foundation, asking her to be on a juvenile-crime task force he's chairing, Joann doesn't make an instant decision.

"It sounds as if it would be well worth my time, Matt. There's an opportunity to have some real impact on the community, but I'm going to have to take a hard look at my schedule. I promise I'll give you an answer by Friday."

Joann does review her own commitments and realizes that the bulk of the task force meetings fall during the crunch period for decisions on several large grant programs. There is no way she can do one without the other suffering. So Joann's first order of business after settling into her office Friday morning is to call Matt.

"I've looked at my own commitments over the next two months, and I'm sorry to say I wouldn't be able to give the task force the time it deserves. But I have a suggestion for you. Namosha Adams is a good friend from college and she works as an assistant district attorney specializing in prosecution of juveniles who are tried as adults. She's had years of experience with the issues you're going to be confronting and she's served on an American Bar Association committee on the same topic. I'd be happy to approach her if you're interested."

In two brief conversations, Joann has been able to protect her demanding schedule from being overrun, maintain goodwill with a coworker, and contribute indirectly toward a solution for Matt's problem. Joann realizes that effective self-management is rarely self-focused. The way she manages her own affairs affects others on a daily basis.

Another flow-sapping behavior common to average performers is the dreaded procrastination syndrome. It's true that when postponing work on tasks and assignments becomes a habit, then procrastination can be a serious barrier to productive flow. Star performers are aware of this and have developed techniques for avoiding the problem.

But the stars realize that procrastination is not, by definition, always a negative. For some workers, procrastination is a way of building in a critical rush period that gets the adrenaline pumping and creative juices flowing. For others, procrastination acts as a prioritizer. What is really important to get done, gets done. What appears to be important on paper or in the emotional rush of a meeting, turns out not to be so when work is called for.

Syed Shariq, a high-level NASA manager and longtime colleague of mine, compares star performers to supersonic aircraft traveling at Mach 2 speed. People are always trying to attach work and requests to them. But when you travel at that speed, only the most important and necessary items—the ones that have been fastened down—will stick.

ORGANIZED SELF-MANAGEMENT: GETTING THE JOB DONE

There may be as many techniques for reaching and maintaining flow as there are stars, but the common theme is that all stars value the process and strive to maintain it.

That said, you need to understand that achieving flow isn't the only step to star self-management. You still must produce—get your work done on time, within budget, and with such high quality that you wow the customer and add bottom-line value to the organization.

To achieve those results, you need to organize your work life to obtain the maximum benefit from the good work produced in flow. The system you adopt must help you:

- plan the entire project
- schedule your time
- keep track of your progress
- store and retrieve important information
- tip you off to potential crises
- provide for a backup plan if problems arise
- communicate your progress and results to important others—customers, bosses, coworkers

It's interesting that in our research work and in running training programs for corporations, we run into so many average performers who are obsessed with the peripheral details of organization. These workers will spend hours developing a color-coded filing system or a computer program to store names and phone numbers. But the minute a crisis hits, their organizational system collapses.

The stars know that the best organizational plans aren't about state-of-the-art filing or whether coworkers can get an uncluttered view of the faux wood-grain pattern on their desktop. Star organizing is built around moving down the critical path and avoiding crises—missed deadlines, for instance—and then ensuring that a plan is in place for dealing with those crises that slip through.

But as we've said before, there is no one way that is perfect for everyone. Each person must find what works for him or her. We often have people in our programs seek out stars they really admire and then ask those stars a specific set of structured questions about how they organize their work. We also suggest they seek out stars who are like them in important personal ways—such as being sloppy-desk people or being phobic about complicated time-management systems—and ask the same questions. The idea is that they are more likely to find and use organizing tools that come from stars that they identify with or admire.

Many workers we studied fell into two categories when asked to evaluate their organizational skills. One group had a quantitative system centered on daily to-do lists. They determined how productive they were by the number of items checked off. The second group took a qualitative view by checking for a "feeling of accomplishment" at the end of the day.

The stars, too, could be grouped into quantitative and qualitative approaches, but their evaluations came earlier in the process.

As we learned from Dan, the Bell Labs design star who struggled with getting on the critical path, quantitative-minded workers didn't just judge their productivity by the number of checkmarks on their to-do list, they rated the items that made it there according to how much the task or assignment contributed to the critical path.

"Rework code section B" to fix a bug in the call-forwarding switching program was rated much higher than "Send out department-wide note on blood donation drive." The same fundamental assessments occurred with qualitative stars. "I felt productive today" was based on a careful analysis of how much a flow session had contributed to the problem or assignment, or to what degree groundbreaking, innovative work had occurred over the course of a project and put the company out in front in some way.

So organized self-management requires that there be some reliable methods to get the work done and an honest, dependable measuring system establishing that the work performed creates value on the critical path. In addition, the stars we studied had an early-warning system and a fallback plan in the event of a crisis. This included a communication link with important others. As April, a star engineer working in videotape tape production at 3M relayed, "Letting your boss know of problems well in advance when something can be done is good planning; letting the boss know after the fact is giving excuses."

Our stars tend to build a lot of forward-thinking behavior into their self-management system. The constant weighing and analysis of the work has implications down the road for both short-term and long-term career choices. The stars, in effect, take control of both daily work routine and career goals, knowing that the days when a paternal hand would reach down from upper management to guide the way are long gone.

ORGANIZED SELF-MANAGEMENT: COMPANY AND CAREER

One of the big differences between average self-managers and the stars is that the average workers aren't proactively involved in managing their own work flow or their own career paths. Whatever projects they're directed to are fine with them. No matter that the projects might not fit well into the critical path. Nor has it occurred to them to think about what they'd like to be doing five years down the road.

The star self-management strategy is to be thinking about what project being talked about would be great to work on, which person would be great to work under, which personal idea might be great to push as a project. Stars begin to think about the next assignment long before the current one is completed. They view pieces of work as if they were pieces in a giant sculpture. Each piece of work is evaluated as to how it will fit into the larger work.

The stars, in effect, are self-managing the career they want by sculpting a piece at a time.

Alan, a benefits processor for a large health care management company in California, has taken a proactive approach to managing his career. His five-year plan is to get enough experience and credentials to become a health care specialist who travels to hospitals and clinics in the field to meet clients and assess quality of care.

Alan has done some investigating and knows that the employees in those jobs have a minimum of two years' experience as a benefits processor and have completed at least half the course load required for a master's degree in health management. But by doing some investigating on his own via his expert network, Alan has discovered a requirement not included on the posted list. All the health care specialists in his part of California speak fluent Spanish. "If we didn't speak the language, we wouldn't get any good information and we'd lose a lot of customers," one of the specialists tells him.

Alan goes to his manager, explains his career plan, and asks for time off on Fridays, because the Spanish course at a nearby university requires a two-hour lab session that starts an hour before his quitting time on Friday. The supervisor says that while he admires Alan's attempt to plan his career, he can't approve a benefit without extending it to others in the department, something upper management is not prepared to do. Undaunted, Alan enrolls in an intensive community-college night course and sticks to the program, achieving a basic conversational ability in the language in ten months.

This example brings up one of the harder-to-control aspects of self-management: dealing with supervisors. An important component of star self-management is to make partners out of those people charged with representing the company's interests in your work.

Our experience has been that many supervisory managers fall into one of two groups—facilitators and dictators.

An active self-manager who lands a facilitator for a boss is generally in a comfortable situation. Supervisors in this group are more secure with themselves, concentrating on big-picture management problems. They have been careful in hiring and they trust those in place to do their jobs well. These managers generally respect brain-powered workers for their intelligence and independence. They recognize that there are many aspects of the work done by their staff that they don't understand, and that is not a situation that makes them uncomfortable. Good self-managers and facilitators are very compatible; they have a strong work relationship based on a foundation of mutual respect and division of labor.

Facilitators are willing to listen to self-management ideas and, when they find them reasonable, go out of their way to make them happen. But good self-managers need to be mindful that facilitators, even though they are not looking over your shoulder, must be consulted regularly about self-management ideas, and whatever advice they offer should be taken seriously. Losing the respect of a facilitator can be a very costly self-management mistake.

Employees with strong self-management skills face a much tougher challenge when working for a boss in the dictator group. Dictator managers are often obsessed with control and a need to micromanage their employees' lives. These managers are usually more insecure than their facilitator colleagues, unlikely to acknowledge that anyone on their staff knows more about the work at hand, and preoccupied with setting schedules and deadlines, even when they affect morale and productivity.

Strong self-managers realize that the dictator-boss's style will cause significant problems if adjustments aren't made. In every interaction with the dictator-boss, the savvy self-manager stays focused on what he or she wants in the long term, well beyond their time with the dictator-boss. As in relations with the facilitator-boss, the goal continues to be making the dictator-boss a partner, but the process is going to take longer and require a different tack.

Good self-managers work slowly to build a rapport between themselves and the dictator-boss, clearly establishing the sense that the boss is in control of the workplace but that the employee has a right to exercise some control over a career path. Dictator-managers almost always love to be consulted frequently, even about small problems that self-managers are capable of handling themselves.

They also respond well to what we refer to in our training programs as the "supervisor interviews," talks that good self-managers have with these bosses that make them feel they're being included in intimate short-term and long-term career decisions.

One of the exercises in our training program is to engage employees in a mock supervisor interview with this type of boss. The issues that should be discussed include the boss's definition of good employee self-management and his or her feelings on a range of issues—work-hours flexibility, what the work environment should look like, the best way to suggest ideas that would make the employee more productive.

If the dictator-boss is committed to getting the best performance out of his or her staff, broaching these issues usually opens the door to a looser working relationship. The best possible outcome would be that this boss takes on the role of mentor to the employee and loosens up the leash considerably. The employee also benefits by having a much better understanding of this boss's point of view and his or her background and goals. At a minimum, the employee will know where the boss stands on these issues and what the limits are. That information can be invaluable in reaching partnership status.

After all, what strong self-managers share with their supervisors, no matter which category, is a commitment to increased productivity and a pride in work that adds value to the organization. If that becomes the foundation of a work relationship, the boss will probably end up encouraging self-management practices in other employees. As individuals take more responsibility for their own work, organizational productivity will soar.

THE CORE SELF-MANAGEMENT SKILLS

Since so many successful self-management techniques stem from individual personalities, it would be counterproductive to set up a single model of self-management. But there are common themes running through the star techniques that we've identified and detailed for you here as guideposts in developing your own individualized skills.

1. The stars find out what the critical path is for their organization and get on it by learning how to add value.

2. The stars choose work that allows them to leverage who they are, use their talents, get into flow, and experience job satisfaction.

3. The stars regularly review their personal productivity—some on a daily basis, others monthly—and devise ways to increase personal effectiveness and efficiency.

4. The stars borrow shamelessly—not ideas and content, but technique and method for better self-management. Stars are careful observers of others' work routines and adopt innovative techniques into their own work styles.

5. The stars aren't afraid to experiment with changes in their work routine to develop more productive habits. They will try new approaches and then evaluate their effectiveness.

6. The stars make a compelling case to management for changing job descriptions and regulations that limit productivity or restrict them from the work they do best.

7. The stars adopt behaviors that allow them to minimize interruptions in their workday without separating them from the group. For example, they will often take a "working vacation"—escaping to another part of the office to complete work. Many try to build meeting-free days into their weekly schedules to give themselves periods of concentration time.

8. Stars work to avoid time-killer crises by planning for problems—building mistake-recovery time into projects. They also write up a personal damage-control plan, a list of general procedures they should follow in any crisis.

9. Stars develop procrastination-busting work habits—to-do lists, priority plans, building enjoyable work assignments around drudge tasks.

10. The stars also learn to accept the occasional unproductive workday, even several weeks' work slump. No one can keep flow going constantly. Productivity, like so much of life,

goes in cycles. Knowing your cycles and how to break a slump are crucial for boosting overall productivity.

11. Stars need to know their own productivity patterns. Some stars are most productive when they give their all in a defined burst of intense activity. They go at their work like a crazed person, often working fourteen-hour workdays until the project is done. Once the project is completed, they will need a lot of down time before they can work back up to that intensity again. Other stars schedule their projects with a steady rhythm, moving easily from one to the next.

Star self-management is not achieved through some fancy one-trick program. It results from coming to know yourself, figuring out what works for you using our concrete guidelines in this chapter, and then doing the hard work of incorporating those skills into your work style. Once you integrate these basic concepts, you will fall off your boss's radar screen as someone who has to be "managed." Instead, by taking the responsibility for your own productivity, you will have attained the power to control your work life and the freedom to head for the stars.

7

GETTING THE BIG PICTURE
Learning How to Build Perspective

When furniture designer William James won the contract to create a conference table and other furniture for Teresa Heinz, heir to the Heinz ketchup fortune, he was beside himself.

The commission was a wood artist's dream. The client: one of Pennsylvania's richest and most powerful public figures with international connections, a pacesetter on national and international public policy issues. The table: planned as one of the crown jewels in a new family-foundation workplace that would take up the top two floors of one of Pittsburgh's newest and sleekest office towers.

But James wanted to make sure he understood the different perspectives involved in the project. There was the perspective of Teresa Heinz to consider; there was the perspective of the architect, William McDonough, a talented but demanding professional with an ecological bent; and there were the perspectives of the foundation officials and staff, who would be using the table even more than their boss.

In all these conversations, James realized he wasn't hired just to build a pretty piece of furniture to seat a large group and hold all their weighty decisions. His main job was to assimilate all the different perspectives and create a table that served both function for the group and image for Teresa Heinz. In both the practical and the aesthetic, James realized he had to turn out a table that not only caught the eye of his client but carried a message to everyone who sat down with Teresa Heinz to talk business.

In the aftermath of the tragic death of her husband, U.S. Senator John Heinz, in a plane crash near Philadelphia in 1991, Teresa Heinz had been thrust into the role of overseer of nearly $1 billion in charitable foundation money and a $675 million personal family fortune.

Three years later, Teresa Heinz emerged from grief to make her mark, and she needed to strike a delicate balance—continue the values and ideals set by her late husband but introduce her own distinct concerns as well.

She would do this in her personal life, eventually marrying Massachusetts Senator John Kerry, though keeping the Heinz name. But she would do it first with the new penthouse offices, especially with the conference room table.

Teresa Heinz had built a reputation as an environmental activist. As vice chair of the Environmental Defense Fund, she was always searching for ways to show major corporations that being a good steward of the land made good business sense. To highlight her own efforts, the new offices would contain only environmentally sustainable woods.

And so would her conference table.

So James retreated to his workshop in the corner of an industrial park on the city's North Side and threw himself into the project.

James did exhaustive research on the larger office construction, talking frequently with the architect to understand how the table project would fit into the larger scheme, interviewing staff members who worked closely with the Heinz family, and getting a sense of the people most likely to sit around it.

On the day the table was delivered—in pieces, on several elevator trips—Teresa Heinz was in the office. When it was assembled and polished she came in unannounced and inspected it from a distance.

After what seemed an eternity to James, she walked the distance across the room to where he was standing and gave him a hug. "It's just beautiful, William," she said in an accent hinting at her Portuguese roots.

But there was one significant problem: the height of the table.

Heinz plopped her thin, medium-height frame into one of the conference chairs and pulled it up to the table. It was true, James thought, that she seemed to be engulfed by it.

But that was understandable. James had done the measuring from the perspective of the largest people who would be sitting around the table.

When he explained it all to Mrs. Heinz, she merely smiled.

It was then James realized he had not spent enough time on a key perspective—perhaps the most important—that of the customer writing the check.

The image Heinz had in mind was not that of a Munchkin in her own conference room. There was no question: The table needed to be adjusted closer to her perspective.

"She was really great about it. I was going on about how some of these very tall men on her board would lose their leg room and she just gave me this little smile. She suggested they could always move their chairs back," James recalled.

Heinz even kicked off her shoes, hiked up her Chanel business suit, and crawled under the table with James to better understand from his perspective the work that would be involved in lowering the table.

A PROSPECTUS ON PERSPECTIVE

James was a forty-year-old star executive with National Steel Corporation, near completing an MBA and one of the youngest department directors in the company's history when he decided to turn his self-taught hobby into a second career.

As astute about business as he is artistic about furniture, James had the brainpowered star attitude in understanding the importance of perspective—seeing his project through the eyes of others connected to it. He also attempted to piece together all those snapshot views to form a mural-sized picture.

In retrospect, James says he learned a valuable star performer lesson when he discovered that the primary customer perspective was lost in the work of getting all the other snapshot views. By missing this one crucial facet of perspective, he was one step shy of star performance.

In the brainpowered workplace, star performers seek out perspective on several levels, even risking their egos to go after the critical outsider view. They do this to better understand how their work relates to the larger group effort. A Boeing flight computer engineer, for example, has to understand that she is only one of hundreds in the project to create the 777 airliner, or an attorney specializing in First Amendment law has to see himself as one of dozens in a large law firm advising ABC News in a libel suit.

A brainpowered worker often plays a central role as a specialist in a complex and often enormous group effort. More and more, brainpowered workers are evaluated by how well their pieces affect the outcome of the larger group effort, how well they understand various perspectives on the critical path.

In analyzing how star performers handled this critical work strategy, we observed that none of them treated perspective in a self-centered way. A star computer engineer at Bell Labs, for instance, would not consider having perspective as merely stepping forward with "Well, from my perspective, this version of the software is not as elegant as what I proposed." While perspective as personal opinion may be the limit for average engineers, the stars are constantly researching outside views, relating their project to both the local and global context in which they are working.

Professionals with broad perspective are able to understand how even small changes in the way they do their jobs affect the group effort, especially in projects that require meshing in with the work of others. The stars with the ability to evaluate a variety of perspectives and prioritize them are better able to evaluate their work honestly in a workplace full of work groups, teams, and interconnected systems.

A jet aircraft computer engineer designing a landing deceleration program is wise to seek out the perspective of the test pilot who eventually will be responsible for its success or failure in the aircraft. But what does the computer engineer do when the software program is a dream come true from the pilot's perspective but a power guzzler from the perspective of the electrical systems engineer?

Where even star performers sometimes trip up is in determining how much weight to give various perspectives on the work at hand.

Bell Labs CEO Arno Penzias, a Nobel Prize winner for his research work on the big bang theory of the universe, believes an inability to consider multiple perspectives is the most frequent reason that many highly intelligent researchers never manage to break from the ranks of the average. They get involved in "work for its own sake, digging one hole, boring in, and getting more and more fascinated by less and less.

"Scientists ask me how I know I'm on a good research project. I say, simple: Imagine what you're going to do will be 100 percent successful; find out how much money it's going to be worth; multiply by the probability of success; divide by the cost; and look at the figure of merit. . . . Everybody gets mad at that, saying, 'How would we know the probability? How would we know what it's worth? What if we don't know who the customer is?' But if you don't know who needs something, why are you going to do it? If you don't know what the chances of success are, why are you doing it? . . . This is a way of looking at the world—the ability to look at the larger context—you don't get that by using a No. 2 pencil between two vertical dotted lines. You gotta come up for air!"

Penzias points to three general perspectives in his example, but what we discovered in our research was that brainpowered workers need to consider many more views, all of them complex. It is a situation that explains why perspective is one of the most difficult work strategies for members of this group to master.

BEEN THERE, DONE THAT

In the early research of the differences between stars and average performers at Bell Labs, I worked with Dick Hayes, a colleague at Carnegie Mellon University who had spent years studying the differences between experts and novices.

Dick, along with Nobel laureate Herb Simon and other colleagues in psychology and computer science, was interested in the traits that defined experts across all disciplines. Experts have a fundamentally different understanding of their field than do novices. When a novice engineer faces a problem, he may generate ten possible explanations of its cause, but his lack of experience forces him to take the time to test all ten possibilities before he can be confident in recommending a solution. The expert, however, will mentally review the ten possible causes, perhaps even expand the list to fifteen. But she can quickly weed out the field to the one or two most likely culprits without having to test each one, saving valuable time. Even more important, the accuracy percentage for experts is also very high.

One study examined the differences between experts, average-but-experienced engineers, and novice engineers during the discovery phase of a project—for example, determining the most efficient way to integrate popular consumer options like VoiceMail into existing phone switches already on the market.

The discovery phase is that amount of project time spent on the front end trying to figure out what needs to be accomplished. Tasks include acquiring new information, creating the basic architecture for the new features, determining the most efficient path to take it from drawing board to market, and committing to a project plan, including a timetable in which to get it done.

The researchers found that expert engineers, the star performers, wasted very little of the important time they spent in the discovery phase when compared with their average colleagues, who might have just as much experience, or with the novices.

Because they were so efficient, experts spent only 20 percent of their total project hours in the discovery phase, while experienced engineers spent 50 percent and novices, 60 percent. Meanwhile, experts wasted only 2 percent of the time they spent in discovery; experienced engineers wasted 30 percent and novices, 43 percent.

Now, most people might expect the experts to cut to the chase more quickly than the novices. The surprising finding is how much faster and focused the experts were compared with their experienced coworkers. These average performers had as much time on the job as the experts, but they performed more like novices. Time on the job doesn't necessarily lead to the perspective of the star performers.

"Some people never seem to learn from experience," a manager of an international engineering firm complained to me. "Every new project that you give them is like the first one all over again, with just as much wheel spinning and going down blind alleys."

In pursuits as wide-ranging as creating art, playing chess, practicing medicine, and writing music, research reveals two skills found in the expert star performer. The first is that they "get it" in the context of employing a variety of perspectives, creating an entire picture from bits and pieces of basic information.

"Getting it" comes not just from superb technical ability, which even novices may have coming in the door, but also from having internalized a process so that it is part of them—nearly second nature. Consider the difference between a novice professor teaching her first college class, tied to detailed lecture notes and outlines, and her expert colleague, who has internally organized the material into a cohesive whole. The expert can speak cogently and extemporaneously on the subject.

Beyond internalization and technical proficiency, the expert has the ability to make judgments. This second skill of perspective puts him or her on a more productive plane than a coworker who may be even more technically adept. By making decisions about what task to take on and how best to get it done, the expert reduces both time spent and probability of failure.

Becoming an expert takes time. Most brainpowered workers start their careers with a defined amount of raw talents. As the individual or the company nurtures and refines those talents, the talents appreciate in value. At some point—ten years, on the average—a few individuals will pull that experience together, internalize it, and finally "get it." The brainpowered worker takes a quantum leap in productive value. These experts are qualitatively different from the merely experienced and the novice. In addition, the talent growth spurts can continue, with expertise and value increasing at a faster rate than those of the others.

Most people, unfortunately, never break into the expert or star ranks, partly because they never develop the necessary perspective. *For too many people, ten years of work experience is merely the first year's experience repeated ten times; there is no learning to move in and out of the basic environment, no leap to the perspective ability that defines expertise.*

During our work, we noticed that practice and experience have a lot to do with turning the potential star performer into an actual standout. How? Constant repetition and familiarity act as hard-wiring mechanisms in the brain to instill pattern recognition. Even highly intelligent people will find it nearly impossible to break into star ranks if they don't practice and have no experience.

No one in his right mind is going to argue that the difference between a superstar, like Mozart, and other composers is simply practice, of course. But even among superstars, practice appears to make a difference. Consider Michael Jordan of the Chicago Bulls.

His first sports love was baseball. During high school, his team won the state championship and he was voted "most valuable player." (In comparison, he was cut from his high school's varsity basketball team during his sophomore year.) During college, however, Jordan chose to play only basketball and went on to become perhaps the best who has ever played the game. Yet, in 1993, Michael Jordan left the arena that had brought him a $45-million-a-year income and worldwide celebrity.

Jordan left his comfortable basketball box to play baseball—minor league, no less—and it proved as unsettling to his ego as it was instructive about the effect of practice. In his first season with the Birmingham Barons, he hit a lackluster .202, with only three home runs. Respectable, yes; superstar, no. He experienced the impact over ten years of practice (or the lack of it) can have on raw talent.

Now, how does this translate to ordinary people who want to gain better perspective in their work world? You see someone who always seems to "get it." How do you become like that person?

When Sarah, one of Oracle Corporation's star software developers, first got hooked on computers in college, she was more interested in e-mail and games than programming. But partway into an introductory computer-skills course, she became fascinated with the logic language of computers and noticed how few of her classmates had that perspective. One incident she remembers involved a group of students who had pulled an all-nighter for a programming project but had forgotten to save their efforts. When a power surge blanked out the screen, they began treating the machine like a person, begging it not to crash.

Other students would swear and bang the keyboard when the machine rejected their commands. Sarah had her share of frustrations, too, but she recognized them as inexperience with the system's logic language, not as the result of some mystical barrier between computers and humans.

In her second semester, Sarah landed a lower-level programming job in the computer science lab. She stumbled more frequently and began to question her ability. But more experienced students encouraged her to stick it out; making mistakes is part of the learning process, they told her. By the end of the semester, she had started catching on.

Sarah helped smooth out some of the learning curve by keeping a notebook to capture the vocabulary and logic of computer programming. She also recorded common problems and their solutions. As Sarah's programming ability grew, coworkers began turning to her, providing valuable exposure to problems she ordinarily would not face in her own work.

Sarah took the software development job with Oracle in 1989 after completing her master's degree in computer science from the University of Michigan. Her six years of classroom and work experience enabled her to develop and then internalize her catalogue of problems and solutions. The combination of practice and experience helped her keep pace with other Oracle hires, but what eventually separated her from the pack was her "intuitive" grasp of software and computer logic. Coworkers recognized this quickly, seeking her perspective to help them over their brick walls.

After her first year, Sarah stunned her colleagues when she requested a transfer to software testing, an assignment often considered second-class, a career dead end. Testers examine the work of others to determine whether the software does what it is supposed to do. They identify bugs and check for quality. There is limited opportunity for the personal satisfaction that comes from creating new products. Software developers tolerate testers, albeit reluctantly and usually defensively, as the necessary bearers of bad news.

But Sarah saw the tester job as a learning opportunity to understand her work from a crucial perspective. She would become familiar with a wider range of the problems that could make software fail. She would gain years' worth of experience in one year's time. She would collaborate with top customers to build testing programs relevant to their perspective.

In the process, Sarah would learn how to avoid mistakes of substance and perspective in her own future software designing. Testing also provided a window into the perspective of her colleagues. She learned techniques her coworkers used in writing software and corrected flaws found during the testing process.

When Sarah returned to software development two years later, in 1992, the testing stint began to pay off. Her colleagues soon began referring to her as the Zen master of software, and she became known as one of the leading software gurus, a highly sought-after talent by firms throughout Silicon Valley.

Star performers like Sarah, who have mastered the nuances of perspective, weren't born to the art of it. They have been immersed in a particular technical field for years, some reaching back to college or high school internships. They learned their perspective skills in the same way Sarah learned how to write brilliant computer code or successful novelists learned how to improve their craft—practice. They sought out learning experiences that pushed the limits of their knowledge. Then they made sure they learned from it by internalizing patterns and forms. In Sarah's case, she kept a log to capture what she learned. At day's end, she would review it, make notes about new insights, and further organize the material. Other star performers use different techniques, such as mental rehearsal of material they have just learned.

For Michael Flatley, the high-stepping, tap dancing star of *Riverdance* and *Lord of the Dance*, his practice came during ten years of touring with the Irish folk band The Chieftains. "That was my training ground," he says. "Going out performing every night in different cities, testing against the audiences, was a great way to find what worked. Doing that for ten years, it became easy to know what would work. So when I went to Ireland to do *Riverdance*, it was a piece of cake."

But the goal is the same for all star performers: to develop a deeper, more well-rounded understanding of their field, which, in turn, leads to pattern recognition skills that form the foundation of perspective. The star engineers we studied didn't always succeed on the perspective front, but what set them apart from the pack was that they put themselves in high-leverage learning situations, created a personal review process to capture learnings and analyze mistakes, resolved to learn from missed opportunities, and actively pushed themselves up the experience curve by practicing new skills of their craft. They also worked harder than most of their coworkers to develop those skills.

Pattern recognition, then, is the essential foundation for star performer perspective, and it can only be attained through experience. Stars—whether they be actors, scientists, or chess grand masters—practice their craft more than average performers. As a result, they run across a wider range of problems with known solutions. They get tripped up less often. And since they have tried more solutions, they have a wider understanding of what works.

But pattern recognition by itself isn't enough. The difference between stars and average performers is whether they incorporate their pattern recognition ability into the kind of perceptive and strategic thinking that leads to expert judgment. That is what the rest of this chapter is about.

BEING THERE, DOING THAT, AND MOVING ON: GETTING OUTSIDE THE BOX WITH THE FIVE Cs

Now that I've preached the necessity of pattern recognition through practice in order to develop a sense of perspective that is second nature, here's one of those infuriating caveats that business professors love to slip into their lectures to drive students crazy:

"Every virtue carried to its extreme becomes a vice."

In other words, once you've mastered the art of perspective in pattern recognition, your next step is to become skilled at breaking away from it. It seems confusing, but one of the higher-level versions of perspective involves the ability to break away from the familiar and seek out points of view that are more distanced. Stars know their field so well that they know both its limitations and when events do not conform to an expected pattern. Stars are better positioned to notice a "surprise" and to determine whether it is just a random blip or a potential breakthrough worthy of further pursuit. Since average performers do not have such a firm grasp of the expected patterns, they either do not notice the novelty or are fooled into thinking it fits into the pattern.

"The first principle is that you must not fool yourself," wrote the Nobel Prize–winning physicist Richard P. Feynman.

"And without a sense of perspective, you are the easiest person to fool."

Often, what separates star performers from average coworkers in the perspective-skill area is the ability of the stars to move beyond the safety of familiar perspectives and place themselves in arenas that are totally foreign. The stars know that the real value of perspective is the ability to see that which is dear to them—a software program, an electric car battery design, a legal argument—from less endearing angles.

In his book *Lateral Thinking*, Edward De Bono writes about how important it is to learn to think outside the box, to seek perspective outside the safe and secure environment where people know us for more than the work we produce.

Figure 2
The Five Cs of Star Perspective

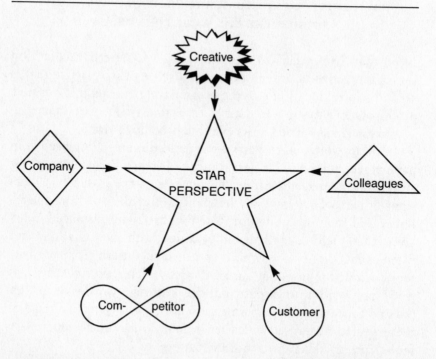

In the brainpowered workplace, star performers are adept at getting outside their specialty box and strategically choosing other boxes to jump into among the hundreds that are open and available every workday. I refer to them as the Five Cs.

1. Colleague Perspective

One of the most important outsider boxes provides the view of experts who are familiar with your type of work but who are not part of your immediate work group. These sources can be coworkers in the same section of the company or outside colleagues.

But many average performers are unwilling to seek these outside perspectives. Mort, a medical research scientist, is working on a medical research project investigating why some Alzheimer's patients experience severe memory loss in their fifties, while others don't show the same degree of impairment until their early eighties.

He is based in Portland, Oregon, but he has heard about a researcher in New York who is taking a different approach to measuring memory loss in her study subjects. Early results suggest that her method may take less time and prove to be more accurate.

But the last thing Mort will do is go to the phone to investigate. He is threatened by seeking out this new perspective. It is easier to convince himself that his way is the best way and limit his focus to his own on the project. How dare anyone suggest that his methodology might be less efficient!

In disciplines ranging from medical research to advertising to law, an aversion to outside perspective is ingrained in many quarters—unfortunate and surprising, given that other segments of the workforce got the message years ago and now even advertise a willingness to listen to other points of view inside their organizations.

A fundamental reason why many brainpowered workers in most disciplines are not nearly so open to outside perspectives has to do with the culture of their work. Years of training in narrowly defined specialties leaves little room for exploring perspectives in other disciplines. And the exclusivity of these professions—evidenced in the jargon used to wall off outsiders—creates an almost willful tunnel vision and an active resistance to differing points of view, even to institutional peer review.

These professional blinders are compounded by personal resistance, as illustrated by Mort in the above example. A common problem for many brainpowered workers is allowing their work to be criticized.

In the Bell Labs workplace, peer review of individual pieces of work on a massive switch-building project was built into the process to ensure that the work passed through the perspectives of other engineers and managers. The process, known at Bell as "design review," was supposed to provide a way of catching harmful errors that could gum up the larger, final product, or to note ways that the code might be written more efficiently. Every piece of work had to pass design review in order to be plugged into the larger project.

Average engineers with limited perspective for the switch had come to treat the review segment as a grueling ordeal, fighting their way through it tooth and nail, resentful of critical points of view. Most often, the process was misery for everyone involved, especially the beleaguered engineer, who would be sent back to his or her work cubicle to make changes.

Compare that with the experience of Claire, a star engineer I observed, who was facing design review on a piece of code she had written for a call-forwarding program that would be tied into a new phone switch device. Claire had a completely opposite perspective on the process. She saw it partly as an obstacle to be overcome, but also as an opportunity to showcase her work and build allies in the workplace by seeking their points of view well ahead of the review date.

"When I first arrived at Bell Labs, I made a point of sitting in on as many design reviews as possible," she remembers. As a new hire, Claire had little to offer in the way of perspective, but she was able to learn much from the perspective of others.

"I noticed that many people went into their reviews either expecting a rubber stamp for their hard work or fearful of cutthroat criticism." Seldom did these reviews go well. "Some engineers stacked the audience with friendly coworkers," she remembers, "and when the criticism began to fly, the defending forces would circle the wagons. In some cases, they might even attack the critics."

During these reviews Claire learned who the players were: the constant carpers; the unprepared, who shot from the hip; and the wise ones, whose opinions brought a hush to the room and whose judgments carried so much weight that their suggestions were almost always adopted.

She also noticed that a few engineers sailed through with only minor changes made to their work, even though the heat generated during the review would have suggested otherwise. Claire talked to these successful coworkers afterward to learn their perspective on design review.

Writing elegant code, she discovered, is only the first step to getting through design review unscathed. Unfortunately, this is where most average performers stop. In particular, although design review is primarily about the quality of the software code, it is also a social and psychological event.

Many of Claire's coworkers have a stake in one particular phone feature, such as call waiting or Touch-Tone dialing. Even more feel protective of the entire phone switch that houses all those features. Many have sweated bullets to get their piece working and have suffered when someone else's "bugs" inadvertently crippled their code. For Claire's work to be welcomed into the larger feature, she learned, it needed the support of key players, and the main way to get this was to invite their perspectives into the process.

Before her design-review sessions, Claire would set up one-on-one meetings with star performers—opinion leaders who are also working on the project. "The truth is that these folks have good ideas, and although I may not always agree with them, because of their background and their own biases they're going to think of things that I don't. And I deliberately go after perspectives from people I know who are likely to be critical." Winning over these skeptics, she reasons, will help ensure passing the review.

Claire's one-on-one meetings before the official session provide an opportunity for meaningful exchange of perspectives. Listening to these critical perspectives in an informal setting allows her time to make changes, or to build the best defense of her work. Claire also made a point of keeping these colleagues informed about changes made after their input. These strategies turned key players into partners on Claire's work rather than outsiders.

Because of Claire's proactive efforts to broaden perspective rather than fight it, she was able to adhere to the spirit of the review process while protecting her work from being pecked to death by others with less-than-noble motives. She became one of a few noted for "sailing through design review" by incorporating her colleagues' valuable perspective into her work prior to the review process.

Bell Labs' design review is not very different from any other review process, whether it be book editors winning support of the publishing staff to launch the book successfully, an ad creator passing her work by the rest of the creative team, or a professor submitting his work to peer review prior to publication. Like Claire, they turn the system around to benefit from their critics' expertise. They adopt useful advice and offer reasons for what they reject.

Stars see the process of soliciting critical perspective as an important way to improve their work. It's also an effective way to enhance professional standing. Moreover, it helps build others' commitment to the success of the work product, as critical players begin to feel a partnership with the star's project.

Relatively few people can sit back with an open mind while others criticize their hard efforts. Even for star performers, this is a difficult skill to learn. But those who found it difficult compensated by finding "buddies"—experts whom they respected, whose personal chemistry was compatible with their own, and whose motives they trusted.

Buddies can become key allies, offering critical perspective in a way that would cause the star to take notes rather than snap a pencil. These buddies would be the first outside audience to react to the work products, catching flaws and offering strategy tips before the work was put to a more public test.

2. Customer Perspective

Star performers always manage to find a way to see their work, and the product it helps to build, through the eyes of the customer. The stars work to understand what customer needs and motivations are, even though they may be far removed from the sales office.

In his effort to design the best possible table for Teresa Heinz, furniture designer William James moved outside his workshop to seek a variety of perspectives. But where he briefly stumbled was in overlooking the importance of the paying customer to the process. He had mistakenly ranked the outside perspective box of how the customer would see herself with the product lower than other boxes. That turned out to be a backward drive along the critical path, a direction that James was eventually forced to correct. Had he spent more time in the customer box, the time-consuming adjustment might have been avoided.

The customer perspective is valuable in every business, even in a health care field that has a built-in customer base, such as dentistry. Most dentists believe that the success of their practice depends on the degree of skill they bring to caring for patients' teeth. But given a certain level of competency, meeting customer-patient comfort needs can be critical.

Despite all the preventive and public relations efforts by the dental profession to turn their customers' image of them around, most people still put off going to the dentist as long as possible. When people do go, the old fears surface and play havoc with both the mind and the body. Blood pressure goes up, as does sweating. Once in the office, numerous cues get your heart beating faster—the bright lights, the Muzak, the chair that puts you in a vulnerable position, the white coats, the cubicles full of pain-inducing tools.

Pittsburgh dentist Owen Cantor paid attention to this customer perspective in the design stage of a new office. After talking to his customers and reading all the latest studies on how to reduce anxiety, Cantor decided on a radical departure from the typical dentist office architecture. He chose a historic downtown building he could renovate as he pleased. He left the high wood-beamed ceiling and exposed brick to give the office a welcoming, homelike feel. Soft, incandescent lamplight replaced the standard medical office fluorescent. A friendly receptionist was positioned out in the waiting room, and a sound system to play soothing, classical music was installed throughout.

In running his kinder, gentler dentist's office, Cantor keeps his appointments on track so patients aren't spending anxious moments alone in a dental chair. The examining rooms contain only a reclining chair that is left upright until the dentist begins the examination. Dental instruments are brought into the room only on an as-needed basis. Before any procedure begins, Cantor chats with the patient to ease any concerns.

Every detail and step is designed to help the patient have a positive experience. If this occurs, then patients are more likely to engage in a positive oral hygiene program, including visiting the dentist's office more regularly. More frequent visits will, in turn, lead to fewer dental problems, as well as a more pleasant experience for the customer and Cantor during office visits.

The customer-centered approach has resulted in a word-of-mouth advertising boom for Cantor; he now enjoys a very successful practice in the city.

This type of customer perspective is what Don Norman extols in his book *The Psychology of Everyday Things.* And he rails against the kind of brainpowered work we have too much of: designed by experts to impress other experts.

3. Competitor Perspective

Pianist Leopold Godowsky once told a reporter, "Do you know the first thing I do every day? I read the *New York Times* obituary page, because maybe a pianist has died somewhere and there might be an opening."

In the brainpowered workplace, there are better ways to get a handle on the competition. The effort in the 1980s to understand how Japanese car companies do so well at designing and building smaller cars, for instance, led American manufacturers to catch up in technology, and in many cases, one-up the competition.

Movie studios have learned that keeping an eye on the release dates of your competitors' movies can make the difference between success and failure. During the summer months, which account for 40 percent of annual ticket sales, a strong opening is critical. Without it, a $70 million investment and three years of work evaporate before they can build momentum.

The ability to see your workplace through the eyes of competitors and objectively assess how your organization measures up is a critical perspective skill, but it's not one easily mastered. Average performers often fall down on this important customer perspective. During our research, we asked people to tell us everything about their competitors that was relevant to their work. While average performers could name their competitors, they could rarely do more. Stars, on the other hand, often had intimate knowledge of the competitors' products and could do a point-by-point comparison with their own product. They also had good clues about what new products their competition had under development.

In the early stages of identifying traits among the best performers at Bell Labs, we mistakenly concluded that they all shared a talent for adopting the correct perspectives for their projects. But even in the star ranks, it was a minority who could effectively set aside their biases and their own experiences to see a situation from a competitor's point of view.

Some engineers were smart enough to recognize their difficulty in getting outside the box, and so they adopted the buddy system to get the perspective they needed. They would find colleagues inside the company, professional associates at other companies, suppliers, or former teachers who had a sharp eye on the competition.

Don, an engineer who worked for one of the regional Bell phone companies in the 1980s, just after the break-up of AT&T, once told me that his company was "on the leading edge of obsolete technology." Now, this was said in a private place, of course, out of earshot of his managers, who were all publicly extolling the company's position as "leading edge." In fact, the company had mounted an internal campaign with that slogan to puff up employee morale.

It didn't work with Don, because he had a broader perspective that his managers were sadly missing. The engineer had done a lot of talking with the company's suppliers and had developed relationships that allowed him to sit in their box, to get their view of the technical reputation of his phone company. "I would quiz them on where our company stood with the other phone companies and the other high-tech companies serviced by these suppliers. Who was buying the latest equipment, what levels of production were they getting, and who was pushing the innovation envelope?"

When traveling, Don also made it a point to develop sources at other phone companies—the eventual competitors—in order to put their perspectives into the mix.

The engineer analyzed all those collected perspectives and was able to inject some hard reality into his company's corporate delusion that it was leading the pack in technology. He gave an informal lunch-bag presentation to his work group, sharing his findings and concerns. With his boss's agreement, he wrote up an internal memo for the technical community comparing a few of the company's core technologies with those of the other phone companies. He invited reactions and encouraged his colleagues to do their own comparisons. He set up a meeting to air people's perspectives on the topic.

Don used this valuable collection of competitor perspectives to schedule a meeting with upper management. This led to a full-blown benchmarking effort of all the core technologies to help company managers get an honest fix on where they stood. His efforts resulted in a plan that actually did move the company to the leading edge, which put them in the dominant position with the lucrative corporate business that spans regional monopolies. It also gave them a leg up in attracting favorable deals with long-distance carriers, such as MCI and AT&T.

4. Company-Management Perspective

The skill of being able to think like the competition is especially useful when it is paired with an ability to take on the perspective of decision makers inside your organization.

A finding from our research that surprised us is that many workers do not know their boss's goals or vision to help guide their work. Most books and consultants fault the bosses for this, giving them poor marks in communication. This is true in many cases, but the boss's communications flaws don't serve as an excuse for your failure to deliver what they expect.

In our productivity improvement programs, we send workers to talk with their boss and then the boss's manager about their work project and how it fits into the bigger picture. The results are always eye-opening. It is common for employees to discover that they are working on something that is not very important to their boss or the company's fortunes. Perhaps it was important when they first got the assignment, but now it has drifted off the boss's radar screen. Another common eye-opening response is that the employee's boss and his or her manager disagree on the project's importance, direction, or progress. These disagreements always fall hardest on the brainpowered worker.

When Phil moved from the small-business part of First Chicago Bank to the larger corporate banking division, his star performer status in his previous department did not transfer with him. Corporate banking has traditionally viewed small business as small-change profit generators—as teller and ATM deposits and small loans. Though Phil had done the same kind of brainpowered work as his corporate colleagues, although on a smaller scale, he realized his reputation depended on switching over quickly.

In his first few weeks, Phil read everything available on the department, from the annual report to regulatory agency filings to stories in the popular or trade press. "I wanted to learn what face we were putting out to the public and what the public thought of us," says Phil.

He also collected departmental mission and strategy statements, poring over past plans and performance reviews to see what had been intended and what had actually happened. He paid particular attention to the measures that were used to determine whether the targets were reached, such as sales revenue, number of new customers, and cost savings. Then he compared those with the compensation system to see if they were tied together. "I was trying to figure out what they said mattered and what really ended up mattering."

When Phil finished reading his way down the bank's paper trail, he turned his attention to the staff, beginning with the two stars of the department. "I told them that I wanted to pull my weight as soon as possible and that I needed their help to make sure that I was in sync with the department. So then I asked them, What are the department's goals and how do they map with the supervisor's or department head's goals? Which goals are most important? How does the work of this unit fit in with the work of the other units that we work with? What do the other units think of us? What do the customers think of us? How about our competition?"

Phil then chose the stars for his first perspective check on the company's written record of itself. "I could also see how good my initial instincts were," says Phil. "If what they told me did not map well with my conclusions, then I asked them about the discrepancy."

Phil's next perspective check was with his boss, asking the same questions he posed to the star producers. In addition, he asked for her perspective on what constraints faced their department, what her goals were, and how his work assignment tied into the goals she had set for the unit. Phil also asked if she had any objections to his scheduling a similar meeting with her boss.

"The point of all this was to get a good grasp of what my bosses wanted and how my work fit into their plans. I also wanted to learn where any trouble spots were that could blindside me."

If Phil's bosses didn't agree on some fundamental perspectives, such as which customers were most important or which new products were to get priority, that information would be critical to Phil's productivity. If the political climate allowed for it, he might even initiate a meeting to discuss areas of disagreement. In any case, Phil can't afford to be out of sync with his bosses and the larger company goals. "Every six months or so, I try to sit down separately with my boss and her boss to assess how things are going for the department, for the project, for them, and for me. I use their perspective to shape my efforts and to determine if I need a midcourse correction."

Although other workers might meet with their manager, what Phil asks about, learns, and uses from these conversations sets him apart.

When Compaq Computer Corporation was being ravaged by competitors who were selling products of the same quality but at much lower cost, the CEO sent word out that costs had to be reduced. Some engineers and managers had fallen into the trap of believing that every important part that went into Compaq products had to be made from scratch by the company. But several engineers who understood the CEO's perspective—that cost cutting was a do-or-die proposition and he was not going to take no for an answer—began scouring the trade fairs and realized many of the parts could be purchased from other sources, significantly driving down the costs of their personal computers.

Not only did the move lead to Compaq's surviving, but the company leapt ahead of competitor powerhouses like Dell, IBM, and Apple to secure the number-one sales spot.

This ability to think with a company perspective can be extended to empowering the entire organization to take an active role; it doesn't have to be limited to scoping out the competition.

Companies legitimately on the leading edge of technology in the 1990s often have arrived there not by accurately seeing themselves through just one or two competitors' eyes but by getting a sense of the entire field—multiple perspectives that give the company an angle no one else has bothered to see.

The number of companies that do this successfully is just as small as the number of employees who do it well. But many more are trying, because the rewards are great. Seeing the business land-scape in broad perspective has brought companies into entirely new technologies, rocketing them years ahead of the competition.

5. Creative Dissonance Perspective

I once asked Tim—a 3M design engineer who created the complex machines needed to make precise cuts for tapes, disks, and paper products—where he drew his inspiration.

"From God—from nature," was his first answer. "If you look at the designs in nature, they are elegant and yet each part of the design has a function. Nothing is wasted."

"Aside from nature, where do you look?" I asked.

"From the special effects done for movies," he said. "Those people make it look so real, so effortless . . . so, well, cool. What they do for movies, I want to do for my machines. I want people to be knocked out of their seats, to be in awe when they see the machine and discover what it can do."

The idea that this technical engineer would be sitting in a theater thinking perceptively about some machine cooked up for *Terminator II* might seem to defeat the work escape that so many of us look for in a trip to the movies, but escape is not the goal for this design engineer.

To Tim, design is everywhere. The difference between good and bad design is a function of perspective. For the design engineer, the ultimate goal is to achieve what people really want but that they believe to be impossible, like a handheld computer that actually works effortlessly or a nonpolluting auto fuel.

Tim, a thirty-eight-year-old avid athlete who has a passion for skiing, has visited factories that make the best skis, snooping around for tips he can use in his work. Do the ski-making machines hold any secrets that he can adapt to his next design?

Tim has vowed not to reinvent any wheels, so he reads widely outside his design area, always searching for ideas to stimulate his own creativity—new-car factory ads and articles on paper mills, amusement parks, and large household appliances all cross his desk.

While many of his colleagues fall prey to the Not Invented Here syndrome, Tim tries to save time by incorporating other peoples' ideas into his work.

"Borrowing shamelessly" is how he refers to it. "I'm not trying to copy their end product," Tim says. "I'm simply melding their ideas with mine to create something new, unique, and elegant. Plus, I always give people credit when I apply their ideas. In a good design, there is always enough credit to go around."

In one particularly difficult videotape machine design involving over ten moving subassemblies that had to be synchronized, Tim borrowed one idea from an automotive designer friend, played off another from an industry supplier, and found inspiration for a key part from a former university professor. Members of his design team said the key part did not exist and would have to be specially made, threatening the schedule and budget. Tim believed the part was being manufactured; he remembered reading about it, and began to check his wide network of sources. A former engineering professor responded that he had used the part—in ready supply for $8—on a telecommunications project.

Tim's teammates were smart and talented. But they had trapped themselves within the confines of their own industry. The ability to think across disciplines—either to see how the insights of other fields can be applied to your area or how your discipline can alter another field—is a distinct mark of the star brainpowered worker.

And it is never too late to develop the skill, building a multidimensional internal résumé. On paper, fifty-seven-year-old Solomon Snyder, the even-tempered director of the Department of Neuroscience at Johns Hopkins University, in Baltimore, is a formidable scientist. He has won twenty-nine scientific awards for his research on brain chemistry; his curriculum vitae runs to fifty pages and includes only the most important of the seven hundred papers he has published in his distinguished career.

But the real mark of his success is the amount of esteem in which his peers hold him. Solomon is a star performer in his field, having repeatedly opened new fields of research and developed new drugs to treat a range of conditions, from psychiatric disorders to chronic pain.

If he were not so likable, many of his colleagues would be put out by someone of such consistently high performance, because he makes the brutally unforgiving work of science seem so effortless. "He sits at his desk, he reads, he thinks," reported one admirer, "and he comes up with an idea that is, to use one of his favorite phrases, 'really neat.' "

So how does Snyder manage to be so productive and make it seem so natural? One of his secrets is to stop acting like a scientist. Solomon goes to great lengths to get out of the hard-science box. He cultivates a network of friends who are not connected to science at all. He gets involved in a wide range of activities that have little to do with his work, serving as president of his synagogue and on the board of the Baltimore Symphony.

And when he is at work, he doesn't let technology become a barrier to human interaction. Instead of working in seclusion in front of a computer or in a lab, Snyder spends most of his day in meetings and on the telephone.

Snyder says his most profound ideas—invaluable discoveries about how the brain works—often come at moments that have little to do with the work at hand. He reads a wide variety of material, staying on top of research that has little to do with studies of the brain. Instead, he says he tries to think about ways in which the findings might be applied to his work. It is this pattern of getting out of the science box that Snyder says led to all his most important discoveries.

Colleagues describe Snyder as a star at making the "intuitive leap" from one field to another.

Consider the evolution of an immune system suppressor drug known as FK-506 as an example of how Snyder uses the perspective of one field to apply to his own:

Reading a newspaper article on the drug one day, Snyder latched onto the finding that tiny amounts of FK-506 bind specifically to receptors in white blood cells. Immediately, he thought that the same binding process might be occurring in the brain. Not only was that the case, his lab staff later discovered, but brain cells were bound to the drug fifty times more tightly than white blood cells were.

Snyder and his team also discovered that the binding process occurred in very specific areas of the brain where an enzyme, calcineurin, is found. Then a Harvard immunologist moved the project further by discovering that in the presence of FK-506, calcineurin is inhibited and proteins retain their phosphate groups.

Looking at his colleague's perspective on what was going on between the two chemicals, Snyder decided to use FK-506 as a tool to find out what phosphate groups do to different proteins. What his group learned was that the key proteins affected the enzyme that makes nitric oxide, the gas that Snyder had become world famous for identifying as the chief neural transmitter in the brain.

The clinical implications in medicine are enormous. Snyder and his colleagues had discovered earlier that nitric oxide is responsible for killing brain cells during strokes. The chain reaction starts when injured brain cells release glutamate, which stimulates production of nitric oxide. But when FK-506 was added to the equation in experiments with animals, they found that the drug prevents glutamate from killing neurons.

Now he is trying to establish whether the drug will have the same effect in the human brain. In the process of doing that, Snyder once again jumped out of his narrow field to read up on a clinical study of liver transplant patients in which some received FK-506 and others got cyclosporin—another immunosuppressant but one that does not interact with the brain.

In the long list of side effects listed at the end of the paper for each drug, Snyder sifted out the nugget that while 50 percent of the cyclosporin patients had "cerebrovascular accidents," only 5 percent of the FK-506 recipients did.

The significance of the drug as an aid to stroke patients could vanish as it undergoes more clinical trials, but Mark Fishman, director of Massachusetts General Hospital and a collaborator with Snyder on nitric oxide research, says it is a credit to Snyder that he is willing to discuss his ideas publicly in an early stage of research, welcoming critical perspectives.

"Many scientists only give their ideas when they are carefully sculpted," Fishman told the *New York Times*. "He's not afraid of being wrong about something and I find that refreshing." In the ranks of star performers, however, that openness to perspective and willingness to make mistakes is the norm.

Synder's creative dissonance, his ability to cross disciplines for perspective, plays a crucial role in boosting him from solidly performing medical researcher to star scientist. Even superstars in nontechnical fields know the benefits of getting outside the box.

Let's go back to the example of Chicago Bulls superstar Michael Jordan, who left his comfortable basketball box to take on the perspective of a baseball player. "The picture painted of Michael Jordan always is, Whatever he does, he's great at it," says Jordan, speaking from the perspective of his public image. "A lot of people thought I wasn't successful at baseball because I didn't make it to the major leagues. Baseball gave me a more humanistic side."

In other interviews, Jordan says his baseball perspective has made him more of a team player now that he has returned to the Bulls. Jordan is producing at the same level as before (the team shattered the twenty-seven-year-old league record for most wins in a season), but the way in which he produces is different and more amenable to team play. For the first time in his career, Jordan is working out regularly with his teammates and embracing a Bulls-developed strength-training regimen.

Where once it seemed his only friend on the team was coach Phil Jackson, a master in the art of dealing with superstar egos, he has now developed a working rapport with each member.

And Jordan's new friendship with costar Scottie Pippen has much to do with their shared perspectives in the team captain job. When Jordan went to find himself in minor-league baseball, Pippen felt the pain of intense pressure to hold the team together and perform. "I really had no idea what he had to deal with until he left," says Pippen.

A FINAL WORD ON PERSPECTIVE

From the superstar ranks of professional basketball to the top medical research labs in the country, the benefits of shared perspectives and of perspectives obtained outside the box are clear. Average producers become stars when they muster the courage and self-confidence to build perspective searches around the Five Cs into daily routines.

In the brainpowered workplace of the 1990s, the alternative is to exist in a self-imposed vacuum. Stars can't be grown in that environment, and companies that don't have a rich flow of perspectives are not long for this economy. The reason is that in the brainpowered economy, the game and the rules are always changing.

Stanford University's Brian Arthur compares the brainpowered economy to a casino, "where part of the game is to choose which games to play, as well as playing them with skill. Over at this table, a game is starting called multimedia. Over at that one, a game called

Web services. In the corner is electronic banking. There are many such tables. You sit at one. How much to play? you ask. Three billion, the croupier replies. Who'll be playing? We won't know until they show up. What are the rules? Those'll emerge as the game unfolds. What are my odds of winning? We can't say. Do you still want to play?"

According to Arthur, the rewards go to the players who are quickest to make sense out of the new games emerging from the brainpowered economy, to see their shape, and to grasp their rules. "Bill Gates is not so much a wizard of technology as a wizard of precognition, of discerning the shape of the next game."

To succeed in a casino type world, you need perspective. It prepares you for the next wave that is coming, helps you figure out how it is similar to or different from previous waves, and gives you a basis for reinventing yourself and your company to take advantage of it.

But you cannot succeed on perspective alone. Just as star-quality perspectives cannot be formed without the practices we've discussed, perspective as a superproductive work strategy needs to mesh with other skills in the productivity model—among them, initiative, networking, and organizational savvy.

Perspective is the major work strategy, however, that reflects on your standing as a brainpowered worker. Whereas initiative speaks loudly about your motivation, and self-management about your ability to get work done, perspective goes a long way in establishing your reputation for brainpower. With the ability to recognize patterns, to think creatively outside the box, to exercise expert judgment, and to discern the changing games and their changing rules, you have the essential perspective keys to gain entry to the star performer ranks.

8

FOLLOWERSHIP
Checking Your Ego at the Door
to Lead in Assists

"SO YOU DID THIS BECAUSE YOUR FRIENDS WERE DOING IT?
THAT'S JUST GREAT! AND IF THEY JUMPED OFF A CLIFF WOULD
YOU FOLLOW THEM? YOU WANT TO BE A FOLLOWER YOUR
WHOLE LIFE?"

—YOUR MOTHER

The notion of being an exemplary follower is one of the most challenging in the star performer skills model, not only because it is so difficult to master but because it is so hard to accept. Average performers are always surprised that star producers, whom many people label as leaders, also are adept at following others.

Followership is the work strategy that guides your interactions with leaders. It focuses on all the relationships you have with people who have organizational power and authority over you. Followership is also different from teamwork, which is most often about brainpowered-worker-to-brainpowered-worker relationships—the horizontal, not the vertical top-down relationships of leadership.

As the opening quote demonstrates, there is a negative image of followership in American work and social structure every bit as powerful as the glittery popular notions of leadership. And I argue here, as I have in my other writings, that it is every bit as inaccurate.

The now famous picture of a sixteen-year-old Bill Clinton shaking hands with President John F. Kennedy during a civics program sponsored by the American Legion in Washington was a powerful campaign image because it supposedly captured the watershed moment when Clinton decided he could someday be president. It would hardly have had such resonance with voters if Clinton had described it as the moment he decided he wanted to be an administrative assistant in the White House. But in reality, much of the concrete successes in an administration can be credited to creative, capable assistants who get only broad policy directives from a president.

In fact, the dogma pounded into us from kindergarten on into retirement is that being a leader is something special to be aspired to, while being a follower is something mundane to settle for.

Consider the unusual experience of Dave, who set himself on a successful career track and made an important contribution to his company when he stepped forward and shattered the traditional image of followership. In fact, Dave is one who would have answered a resounding yes to his mother when she asked him if he planned to be a follower his whole life. But he's done it in a way that would make her proud.

Now a vice president of one of the country's top pharmaceutical firms, Dave began his career with the company fresh out of college, thrown into a highly competitive management training program with twenty-eight other employees. After two years, the twenty-five who remained graduated from the program and were pitted against one another in a horse race to determine who would win top management jobs. In the end, only Dave and nine others remained on the company's fast track.

Dave recognized the brutal nature of the leadership race early on. He decided to continue with the program but with a radical change in course. He decided to move to the follower track and leave the leadership contest to others. At a company ceremony marking graduation from the training program, many in the group talked about their plans for reaching the highest ranks of management—how their ideas and skills would see the company through the next twenty years.

Dave's talk caught the group by surprise. Yes, many of his fellow trainees did have great ideas and brilliant minds, he said. But for any of them to reach the highest leadership positions in the company, they were going to need sharp, dynamic, independent-thinking followers working along with them. Dave was putting them all on notice that he was aspiring to be that kind of follower, rather than racing against them for the leadership slots.

The pitch had such an impact that Dave heard from every one of his fellow graduates by the next day, all asking for his assistance. And the strategy has paid off in his long-term career. His vice president's job carries leadership responsibilities, and he fulfills them well. "But I have never coveted a leadership role," he says. "My career goals were to contribute to, rather than compete with, my colleagues—to earn their respect and trust. My promotions have resulted from good followership."

The added benefit of taking the followership route is that Dave has avoided the dark side of the glitzy leadership track. Of the ten management trainees still with the company, Dave is the only one who is on good terms with each of the others. Some are higher in leadership positions than Dave, some are lower. There are even people younger who have passed him by, and he has gone out of his way to help them in their climb. "My strategy paid off for me," says Dave. "I avoided the struggle for leadership, kept my friends, and did a good job without constantly guarding against power and politics."

Our research shows that star brainpowered workers have figured out how much they want to play the followership role in their day-to-day work. They have waved off the negative popular notions and concentrated on developing a definition that elevates followership to its proper status:

Brainpowered followership means being actively engaged in helping the organization succeed while exercising independent, critical judgment of goals, tasks, potential problems, and methods. Star followers have the ability to work cooperatively with a leader to accomplish the organization's goals even when there are personality or workplace differences. They are key players both in planning courses of action and in implementing them in the field. They use other productivity-model skills to choose the manner and timing.

This definition contrasts with what average performers think followership is: A work behavior that shows managers and coworkers that "I know how to toe the line and not threaten the leader, and I promise to stick to the boundaries of my job description."

The stars have figured out that the day-to-day realities of the workplace put the lie to societal snubbing of followership. While this is a relatively new field of research, my work shows that 90 percent of most brainpowered workers spend 90 percent of their time as followers. And followers actually contribute about 90 percent to the success of any organizational outcomes, while leaders account for 10 percent. It is the way the business world is set up, but the glamour bias pushes workers to devalue what they spend most of their time doing. For every committee where a brainpowered worker holds court as chairperson, there are dozens more, over the span of a career, where she or he is merely a member.

When I pointed out the followership-leadership ratio in a consulting session with some General Motors executives, the reaction was predictably hostile, so I had them crunch some numbers, which many business leaders love to do.

"Of the 400,000 employees at General Motors, how many would fall into the leader category—the people who you think make things happen?" I asked. The group agreed the number was about 2,000. So I told them to do the math. Half of 1 percent are leaders, and if you follow models of effectiveness already established out there, this group has an impact equal to 10 percent of the workforce, which is a lot of power in proportion to their numbers. Yet it is still not enough to account for or to guarantee success.

That calmed them somewhat, but I think these seasoned executives wanted to believe their leadership accounted for as much as 50 percent of the productivity in the organization. They had to confront the fact that 90 percent of the success is coming from people who implement the directives of leadership. While leadership skills are important, follower skills are probably more important when it comes to adding bottom-line value to the corporation.

In the course of my research on another book, *The Power of Followership*, many well-known leaders and followers reacted in extremes to my ideas on cultivating bright, creative followers in the business world. Most were wildly enthusiastic, but a few were surprisingly hostile to the concept.

One of these was Red Auerbach, coaching titan and past president of the Boston Celtics basketball team.

"Can you imagine a team in which players picked other players and decided on the substitutions? It is absolutely ludicrous," Auerbach said after reading a *Harvard Business Review* article based on my book. "Can you imagine a business run by people without authority or by people who are not in a position to assume the responsibility of failure? It would undoubtedly flounder."

Now, Auerbach may very well be correct that in a few limited situations—military operations, for instance—the only call is for one leader to bark out orders, with followers carrying them out precisely as directed. And although there are many in the Auerbach mold who would prefer all of life's endeavors be run that way, very few are.

Even on Auerbach's most successful squads, the creativity, innovation, and spontaneity on the court seem to belie his words. Perhaps he issues the overall commands, but team members carry them out with independence and their own distinctive style. When they lose, they appear as downcast and self-reproaching as the coach.

There are very few situations that depend on robotlike conformists to achieve a goal. In fact, there is a lot of evidence to suggest the opposite. The domineering, ego-centered style of management—introduced in the chapter on leadership as the "Big-L" attitude, where the manager defines the role—brings far more failures than successes. Many societal disasters, ranging from the Iran-Contra scandal to the O-ring failure in the space shuttle Challenger, result from conformist following.

If you were to jot down the name of every supervisor you've had in your career and rate each according to his or her ability to lead, it's likely only a few would get high marks. My surveys show that workers admire less than 20 percent of the bosses they've had. The same would be true of the number of coworkers you've known who make dynamic, effective followers. There are a lot of people you work with every day who go through the motions of completing assignments but don't add anything to the process.

At different points in their careers, even at different times of the workday, most brainpowered workers have to play both roles, though seldom do they perform equally well in each. Part of that has to do with awareness and training.

There is a clamoring for business-leadership seminars and specialized courses in graduate schools, but when was the last time someone in your workplace came up to you and said, "Hey, I just finished this great training course on how to be a star follower. You really should get in on this; it's hot stuff."

So followership dominates our work lives and the organizations that coordinate them, but it is rarely discussed. Star performers are keenly aware of both the importance of followership as a developed skill and the lack of information about it. As a result, many have developed their own systems for sharpening followership ability. But our research has uncovered some common themes that account for much of the increased effectiveness.

THE FOLLOWER STYLE CHART: STARS SURROUNDED BY SHEEP

There are two primary factors that distinguish a star follower from an average one: independent critical thinking and active participation in the destiny of the enterprise (see Figure 3). The stars we studied bring enthusiasm, intelligence, and self-reliance into implementing an organizational goal. They are actively engaged in making the organization a success, while average coworkers are more passive, withholding their best thinking and efforts.

Many of these stars choose followership as their primary role at work because it is more closely tied to the actual work than the leadership role. Yet the jobs held by most brainpowered workers also have a leadership component that demands workers fill the role of follower temporarily, often on a moment's notice. The stars become adept at moving back and forth. They know the appropriate times to turn their respective followership and leadership switches on and off.

Some star followers enjoy the challenge of dual roles and have a talent for switching hats as situations demand. Others treat followership as a temporary proving ground where they log experience that will qualify them for upper management. Whatever the motivation, followership is seen as a critical skill by stars.

Just as there are different leadership styles, people have separate styles of followership. As seen in Figure 3, our studies show that followership style is determined by how well the worker performs on two behavioral dimensions: a measurement of independent, crit-

Figure 3

Followership Styles

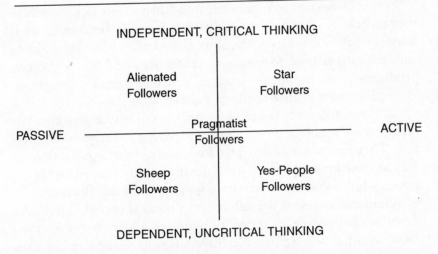

INDEPENDENT, CRITICAL THINKING

Alienated Followers	Star Followers

PASSIVE —————— Pragmatist —————— ACTIVE
Followers

Sheep Followers	Yes-People Followers

DEPENDENT, UNCRITICAL THINKING

ical thinking and a ranking on a scale from active to passive. These factors then yield five separate styles of followership.

When your mother, father, or other role models warned you, the child, about blindly following your friends, they probably recognized better than most the reality of this world—that most of our lives are spent following others' directives. The worry in their minds was "What kind of follower are you going to be?" The point was to dissuade you from the most negative type—what I refer to as the sheep follower.

One reason ranchers prefer sheep over other animal stock is that they're passive and completely dependent—there's usually not an upstart, critical thinker in the flock. Because of their herd instincts, they can be trained to perform necessary simple tasks and then wander around while awaiting further direction.

Yes-followers are also in the negative section of the critical-thinking section of the Followership Styles chart. They are more enthusiastic and involved than their sheep coworkers, but they are aggressively dependent on leaders for direction. If they are not led, they look for a leader to tell them what to do. They will do whatever the leader says, but they need the leader to say it.

Yes-followers can be more dangerous than sheep, either because they do exactly what they are told and no more, or because they tell leaders what they want to hear, not what they need to know. Insecure executives tend to surround themselves with yes-followers, producing a management structure that operates in a dangerous vacuum, without critical thinking and new ideas.

Alienated followers are critical thinkers and very independent in relations with management, but they're passive in carrying out their role. They have a personal dislike for leaders in the organization, or they are unhappy with their work situation. Most started out as exemplary followers, but someone or something turned them off.

Alienated followers are often cynical and skeptical. They tear down what the leader is trying to build up. Their energy is channeled into fighting against the leader or organization rather than toward their work or a mutually desired future.

In the center of the Followership Styles chart is the pragmatist follower. Pragmatist followers are capable brainpowered workers who eschew their independence for political expediency. Or they are system bureaucrats who carry out directives to the letter, even though they might have valuable ideas for improving things. They are constantly monitoring the wind direction, and their motto is "Better safe than sorry." They manage to survive even the most sweeping changes in the workplace.

The last section of the chart is the most valuable—the star followers group. Workers in this category never stop thinking for themselves. They do not follow blindly, but when they disagree with the leader, they do so constructively and with the organization's best interest at heart. They also carry out their assignments with great energy, paying attention to policy implications down the road as well as the details of implementation. Star followers are self-starters and creative problem solvers, applying their talents for the benefit of the organization even when confronted with bureaucratic inanities or nonproducing colleagues. And because they have these qualities, they get consistently high ratings from peers as well as from supervisors.

Star followers are those who can take on a project with minimal preparation. As a supervisor, you can trust them enough to turn your attention elsewhere and know the project will get done in the best way possible (even if it's not the way you originally had in mind). A leader who has a star follower on staff doesn't need to worry about hands-on supervision, time-consuming explanation of assignments, or being visited with problems along the way to implementation. Star followers are independent and responsible members of the team, and they add as much value to the organization as anyone in upper management

Work Strategies of the Star Follower

The late Frank Wells played the follower role to Michael Eisner when they were enlisted by the Walt Disney Company board of directors to help rebuild the moribund company in the 1980s. Disney had originally recruited Wells for the CEO slot, but he turned it down. Instead, he suggested that Eisner was a better choice, and he offered to be Eisner's number two. "[Frank] is a great devil's advocate. I mean, he will ask questions that nobody's ever thought of, and he will take the opposite side of everything," Eisner said in describing Wells's followership style. "But he's a deal maker, not a deal breaker, and that's very unique." Wells's value was that he thought for himself but always with the goal of producing successful outcomes for the organization. Wells's untimely death in a helicopter crash left a void in the company that even the likes of one of Hollywood's most formidable power brokers and leaders, Michael Ovitz, could not fill.

Like Wells, the star followers we observed fell under the broad behaviors outlined above, but they also exhibited some common specific behaviors that propelled them to a followership-skill level well beyond that of their average coworkers. These followership skills complement and draw upon previously discussed star work strategies like initiative, self-management, and perspective.

1. The stars know how to lead themselves well.
2. They have focus, commitment, and incentives beyond personal gain.
3. They build competence and credibility in order to have maximum influence in the workplace.

4. They exercise an honest, courageous conscience when carrying out assignments and implementing policies.
5. They control their own egos to work cooperatively with leaders.

Self-Leadership

Many of the brainpowered workers in our productivity-improvement course are surprised to learn that a key behavior in being a star follower is to show some self-leadership, which is different from the leadership of others, discussed later, in Chapter 9. The best followers know how to lead themselves, and they've demonstrated personal reliance that makes managers comfortable in delegating responsibilities to them.

Another surprise to our participants is that star followers do not see themselves as underlings of the manager doing the delegating. More often than not, they see their work as different from but equal to the manager's in any given work situation, because they know how critical the implementation role is to the overall success of the assignment.

"The decision as to whether an order has authority or not lies with the person to whom it is addressed," not with the boss issuing the assignment, Chester I. Barnard wrote half a century ago in his seminal business-management study *The Functions of the Executive.* Leadership authority is only on loan from the followers, who can demand its return at any moment.

That assessment is even more true in today's stripped-down organizational flowchart, where the brainpowered worker in the benefits section of a major corporation is likely to report directly to a senior vice president. No longer are there the layers and buffers of management that once regulated the flow of assignments and criticism. Followers have more direct involvement in receiving assignments and reacting to them.

A large Midwestern bank redesigned its personnel-selection system to attract self-leading workers. Those conducting interviews began to look for particular types of experience and capabilities—among them creative thinking, critical analysis, self-starting, and self-monitoring—and the bank revamped its orientation program to highlight self-leadership. Even at the executive level, self-leadership role playing was introduced into the interview process: a scenario in which a job candidate shows how he would disagree with a supervisor, or one that shows what five steps the candidate would take as an executive returning from a two-week vacation. In the three years since overhauling the interview/orientation process, employee turnover at the bank has dropped dramatically, layers of babysitting supervisors have been eliminated, and administrative costs have dropped markedly.

Many of these improvements would not have happened if there hadn't been star followers who took their responsibilities seriously. They openly and unapologetically disagree with leadership if it becomes necessary, and they are less likely to be intimidated by titles, since they view it as more of an interactive partnership. At the same time, they are careful not to develop a reputation for challenging every assignment that comes down the pike. Star followers choose their battles carefully, weighing the necessity of panning the entire idea against working to modify parts of it. With organizational perspective, they realize that the people delegating an assignment to them may have been directed to do so by someone above them.

Focus/Commitment/Incentive

Star followers are often purposefully committed to something—a cause, a product, an organization, an idea, a person—in addition to their own lives and careers. For some, this commitment is a passion that engages their hearts as well as focusing their minds, emotionally fueling their everyday work activities.

Jessye, a star medical researcher in a Chicago hospital, told me during a training seminar that her career goal was to help eradicate diabetes. She had a personal connection, she said, watching her mother struggle with the disease for twenty years and then die from it. She was willing to work with any leader who could help find the cure to diabetes faster than she could alone.

Some leaders mistake a follower's commitment to their goals for personal loyalty. While in some cases it may be true that the follower is personally loyal, and this may end up benefiting the organization nonetheless, star followers like Jessye are almost always devoted to something beyond an individual personality or personal gain. There may be a principle at stake, or perhaps the worthy goal of a new product that will change lives, or their dedication may be bottom-line oriented—toward increasing profit and publicity for the organization.

Since most star followers see their managers more often as equals in the process of reaching a goal, the work is considered important enough that titles and protocol are not necessary to achieve results. Star followers consider their leaders part of the team, but if they sense that a leader has so much ego that it conflicts with their mutual goal attainment, or if the leader starts to swerve away from the goal, they will strive to get the leader back on track. If they cannot, then they will end the working relationship with that leader, even if it means undermining the leader or leaving the organization.

For secure, intelligent managers, the advantages of having star followers on staff are enormous. On the plus side, the high enthusiasm generated on projects that include these workers is infectious. The work is generally more creative and of higher quality; morale is higher and schedules stay on track.

On the downside, conflict can arise when the goals of the leader, who must represent the company's interests, are at odds with those of the follower. Sometimes the commitment of the star follower pushes for a higher standard than the boss thinks is necessary. In this case, the follower must understand the boss's perspective while not letting either of them lose sight of the overall goal.

In many brainpowered companies, a fine line must be walked between what the company believes the customer wants and what the workers think is best. I often hear bosses complain that their brainpowered workers are building a Rolls-Royce when the customer only needs a Dodge. Enamored with their ability to build the best, workers want to attach all the latest bells and whistles, which can lead to delays or budget overruns.

In one such exchange, a star follower at Bell Labs had to confront the boss's nagging about his extra efforts. The boss wanted to ship a stripped-down call-routing feature for the telephone switch in order to come in ahead of schedule and win points with the customer. "Forget about all the extras. The customer would rather have a basic model today than the greatest model one month from now," she said.

The star follower sat down with the boss to review the short-

and long-term goals of the product for this specific customer and for other customers in the marketplace:

"Sure, there might be some short-term gains with this customer," said the star follower, "but there are some risks, too. These risks may relegate us to the low end of the line, when the company has staked out the high-end market. If we do the extra work on this customer's product now, we'll save significant product-development time on other customers already in the pipeline. But let's sit down with the customer to see what she prefers."

Our star follower understood the boss's immediate concerns. At the same time, he tried to shift the boss's perspective to the larger overall goals they shared. When possible, star followers temper their own efforts so that they fall in the range of company objectives—or they find an organization that is a better match.

Erik, a physician's assistant once employed by a national health care maintenance organization, was as furious as many of his patients when he discovered that the CEO of the company had received a huge bonus in a merger deal with Aetna Life and Casualty Company. He had become a physician's assistant, he said, because of his commitment to the idea of general-practice health care. The front-line position was the closest he thought he would come to the role played by his grandfather, a family-practice doctor in a small town in upstate New York.

But as Erik watched tighter and tighter management controls exerted on health care decisions for his patients, he voiced his concerns to executives on the business side. When they told him that he too would benefit financially from the cost cutting and the increased stock value as a result of the merger, Erik told them that wasn't the point. Eventually, he decided to leave and join a large physicians' group practice for less money. "They thought my commitment was to the company and the idea that I could make a lot of money. They were shocked when I walked away, and maybe that says it all."

Competence That Leads to Credibility

Star followers are keenly aware of a harsh but important reality of the brainpowered workplace: Some of the most enthusiastic, most committed, nicest workers can also be the most incompetent, the most lacking in useful work skills. As I repeat to all my clients and students, "Highly committed and motivated incompetence is still incompetence."

The stars almost always have higher competency standards for themselves than those in the general work environment. As masters of perspective and self-management skills, they also are sharp observers of new technology and societal trends, working to stay up to date. They are the first among their peers to take advantage of continuing-education programs and performance improvement seminars, even suggesting programs that managers don't know about.

Average followers are not nearly as proactive. They may sign up for a course if it's pushed by management, and they're likely to be competent only in those skills that bear directly on their day-to-day work. They require frequent hand-holding sessions in the boss's office when problems arise. They are reluctant to take on extra assignments that improve their expertise, often pointing to the clock or the boundaries of their job description as excuses.

Jenne, a middle-management editor at one of the country's largest and most important newspapers, was attending a company picnic and fell on a slippery hillside, breaking her leg. The doctor ordered her to spend several weeks at home, and the editor was asked by her boss to divide her staff of follower reporters into two groups: those who were highly competent self-starters, who needed only occasional consultation, and those who were going to demand a lot of direction and nurturing.

As she made up her list, she was shocked to discover that only about a third of her staff were able to do their jobs with minimal management. "Half the time it came down to a competence problem: They needed specific directions on where to go to find information or how to get around some obstacle. Then the work they eventually turned in needed a lot of editing. And between the reporting and the writing, they needed a lot of confidence-building sessions. When I realized how much hands-on managing I had been doing, I thought about going into the office on my crutches and demanding a raise," she said after compiling the list.

But Jenne's second reaction to the list was perhaps more telling. "I had a newfound appreciation for those reporters who had their act together. They weren't just sitting at their desks waiting for me to tell them what to do. They were thinking about story ideas, investigating on their own. And when they were given an assignment that wasn't their idea, they researched the hell out of the topic before coming to my office, so that when we talked, it was a very efficient, productive session."

Jenne also has a new appreciation for the value of good followership, and she's now working on ways to instill the traits of her stars in other members of the staff. One behavior she's discovered that stands out as a paradox is that the most competent followers know their weaknesses well.

They also are aware of their strengths, of course, but the sense of knowing in what areas they may fall short prompts them to take action to compensate. If they're asked to produce in an area where they don't feel qualified, they look for assistance on their own. If they can't find help on their own, they don't waste the company's time going in circles. They speak up and work with the lead editor on a solution.

Jenne has discovered that star followers are also invaluable as members of project teams. Unlike the prima donnas of the newsroom, who must stand out in front of other team members, the best followers treat their coworkers as colleagues, not as competitors.

The Courageous Conscience

In my experience, star followers spend considerable time and effort worrying about the ethics of their actions on the job, often more than leaders do. There are some exceptions to this, but I've discovered that in the vast majority of cases where a star follower is directed to implement a new policy or take on a controversial assignment, the dictates of personal conscience come into play. In the traditional leader–follower dynamic, the leader makes the decisions and sets the ethical framework for the group, while the follower is expected to do as he or she is told. But that is not how it works with the best followers.

In some cases, leaders are forced to choose from among a series of bad options, or forced to make their decisions within sharply defined boundaries and under enormous pressures that followers don't have. In these cases, ethics is seen as just one of many factors that must be considered in the final decision; it can get lost in the pack. But that is precisely why conscience is included in the range of skills that make up star followership. Even though there are times when it can be very inconvenient, leaders need their star followers to fulfill an ethical watchdog role. The organization's future can depend on how effectively followers heed their consciences more than on the leader's image. A lot of evidence suggests that this aspect of star followership needs more attention.

A study by University of Pittsburgh business-management professor William Frederick found that 70 percent of middle managers reported organizational pressures to conform, and they often compromised personal principles. These ethical compromises occurred even though managers rated honesty, responsibility, and independence as the most important personal attributes, while relegating obedience last on their lists.

In a survey I conducted involving 250 brainpowered workers and managers, 30 percent responded that they "often" or "always" accept what authority leader figures tell them without any questions. And 30 percent also reported that when the leader asked them to do something that was not right for them, they usually did it anyway. After analyzing ten studies of ethical problems in business, Rick Wartzman of the *Wall Street Journal* concluded, "Even the most upright people are apt to become dishonest and unmindful of their civic responsibilities when placed in a typical corporate environment."

When the courageous-conscience skill comes up for discussion in training sessions, most participants bring up the obvious first-level responsibility of avoiding or correcting existing wrongs. Stopping there would provide organizational benefit, but there is more to it.

There is a corresponding duty—to use the courageous conscience to make positive contributions. The stars champion a worthy idea even in the face of strong organizational resistance, or they deal with a problem before it grows into a crisis. In the example of Post-it notes creator Art Fry, in the initiative chapter (Chapter 4), there is a courageous-followership component worth noting here.

Although the organization discouraged, even resisted, his efforts, he kept at it. The courageous conscience provides the emotional support for initiatives that don't initially win organizational approval.

Consider the sharply different cases of two strong followers, both high-ranking executives at Alcoa Corporation, the world's largest manufacturer of aluminum and related products.

In 1989, Timothy Mock, the operations manager of the company's upstate New York plant, discovered that a manager in charge of environmental monitoring reported only some of the water sample tests performed by Alcoa, but not all of the tests results, as required by state law.

Under the old management system at Alcoa, the plant manager would have consulted with a company vice president and then taken steps to stop the environmental violations, but it is unlikely that the company would have owned up to them by telling regulators. But Alcoa had been revamped by a new CEO, Paul O'Neill, who had made it clear early on that environmental responsibility was going to be one of his top priorities. Mock went directly to O'Neill to notify him of the violations and argued that the company should take a proactive stance by informing state officials. But O'Neill needed no convincing.

They went directly to the state and triggered a broader investigation and review of environmental issues. It was then found that Alcoa had allowed thirty-three railroad cars full of PCB-contaminated soil to sit idle for more than ninety days and that caustic waste had been poured into utility holes at the plant.

Alcoa paid a stiff price—a total of $7.5 million in criminal and civil penalties—but it was the plant manager and O'Neill who notified state officials that the violations had occurred. While the environmental engineer was dismissed and told to hire his own lawyer in the event he faced criminal penalties, Mock was praised in management meetings by O'Neill for an honest, courageous, and proactive response to the crisis. Mock was eventually promoted to head the company's business operations in Italy.

Not so fortunate was Robert H. Barton III, the top officer of Alcoa plants in Mexico, who as a top follower of O'Neill's knew well his leader's convictions on environmental and safety issues. Despite that, three accidents at his plants in 1994, in which workers were exposed to noxious gases, were not reported to headquarters.

It was at a stockholder's meeting in May 1996 that a Benedictine nun working in Mexico, whose order owns fifty shares of Alcoa stock, made allegations of accident cover-ups. O'Neill cited the company's track record on environmental and safety issues but promised to investigate. And when he found out about the accidents—in one, about two hundred workers required hospital treatment for exposure to carbon monoxide gas—he removed Barton from his job.

"Some of you may think my decision is an unduly harsh response for a lapse in communication," O'Neill wrote in an e-mail message to Alcoa employees. "I felt constrained to make it because of the effect of these matters on our values and the possible misperception that there can be tradeoffs in these areas."

In January 1996, Alcoa was awarded the gold medal for International Corporate Environmental Achievement given by the World Environment Center for "exceptional performance in environmental policy and leadership."

Disagreeing Agreeably: Seven Steps for Controlling Your Ego to Work Cooperatively with the Leader

Star performers fulfill their followership obligations by first trying to work cooperatively with the leader. They try to make the leader's job easier rather than be a constant thorn in the side, like alienated followers. They proactively try to support the leader and to fill in gaps that the leader might have.

But in any work situation, conflicts will inevitably arise. When they do, star followers try to curb their own egos so they don't get in the way of progress. They distinguish between their own preferences and an honest assessment of the ideas under discussion. Drawing upon their multiple perspectives, they try to understand the leader's view while being sensitive to the leader's public image.

After all this, they may find they are still in disagreement and do not feel that it is in the organization's best interest to acquiesce to the leader. The issue might be over a positive contribution, such as new-product strategy, or an ethical concern, such as targeting problems that could compromise company values. Whatever the conflict, they do their homework and argue persuasively without being threatening or self-righteous.

Not even the best followers win every battle, but by taking the seven steps developed from our observations of star followers, you can substantially increase the chance that your view will carry the day and limit any negative fallout to your career.

1. Be Proactive

Star followers assume that the leader wants the best outcome and operate from that assumption until it is proved false. In addition, they believe that leaders would rather have input before the fact when there is still time to act on it.

Star followers are experienced enough to know that leaders often make decisions without complete information (or different information from what the followers have). They appreciate that leaders cannot see some problems brewing because they are farther removed from the front lines. Or leaders might miss some downside ramifications of their decisions that followers can catch. Also, being more closely attuned to other followers, star followers can sense how their colleagues are reacting to the leader's decision or situation. Given access to this information, leaders can often self-correct before going off a cliff.

When a large West Coast textile manufacturer committed over $100 million to "reengineer" most of its operations, the company leaders were convinced they could shave weeks off the production process, saving money and creating higher customer satisfaction. In theory, they were probably right. In actual practice, it took a star follower to avert a disaster.

The first step began innocently enough when consultants were sent to solicit ideas for improvement from the workforce. The employees gladly shared their ideas on how to clean up and consequently speed up the operations.

The complications began at the next step, however, when 1,500 workers were notified by company memo that their old jobs and departments didn't exist anymore. Instead, the affected workers had to reapply for jobs in seven newly reorganized "process" departments. Details would follow in a series of meetings with the workers.

Maya, an accounts receivable manager, heard the grumbling from her fellow managers and the rank and file. "This is so typical," a coworker complained. "Pump us for our ideas and then use it against us. Do consultants or top executives ever get reengineered or downsized?"

Maya wondered if top managers were aware of the growing resentment and potential backlash—some workers were talking about starting a union-organizing drive. She met with her boss, who said nothing could be done. But Maya asked to meet with the executive in charge of the reengineering effort before the meetings started. Although her boss wasn't thrilled, he agreed.

"Before you begin your meetings with the employees," she told the executive, "I thought you ought to know the mood of the troops. Although the new effort got off to a good start, I wasn't sure if you knew how it was going over now. The truth is that people are really upset."

"Oh, we expected that. People always resist change, but they'll get used to it. After all, we're using many of their ideas," the executive explained.

"Well, the employees have seen what's happened at other companies that have reengineered and they are afraid for their jobs. They're talking work slowdowns and unions."

"But we don't plan to lay anyone off," said the executive. "We're trying to reorganize to save jobs, not cut them. If we don't act now, then we might actually have to downsize in the future."

"Well, none of the employees know that," said Maya. She then suggested that top executives issue a memo emphasizing the reorganization as an effort to save jobs, get it into the hands of employees before the first meeting, and reiterate it as the first step when the meeting began. It would help people focus on the effort rather than on losing their jobs. She also recommended some educational meetings about the company's competitive situation, its standing with customers, and why the reengineering effort was necessary to help improve both.

Although the executive was exasperated that the employees didn't trust the company's good intentions, she listened to Maya's advice. The first meeting began with a clear mood of resentment evident among employees. But as the executives spoke, each assuring workers that jobs weren't in jeopardy, the tension eased.

As a result of the training sessions, employees began implementing the program with enthusiasm. In the end, the company was able to speed up the processing of orders by 200 percent, winning renewed customer loyalty and significantly reducing costs. They also had a more dedicated workforce who trusted the company to keep its word.

2. Be a Fact Finder

Only a foolish follower champions a cause with incomplete information, or worse, with allegations based on rumor and innuendo. Star followers take time to get the facts of a situation before making a case to leaders. Columbia University business professor Harvey Hornstein did a study of two hundred brainpowered workers and found that nine out of ten who had to summon the courage to challenge managers—on everything from pursuing radically innovative product ideas to revamping nepotism-riddled hiring procedures—said they felt comfortable doing so because they had the facts on their side.

Once the star followers we studied had convinced themselves that their arguments were grounded in strong evidence, they proceeded on the assumption that management did not have access to the same material. They began their conscientious response with an informational talk or memo to a supervisor.

3. Be an Advice Seeker

Star followers trust themselves to gather facts, but in controversial areas, they know better than to try to interpret those facts without benefit of a second opinion. Instead, they seek wise counsel. Followers who want to be sure of their findings rely on the perspective skills of those they respect to get a fresh outlook. When the star followers sought assistance, they were looking for someone—a respected business executive or a recognized expert colleague in another department—who could view the situation from both their own position and that of the organization's leadership and make an informed judgment. A follower's adviser should have a track record for keeping confidences, be knowledgeable about the responsibilities of leaders, be experienced in the ways of office politics and protocol, and be willing to play devil's advocate to test the strength of the follower's position. If they know the particular department, problem, and players, all the better.

4. Be a System Player

Most organizations have norms and protocol for airing disagreements. Star followers realize that company leaders take the procedures they've put in place to deal with these issues very seriously. So they find out what these are before taking any action. Then they go the system route first, usually trying to work the issue out privately with the leader who is directly involved. When that fails, each step in the system is followed until there is a resolution to the problem. The key point here is that the star follower always wants to be perceived as part of the community working within the framework, not an outsider trying to tear it down.

5. Be Persuasive: Speak in the Language of the Organization

Star followers always orient their position according to the values and vision dear to the organization and its leaders. They make their arguments based on what they'll do for the organization, and more rarely, what the organization stands to lose by not accepting the argument.

Proactive followers at the health care products giant Johnson & Johnson were alarmed when one faction of corporate leadership made plans to market the company's baby oil to adults as a suntan product. The followers grounded themselves well in research linking sun exposure to cancer and also referred to the company credo, which corporate officers take seriously: "Our first responsibility is to the doctors, nurses and patients, to mothers and all others who use our products and services." The followers also came up with other marketing ideas for adult use of the baby oil. Putting the whole package together in the language and methodology of company leaders' decision-making process eventually won the leaders over. Viewed in the light of current medical research, the decision to end the suntan marketing campaign saved the company a confrontation with health care professionals and possible lawsuits from consumers.

The key to star follower behavior here is to change a bad leadership decision through conversion, not intimidation. Leaders are more favorably moved to accept an argument framed in terms consistent with the values and vision of the organization and backed up by solid, objective information than one that is not.

6. Be Courageous: Go Over Heads When Absolutely Necessary

No star follower operating in the quick-changing business environment of the 1990s, and likely to be working for several organizations over the span of a career, can expect to breeze through the years without facing at least one crisis of conscience over a disagreement with a leader.

Corporate leaders do not always take well to brainpowered workers who challenge policies and directions forged in top officers' suites. Hal Sperlich, who moved from Ford to Chrysler when top executives blasted him for repeatedly pushing his idea for a new vehicle—the minivan—says corporate life is much easier in the short-term "if you go with the flow. . . . The corporate environment just doesn't reward people for challenging the status quo."

But the long-term effects of going along and getting along can be very hazardous to career health, especially in situations that involve serious ethical and legal issues.

Star followers work on their confrontation and courage-building skills on a daily basis, practicing insightful, positive challenges to small directives in order to establish both a reputation and an experience level that prepare them for the heavy crises that will eventually present themselves.

Consider how much the lack of ethics-based skill development eventually came around to haunt Jeff Nobers, a public relations director for the Pittsburgh Brewing Company:

Approached by a reporter for a local newspaper doing a story on the brewery, Nobers offered the latest employment figures, a healthy increase from several years before, to show how well the business was doing under financier Michael Carlow. When the favorable story appeared, Nobers was summoned by his boss, the vice president in charge of human relations, who berated him for giving out the figures. Nobers was shocked, since his job was to encourage the kind of favorable publicity Pittsburgh Brewing had received in the news story.

It all became clear when another company official dropped in on the meeting and tried to calm Nobers' boss, assuring him the company's insurance agents in Philadelphia wouldn't be reading Pittsburgh newspapers. As it turned out, the accurate numbers Nobers was giving to the press were not the same numbers company officers were reporting to the company's agent for workers' compensation insurance.

Nobers realized that company officials were engaging in criminal fraud—saving $1 million in premiums—but he kept quiet because he feared for his job. As it turned out, the insurance scheme was just the tip of the iceberg. Federal officials began investigating CEO Carlow and discovered a $31.3 million check-kiting scheme.

Carlow was indicted and pleaded guilty to several counts, and Nobers' boss and several other top officials were charged in the insurance fraud. If Nobers had refused to go along and reported the fraud to board members, or, if necessary, to the U.S. attorney, he would have put his courageous conscience on public record.

As it turned out, Nobers lost his job anyway, was forced to hire an attorney, and ended up having to testify against his former boss in court under a grant of immunity.

Very few leadership teams are as unprincipled and corrupt as that Pittsburgh Brewing Company group. In fact, we would hope that any CEO with the smarts to have risen to the top leadership position would be keenly aware of the devastation that can be caused by lack of attention to ethics and policy disagreements.

This hope doesn't let followers off the hook, however. They still have a responsibility to come forward to defend what they believe is right, whether for a different product strategy or to disclose illegal actions.

Those who take it to a higher level in the company, or to an outside authority, should be aware that they are taking a tremendous career risk. Differences of opinion and personal gripes are not meant for this level of action.

7. *Be a Collective Follower or Plan Well to Stand Alone*

It is easier to find courage to take a conscience stand when others are with you. Star followers know their voices are stronger when blended into a chorus of colleagues all singing from the same page. While the group approach can be threatening to some leaders, star followers have been successful at making changes when the go-it-alone approach fails.

In those cases where star followers have been forced to stand alone, wise planning has helped cushion the blow. Some have lined up other job options in the event there was retaliation against them. Others have established special savings accounts as a financial cushion should they be forced to find another job or have to hire an attorney.

. . .

"The brave carve out their own fortune," Cervantes wrote in *Don Quixote*. Followers may agree to suspend their decision-making power and vest it in a leader. But star followers make sure leaders understand that their control has only been suspended, not surrendered. By following the seven steps of star followers who have learned to disagree agreeably, you will greatly increase your chances of success in the leadership confrontations all star brain-powered workers are bound to face.

9

◉

SMALL-L LEADERSHIP IN A BIG-L WORLD

Marianne Jennings, a business-management professor at Arizona
State University, speaks from painful personal experience when she
pokes fun at American business's obsession with leadership and the
seminar-training program craze that feeds off it.

"I have attended a few leadership seminars in my time, most
under the threat of pay reduction," she said in a recent National
Public Radio commentary. "It's a little-known historical fact, for example, that George Washington left Valley Forge for a week to attend a leadership conference held on the isolated island where Fort
Sumter is located. And most historians have missed the fact that
General Douglas MacArthur actually said, 'I shall return—after my
seminar.' "

Jennings' tongue-in-cheek retelling of history also skewers the
tools of the leadership seminar trade—the flip chart stand and the
flip chart. "Margaret Thatcher was never without one," she says.
"An overhead projector—General Patton always had one with him

in North Africa; and tape, because you will develop lists on the flip chart that will be taped to the walls for the entertainment of the custodial staff on the graveyard shift."

During their breaks, says Jennings, "they will read the leadership qualities you've developed and wonder why they can't get a job like yours."

Her sarcasm lays bare the obsessive love affair that American corporations have with this notion of leadership. The signs are everywhere—front-page feature stories and TV talk-show gabfests on celebrity CEOs; $1,000-a-day cult seminars; best-selling autobiographies that highlight swagger over substance. We are drawn to these leaders because they are packaged as larger than life. If we could learn their secrets, be more like them, then we too could advance to chair of the board or CEO, get our picture on the cover of *Fortune* magazine, or collect on stock options worth more than the government budgets of some foreign countries. Sure, we wouldn't be able to end world hunger, but at the very least, we could assign ourselves a coveted space in the company parking lot.

We adore what I call leadership with a capital L—even though that big-L leadership style has the same relationship to organizational success as, to paraphrase the science fiction writer Robert Heinlein, "history has to truth, i.e. none to speak of." Certainly much of what has been written and taught on leadership over the past decade feeds the popular culture myth of the hard-driving, high-living CEO. In reality, much of the material is filtered through a sophisticated public relations strategy that seeks to market CEOs as much as the products their companies make.

Many training seminars and business "self-help" books also embrace this cult-hero worship as the best way to teach business leadership. But consumers who hope to take on the traits of these titans end up with a mythological, rock-video version of leadership that can't possibly succeed in the workaday world.

Charles de Gaulle must have been thinking about big-L leadership when he quipped, "The Great Leaders always stage-manage their effects . . . while the real leaders are down in the ranks, quietly changing the world."

Big-L leadership traits may make for an impressive show at times, but they're of little productive use to the 99 percent of brain-powered workers who have to deal with vexing problems in the trenches and those who aren't charting their careers with an eye to the CEO suite. Brainpowered workers know they need no-nonsense leadership skills to be more productive, but they also know the big-L stuff being offered isn't going to help them much.

And that is where the star performers we studied came down on the definition of effective leadership—not the puffed-up version practiced by the big-L executive whose camera-friendly style is mistaken for charisma, whose unbridled ego is misunderstood as constructive ambition. The stars we studied were able to see big-L traits as unproductive posturing. They concentrated instead on a set of skills I have identified and labeled as small-l leadership behaviors.

Where big-L leaders noisily preside with an ego-centered, management-by-me leadership style, small-l leaders work quietly and unceremoniously side by side with their coworkers inside the system. The small-l leader usually has no direct supervisory authority; no staff depends on his or her good graces in order to get a paycheck. Colleagues voluntarily cooperate with small-l leaders, because they trust that if they work together, important things will get done.

This starkly different style of leadership is a response to the shift in management from the industrial to the informational era.

The small-l style must not only acknowledge the limitations of previous management but also recognize that knowledge-intensive businesses require a whole new form of leadership. Highly complex, specialized, and long-term projects performed by teams of brainpowered workers, whose members are often in different offices and different cities, define the environment in which small-l leaders operate. In addition, the heightened powers that brainpowered workers have been given in the workplace require a broader range of leadership skills.

Small-l leadership is practiced among peers, most often in teams. The degree of success has less to do with the power of a job title than the power of expertise, a credible reputation, influence, and persuasion. The small-l leader may run the entire effort or a portion of it in a roomful of coleaders and cofollowers. She may be a leader for a one-hour meeting or a six-month project, but it is clear to her and those who follow that this is a role she is filling temporarily. The small-l leader is a role, not a person, and the workers who assume that role know they don't own or define the job, as some big-L leaders pretend to do.

So imagine such a situation in your workplace, where the employees match their particular technical strengths and personality styles to a leadership spot that presents itself. No jockeying for the spotlight, no posing as a leader to impress the boss, no power tripping. If these do occur in your imaginary workplace, every worker realizes these are acts of false leaders who must be politely detoured around on the path to higher productivity.

Aida is a star reporter with a large metropolitan daily newspaper. She is one of four reporters assigned to a year-long project investigating companies that violate child labor laws. Aida is forty-eight and a twenty-year veteran of the paper who has won several national journalism awards for her work on similar projects.

She has been assigned to the project's team because of her experience but she holds no special rank and she behaves as an equal with fellow team members. When the group gathers in the project editor's office for weekly meetings, Aida does the speaking for the team—but only in the portion dealing with strategy planning, where she is the acknowledged expert. When it comes to synthesizing the reporting that has already been done and organizing it into a framework for stories, Micah, a team member who has been at the newspaper only three years but who demonstrates superb organizational skills, takes over.

This delineation of leadership duties among team members is not always orchestrated successfully by management. In fact, in situations where managers attempt to impose a leadership structure on a team where it doesn't make sense to its members, we observed an underground reassigning of leadership roles. The management-assigned structure remains in place but the productive leadership roles are assumed by others in order to get the work done successfully.

Back when we began our research at Bell Labs, our first task was to identify star performers. As we discussed in detail in Chapter 1, a natural starting point was in managers' offices, where we asked the managers to name twenty of the most productive workers. In defining productivity, we looked at evaluations, merit raises, and awards, but we also suggested characteristics like leadership.

There was surprising consensus among managers about who

these stars were, but when that list was compared with one generated in similar fashion by the brainpowered workers themselves,
the choices were strikingly different.

The workers weren't surprised. Many of them said it's a given
assumption in the workplace that managers who are removed from
the day-to-day interaction often miss important components of star
performance, such as who originates an idea and leads it through,
or who helps colleagues the most when it comes to solving critical
problems. And also because of their distance from the workforce,
managers are sometimes taken in by the big-L wanna-bes who offer
more show than substance.

In the newspaper example, both Aida and Micah are practicing
the essence of small-l leadership. Each wears the mantle only for as
long as her or his special skills apply in the meeting's agenda, not by
virtue of any supervisory power. Coworkers move in and out of the
small-l leader position on the same basis—proven expertise or some
specific talent that is needed at the time. Authority isn't an issue because credibility already has been established in previous interactions.

To be an effective small-l leader, a team member must secure the
respect of coworkers in at least one of three areas covered by this
critical skill:

1. *Knowledge Quotient*—respected expertise and proven judgment in areas relevant to the group's goals
2. *People-Skills Quotient*—that you care about your colleagues
   and that their goals are as valued as your own; as a result your
   coworkers are moved to work voluntarily with you to accomplish the goal
3. *Momentum Quotient*—that you will do those leadership activities that help the group actually achieve the goal

THE KNOWLEDGE QUOTIENT: STAGE I OF SMALL-L LEADERSHIP

When I began my consulting career over twenty years ago, most
firms used a hierarchical approach to monitoring projects. A manager was assigned to be all things to the task, from overseeing ad-

ministrative details such as work schedules and assignments to coming up with the creative spark. In the end, this one manager rose or fell according to how the results were judged. The leadership structure mirrored the command-and-control model of the military, which was an important influence in the lives of many top managers in these firms. The one-leader method helped those who weren't in touch with the project feel more confident that it was going smoothly. This 1970s version of small-l leadership, then, was merely big-L leadership on a smaller scale.

Since then, I have learned that this hierarchical approach is fine for organizations involved in traditional, routine work, but those in brainpowered careers don't take well to one-leader commands barked out from above. In a marketplace that expects groundbreaking creativity and innovation from brainpowered employees, and that places such high value on them when they deliver, the small-l leadership style developed by the star producers we studied is the most effective system.

Most brainpowered projects—whether consulting, legal, engineering, or advertising—require teams of experts who complement one another in talent. Although clients may see one individual as the project leader, they expect that each of the team's members is capable of leading and following when appropriate. Most important, they want assurances that the team has the right mix of knowledge leaders who will drive the "content" of the project.

Once I had the opportunity to observe managers of a large natural gas company choose and work with an outside consulting firm. The company needed help with the upcoming deregulation of the industry, so they solicited proposals from several well-known consulting firms. All the firms but one responded similarly, offering a team staffed by consultants with natural gas industry experience.

The maverick firm offered a different approach: their team consisted of consultants from diverse backgrounds. The project leader had deep industry experience; another was a specialist in deregulation, having helped airline, banking, and telecommunication firms move from government-authorized monopolies to competitive environments; the final member was a marketing strategist who understood how markets were changing.

The gas company chose the maverick firm. "We know our industry well enough and we don't need consultants for that," one of the decision makers said. "What we don't know is what the industry will look like ten years from now. For that we need people who can see it differently." The value of the project leader with industry experience was primarily to bring the rest of the consulting team up to speed on the history and nuances of the gas industry.

During their first full day together, the leadership of the meeting rotated several times as different areas of expertise were required. One company manager had the best fix on the ins and outs of the company bureaucracy and corporate culture; the marketing consultant weighed in on future trends that would impact industrial and consumer market behavior. They all took turns going to the whiteboard to sketch out an idea, to make a point, or to give a quick tutorial to the rest of the group. At various times, when the group got stuck, one of them would step forward with a fresh approach.

Toward the end of the day, no one on the team was quite sure what the next step should be. Pages of ideas had been generated, but they were not coming together. At that point, an approach came to the deregulation specialist that tied together much of the day's work. Her synthesis and integration provided the basis for the multiyear project that led to the gas company's shifting its strategy and altering its core competencies.

As an outsider, I had a difficult time identifying *the* "leader." The lead manager and the lead consultant had represented their respective sides during the morning introductions and in the administrative aspects of the day's work. But they were not the knowledge leaders throughout the day. The team rotated the knowledge leadership roles at different times during the project. As the lead consultant confided to me, "For anyone, particularly me, to declare him- or herself leader would interfere with the process and the peer relationships that drive the group."

But one thing was clear: The group paid attention to members whose expertise was relevant to the problem and was helping the group move forward.

Knowledge leadership comes in many forms, as it did on this project team. Some people have amazing expertise in a specific field; others are experts in processes—they know how to work the system. Still others are expert practitioners of perspective, one of the most important work strategies in our star performer skills model. Perspective knowledge leaders can play the current game, but they also understand how the game and its rules are changing. They are known to have good instincts and intuition—their hunches are often right on target.

Perspective-knowledge leaders can be extremely effective in rising to the task during a crisis.

In the mid 1980s, the Federal Home Loan Bank Board (FHLBB), the federal agency overseeing the savings-and-loan industry, asked me to help reorganize the agency so it could better supervise the industry.

FHLBB was modeled after the Federal Reserve—twelve presidents, each in charge of a regional office. In reality, the chair of FHLBB and the bank presidents were from the big-L leadership mold. Collectively, they were charged with providing liquidity, supervision, and insurance to the country's S&Ls.

In theory, all these leaders were experts in the industry; in reality the industry was changing too fast for them to keep pace. Most of them were boxed in with outdated notions of how the industry operated, and they were using monitoring techniques that had been in vogue decades before when they began their careers. These big-L bosses were comfortable doing business the old way and stubbornly refused to change, even though the old ways no longer worked. It was in this context that the $300 billion S&L crisis of the late 1980s began.

In the midst of this was a star performer named Tera, an assistant in the chair of FHLBB's office. She, more than any of the top officers, understood the significant changes occurring in the S&L business and what new problems were emerging. Tera made it a point to stay a step ahead of her big-L bosses. While they would sit in long meetings trying to understand the extent of the growing S&L mess, she had already submitted memos detailing the problems and giving action plans to solve them. While top managers were trying to catch up, Tera took it upon herself to go into the field and begin applying the necessary emergency solutions.

What caused the agency's top leaders to lag so far behind? Part of the answer is that Tera's age—she was thirty-one—and relative inexperience made them leery about trusting her judgments. She lacked the "gray hair" necessary for them to grant credibility to her.

But it was because she wasn't part of the agency's tired, long history that she was able to see the revolution occurring more clearly.

It was only when events began to unfold as she predicted that her credibility grew. Tera never became a highly visible big-L leader, though. The hierarchical, bureaucratic system wouldn't tolerate that. Instead, she quietly became an influential small-l knowledge leader who helped detail the FHLBB's strategy to contain the mess. After two years of fighting the uphill battle against the mushrooming problem and the bureaucracy, Tera was wooed away by Wall Street, which valued her talents and paid handsomely for them.

A brainpowered worker's knowledge quotient, then, plays a central role in small-l leadership. It can provide the initial credibility that opens up other brainpowered peers to listen to you in the first place. It also provides the "content" that separates success from failure. Finally, it is shared throughout the group, rotating as necessary to meet the demands of the work at hand.

THE PEOPLE QUOTIENT: THE TIES THAT BIND

The knowledge quotient is a critical pillar in building an effective small-l leadership style. But it is only a piece of the support structure. We all know very smart people who couldn't lead a one-car funeral. There are other critical skills involved in the leadership process. Small-l leaders understand the human relationships that connect people to one another, while big-L leaders are too self-focused on their ideas, their work styles, their goals. Small-l leaders know they need to take into account coworkers on a project or team—their coworkers' needs, skills, aspirations, and power.

This out-of-self focus is productive because of a brainpowered workplace reality that traditional big-L leaders often overlook. Small-l leaders usually have no formal authority over those they want to lead. Peers will go along only if they believe a member of the group who wants to lead is acting in their interest as much as his or her own. Accomplishing this requires the kind of time-consuming interaction that big-L leaders believe is a waste of precious leadership time. The small-l leader who bonds with coworker followers by slogging through the daily project grind and sharing late-night pizzas while meeting deadlines earns more loyalty and credibility than even the most charismatic big-L boss.

The big secret here from our star performers—the secret that

separates them from big-Ls and other average performing leaders—
is that they don't assume they know everything about other people.
Most big-L leadership hype portrays the leader as omniscient. The
big-L leader knows what's best for the followers and for the situation. In fact, one popular leadership theory states that the leader
should figure out how mature each subordinate is and manage accordingly. The leader unilaterally determines whether any individual needs close supervision or can handle more freedom. Never is
the subordinate consulted about his or her views or desires.

Our star performers make a habit of asking first, even when they
think they already know. When Anithia, a U.S.-based software designer for a German-owned business, begins a new project, she
tests her assumptions about her coworkers. When she and six
coworkers were assigned to develop a new software program for the
Internet, she took time out from the first meeting to ask about work
roles and assignments.

"John, during our last project together, you said that you wanted
more hardware experience. Is that still the case? Because this project has a strong hardware component to it."

Like a perceptive psychologist, Anithia suspended her own assumptions and asked empowering, open-ended questions that allowed the project members to define their own personalities and
offer what they wanted from the project. In this way, she got people
talking about what skills each brought to the table and what each
one wanted to take away. As a result, she was able to make sure that
the work assignments more closely matched individual skills and
interests. She wanted to avoid pigeonholing her coworkers the way
Hollywood producers tend to do when they lock actors into a specific character role.

Now, even in a brainpowered workplace, employees don't always
get everything they want. But the mere opportunity to be heard
and the attempt to meet some needs carries a lot of influence for a
small-l leader who has no formal authority. It also provides the positive platform needed when the inevitable stresses hit during the
project's crunch times. Some small-l stars may be justified in assuming a temporary leadership role based on demonstrated superiority
in a technical area, but that stratification does not extend to the interpersonal side. Instead, they try to create a we're-all-in-the-
trenches-together attitude.

The focus is on getting the job done, and so there is less of the social-political jockeying that overwhelms some projects. If there is grunt work to be done, no one is spared his or her fair share; there are no free riders, least of all the small-l leader. The emphasis is on meeting responsibilities to those customers benefiting from the project and to one another.

In this mode, small-l stars are just as likely to be at the copy machine or running to the mailroom to meet a deadline. Even in environments where official leadership roles are established, the small-l style can pay big dividends. Leaders can reap benefits that go well beyond the project at hand by taking time to consider the individual needs of followers.

Jorge is one of five associates reporting to one of the partners in a large law firm that is defending a national producer of wire fencing in a $400 million antitrust case. Jorge, as the informal lead attorney among the associates, has a reputation as an excellent litigator and small-l leader. Because he has that rare combination, younger associates trip over one another trying to get assigned to Jorge's case teams, even though they have full workloads of their own.

As the judge is set to hear arguments about whether the corporation's stake in a national chain of discount hardware stores might give it an unfair advantage in the fence market, the team needs a legal brief supporting its client's position. The managing partner tells Jorge to get the team on it.

Jorge calls the team together to discuss the assignment, each member's professional responsibility to provide the very best work to the client, and how best to get it done.

During this process, Arnie, one of the younger associates, volunteers to write up the section on similar cases in other state jurisdictions. Although Jorge has never worked with Arnie before, he has heard the office rumors about his past troubles with research tasks, failing to locate key cites in other cases, or bringing them in late.

Instead of keeping Arnie off the critical path, Jorge takes a bigger view: What is best for this project and how can he help Arnie put the negative rumors to rest?

In a private face-to-face meeting with the associate, Jorge is candid about the demands of the project and what he has heard about

Arnie. Jorge tells Arnie he doesn't want to prejudge his performance, that he plans to give Arnie the chance if Arnie feels capable, and that he'd like to get Arnie's viewpoint. During the conversation, Jorge learns that, yes, Arnie had some difficulties in his first few assignments. But he has been through research tutorials on his most recent cases and feels confident about handling any research assignment. He also appreciates Jorge's candor and would appreciate any tips that Jorge might offer.

Together, they devise a plan. Both Arnie and Jorge will independently research the applicable case law, but only Arnie will write up his research. Jorge will check Arnie's work against his own. If Arnie does a great job, Jorge will let it be known both to the team and to the other senior associates. If Arnie doesn't, then Jorge will be in a position to help him improve his research skills for the future. In either case, the project won't be in jeopardy.

So Jorge backs off and allows Arnie to research the applicable case law. During his own research, Jorge remembers a California case on a similar issue where the ruling was for the defendant company. He makes a few phone calls to sources in California and has the decision faxed to him. When he reads it, he realizes this could be the winning point in their case. He wonders if Arnie will come up with it.

When Arnie discovers the important California case and rushes into Jorge's office waving a printout over his head, Jorge praises him lavishly. In a team meeting called after the judge cites the case in ruling for the law firm's client, Jorge also gives credit to the associate.

Jorge, our small-l star, was able to avoid a common leadership pitfall—big-L paternalism. It is the mindset that assumes "leader knows best" for each team member, as opposed to the unset mind that allows team members opportunities to chart their own courses within the bounds of the project. These small-l stars create that environment by posing questions like these:

- How can you best add value to this project and how can this project best add value to your development?
- What do you want to do, what do you need to perform well, and what are you willing to give?

Many small-l stars we have observed take it upon themselves to use their temporary leadership role to shore up team members in areas where they are weak. The assistance is always offered in the framework of helpful tips from one colleague to another, not as the omniscient big-L dispensing wisdom to a hapless underling.

Small-l stars also know that presuming to be a leader is often far less productive than filling the actual leadership role of facilitator; they are the rank-and-file workers who step forward at key points, pull out their oil cans, and lubricate the process to get the engine up to speed. As we will see in the teamwork chapter, Chapter 10, the lubrication can take many forms—from interpersonal skills that smooth out factions to technical skills that ease a group through a complicated problem on a project. The small-l facilitator usually has no lofty ambitions to a management position or special recognition. The leadership interest comes from a desire to meet a need or solve a problem.

Big-L behaviors can also creep in when it comes time to assign credit for a successfully completed assignment. No matter how much individual work the small-l leader does to realize the team's goal, the spotlight always must be extended to the team. When performances warrant, individual members are singled out for praise, as Jorge, the antitrust attorney, did with Arnie.

Indeed, our research shows that a fast way to a star leadership reputation is to be overgenerous in crediting others; the fastest way to wreck one is to horde the credit for oneself. Coworkers understand better than managers those in their ranks who have trouble parting with their egos—and they don't forget.

The most effective small-l leaders we studied were profuse thankers and sharers of credit, especially with team members who have chosen not to play any leadership role but whose work as followers meets a vital need. Small-l leaders treat these team members as equals, recognizing that in other assignments the roles could easily be reversed.

To software designer Anithia, the Internet project in which she acted as small-l leader turned out to be a huge hit with customers. At the annual awards banquet, the president of the North American division praised its success by describing it as "vintage Anithia." Inviting her to the stage, the president then compared it with other successful past projects that Anithia had led. If the company had five hundred more like her, he said, domination of the U.S. market would be assured. Then he summoned her to the podium to speak.

Like so many self-important actors clutching their Oscars, Anithia could have rushed through the standard nice words about her boss and project members. Instead, she invited them all on stage with her. She then asked one of them to introduce each member of the group. Finally, she stepped to the microphone and said, "This project was the result of *our* effort; without each person's contribution, it would not have been the success it is. We were proud of it and glad that you are too." Then they took a collective bow.

FLIPPING THE MOMENTUM SWITCH AND OTHER STEPS OF SMALL-L LEADERSHIP

Khalifa often felt isolated in the public relations firm where he worked in Chicago. Having parents from the Middle East country of Oman was a powerful strike against him in a country still reeling from the bombing of the World Trade Center. In every corner of popular culture—from newsweeklies to big-budget Hollywood films—Middle East Muslims had replaced the Soviets as the evil enemy stalking Americans. His University of Texas education and his U.S. citizenship by birth didn't matter. In the eyes of much of America, he was not to be trusted, a suspect by association. Because he was a public relations specialist, his success on the job depended on his ability to be perceived as trustworthy and credible, and so the ethnic stereotyping was a real threat to his performance.

Khalifa decided to meet the problem head on and do careful research to find a solution using the same star strategies he used for clients on the job.

He began with a thorough search of his profession for colleagues with the same Middle Eastern roots and put out invitations to bring them all together to discuss the credibility issues he suspected they faced on the job, too. He asked them to think about the issues and to come with productivity ideas that they could share with one another.

Khalifa brought together the twenty who responded at a dinner at a Middle Eastern restaurant and opened up the discussion about the meeting's purpose—to determine whether the credibility problems he was experiencing were shared by others in the group and to work on solutions. By meeting's end, the group had shared painful personal experiences, developed a list of solutions, and even agreed to work toward starting a formal organization.

Khalifa not only ran the meeting and recorded action plans, he also offered to put together a directory of the participants so that members could rely on one another for advice.

The membership has since grown to about sixty—from both PR firms and departments in large corporations. The members give one another tips on projects, serve as resources, and refer business to one another. Khalifa also started a mentoring network within the organization. This incredible resource group would not have happened without Khalifa's organizational leadership skills. Khalifa himself has become more productive and has brought in substantial business from contacts he has made in the group.

Khalifa knew that an important step in exercising small-l leadership was to move from standstill into momentum mode. Whether it be a meeting, a memo, or the first piece of work on a large project, a primary star-leadership skill is learning how to create momentum.

Much has been written about leaders creating visions or being change agents. Leaders sometimes do these things. But when someone steps forward to "take the lead" on an assignment or a project, we don't assume that person is going to be charismatic, have a grand vision, or shake things up. These notions tend to overstate the case and to miss what really happens. Leadership is most often about the mundane everyday job of creating momentum to get things done. Generally, these things are incremental steps in getting through our individual and collective to-do lists. Rarely do these things change the world.

In the reality of most brainpowered workplaces, we expect those who play the leadership role to ensure that the activities we associate with leadership get done—activities ranging from scheduling meetings to representing the team before upper management. We expect leaders to create and maintain momentum for the project. It's a skill similar to the initiative strategy in our star performers model. It begins with jump-starting the project and continues through to completion. It also involves communicating personal enthusiasm to others so that they want to contribute their energy as well.

Some small-l leaders who are not stars go in the opposite direction. Just as Jorge, the lawyer, was tempted to do, they decide that the safest route is to do all the critical-path work themselves. Rather than working to build up the involvement of team members and then delegating work in fair portions, they opt for taking on extra loads and carrying it through on their own.

Some of this unproductive behavior has less to do with the leader's failure to shore up or delegate than with the proliferation of teams in the work culture of large corporations. We observed, in fact, that the lead engineer on a five-member project team ended up doing most of the work because her four coworkers were backed up with assignments as leaders of other project teams. Each person was doing individual work under the guise of teamwork!

But the star team leaders we observed were able to break out of that on the strength of energy, conviction, and persuasion. Like Khalifa, they tied the project into colleagues' self-interest. Because small-l leaders often know their colleagues, they know what turns them on. When they are really fired up, they make the project seem so hot, so critical to careers and company fortunes that each member can't help but give the work priority. Star leaders also form one-on-one relationships with each team member, providing the close, personal touch that makes the members feel an emotional connection to the team and the project.

But before most of the stars we studied opened the momentum-and-energy spigot, they had an organizational framework set up to manage the flow. There is nothing as counterproductive as a brain-powered work team primed with momentum whose members then race off in a dozen different directions. Creating momentum carries the additional leadership responsibility of developing a direction plan with at least a clearly defined beginning, even if the middle and finishing process are still ambiguous. This plan will probably change as the project unfolds, but the leader provides enough of a solid first footing to start the momentum.

Also, we generally expect leaders to carry a heavier administrative burden for the project. They provide the agendas, the rough drafts, and the initial schedule. They deal with the bureaucratic red tape. They handle the documentation and correspondence. That doesn't mean that they have to do it themselves (although it often turns out that way); they must, however, make sure it gets done.

The small-l star leads through the momentum-building process the way successful player-coaches lead a team through a season—by example and by bonding. A player-coach needs to be more sensitive to team members' experiences than someone who fills the coach role full-time and is viewed as solely management. The player-coach must also be more proactive in defending the team—acting as an effective advocate in a hostile management situation, for instance, or preventing other departments from poaching on the team's turf.

But there is a positive communicator duty as well. Small-l stars keep team members involved in decisions and incidents that affect their work. Small-l leaders go out of their way to listen to team-member complaints, even if on the surface these complaints may seem trivial. And they help devise a solution, or explain honestly why one will not be forthcoming. Overriding all this is the leadership activity of keeping the team thoroughly informed and facilitating the communication flow in all directions.

Momentum leadership, then, is a whole collection of activities required to move a project from beginning to completion. In some cases, like that of Khalifa, the small-l leader simply undertakes these activities. Other times, star leaders will raise the topic of momentum early in the project by asking the team to decide who will do which momentum activities. Is the team expecting the leader to moderate meetings, or will that be a rotating responsibility? Is the leader the hub for all communication, or will there be a phone tree? Who has the group's authority in discussions with upper management? Whose job is it to make sure people are getting their work done on time? The goal is both to make sure that the momentum activities get done and to know who will do them.

In many ways, momentum leadership is like the star work strategy of initiative, but taken to the group level. Your team can have all the knowledge and people leadership skills, but if the job doesn't get done, then failure occurs. Without a lot of fanfare or power-tripping, small-l leaders minimize failure by maximizing momentum.

THE REALITY OF SMALL-L LEADERSHIP

These small-l leadership quotients—knowledge, people, momentum—were not simply pulled out of a hat or identified because they fit some theory of what leaders should do. These are the leadership activities that our star performers used on the job day in and day out to gain their productivity edge. Sometimes one star would engage in all three; other times these activities would rotate from team member to team member. The bottom line, though, is that the stars made sure that all three activities were in play when needed, by the person most appropriate for the role.

In the midst of one of our productivity-improvement programs at Bell Labs, the engineers were confronted with a memo from upper management criticizing the quality of their software and the high cost of rework errors on a just-completed telephone-switch project that the participants had worked on for a year and a half.

On the day the memo came out, the program session's agenda was pushed aside so team members could talk about how hurt and angry they were. When the discussion turned to what the team could do about the situation, there was heated disagreement. A few said the memo should just be ignored; any response would be a waste of time. Management just didn't "get it" and never would. Others thought a response would simply lead to greater antagonism and worsen the situation. The majority, however, believed that a response had to be sent back, informing managers how upset the team was and correcting management's assumptions about the work.

While the situation itself was unfortunate, the timing of it was perfect for a realistic workplace test of all the small-l leadership skills. Instead of the group's settling on its highest-profile member to direct the response effort, several of the quieter, more thoughtful members began assuming the leadership role.

One began to develop influence with reasonable suggestions that seemed to bridge the two extremes of the group—those who resented the memo but feared a group response might make the situation worse, and those who favored storming the executive's office with a demand for an apology.

A response was critical to the future success of the project, another emerging small-l leader argued, because management's assessments would be taken as true and the negative criticism would color future evaluations of the work. But the form of the response would be just as important. "I think we really need to do our homework," this small-l leader argued. "We need to nail down all the facts that support why we think this memo is so insulting, but we need to present it in a polite and professional way. If we don't, then we'll lose credibility even before they get to the first sentence."

By bridging the extremes with inclusive language like "Does this make sense to you?" and "Do you feel comfortable with this?" this unassuming team member became the facilitator/leader of the response effort. But even in that capacity, she did not control every facet of the process. Other members held the floor at various points; one technically talented engineer stepped forward to coordinate the research work that would be required for a point-by-point rebuttal of management criticisms. Another team member widely recognized for his writing skills offered to begin working on a draft. A third took on the momentum role, offering to coordinate all the administration, such as getting the draft distributed and collecting people's comments.

By the end of two weeks, the team had come together to forward a compelling, professional response to management, one that quickly resulted in a series of meetings in which the managers backed off from the memo's accusatory tone. While the offending managers had thought that they had simply been raising consciousness about quality, they hadn't realized the negative effect the memo would have on the engineers. Satisfied with their defense and management's clarification, the engineers then went on to complete the project with fewer quality problems.

They also came away with a dramatic object lesson in the effectiveness of small-l leadership. No single leader on the team was charged with bearing the entire weight of the response memo and the responsibility for picking up the pieces of the project. There was no larger-than-life dynamo mixed into the process; team members were able to exercise leadership in small bursts, rotating from knowledge gurus to people facilitators to momentum leaders as the need arose—no more, no less.

In this case, our star performers were more concerned with successful value-added outcomes than with whether they were the leader. What was most important was that a competent person take on the leadership role and that the job get done right. That is an important reason why star producers in our research developed the set of skills I've bundled together under the heading of small-l leadership. Another is that the amount of time and energy required to employ these skills on a daily basis is a fraction of what is demanded of the big-L leader who starts at the crack of dawn and finishes late because she thinks she's so critical to the company's success.

In a brainpowered environment where the workers often have more technical knowledge than the big-L leader, big-L leadership may be anachronistic. Instead, small-l leadership, with its grounding in the day-to-day realities of the brainpowered economy, responds better to the demands of this fast-changing world.

In the end, it all comes down to which type will both attract the right kind of followership and succeed. As a brainpowered worker, ask yourself: Who would you rather follow? Do you want a big-L leader who thinks he or she has all the answers? Or do you prefer someone who has no formal power over you but who has won your support with a track record in getting things done in a way that includes you? What group of employees will come out ahead on the productivity scale? The small-l star performers or the big-L wannabes?

The stars we studied found that an easy choice and were rewarded with striking increases in productivity.

10

TEAMWORK
Getting Real About Teams

Some of the greatest achievements and greatest abuses of unfettered free enterprise in American business in the 1980s were individual efforts and led social commentators to label it the "me decade."

As we move into the next millennium, individual effort is still critical, but the nature of work has changed. The one-person show has given way to casts of tens, hundreds, even thousands of brainpowered workers required for massive, technically complex projects. We are in the "we decade," a nation of teams employing team spirit and teamwork to realize mind-boggling achievements and, unfortunately, the occasional spectacular failure.

At Boeing, more than a hundred separate teams joined together over a six-year period to create the 777 jetliner, an achievement that boosted company profits by 20 percent the year after production began and doubled the stock price. In similar fashion, the movie *Apollo 13* displayed a team of engineers working around the clock to improvise a carbon dioxide filter to save the astronauts' lives, thus demonstrating the power of teams to accomplish extraordinary tasks under less-than-ideal circumstances.

Yet the project-team method has also become the bane of almost every brainpowered employee's work life. Most of us are spending too much time as team players. Many of the teams we're on are a waste of our time. Either we are not enthusiastic about the team's goals or we're forced to partner with coworkers who have poor teamwork skills, further souring the work experience.

In our productivity studies, we interviewed workers in detail about the reasons they felt unproductive on a given day. "Too many team meetings" tied with "coworker interruptions" for the spot of lead productivity robber.

In fact, in my consulting work with corporations and in our training sessions, I never fail to get laughs when I tell groups of brainpowered workers, "You're probably very concerned about not getting enough invitations to join teams."

Despite all the hype and hoopla over the "wisdom of teams," they are neither a panacea nor a universal success yet. Based on my experience with brainpowered companies, the team concept falls flat with many corporate workers for three reasons:

1. Top executives don't practice what they preach. Upper managers who extol the virtues of teamwork and expect their employees to embrace them don't always take very well to teams themselves. The culture of many upper managements is the culture of individual style and ego. The factors that land many fast-trackers in the executive suite and help them stay there depend on their besting others in individual turf battles. The dismal lack of executive-level team play sends a confusing message to subordinates.

2. Teamwork is not rewarded. When we analyzed compensation benefits to employees for each work strategy in our star performer model, teamwork proficiency was the least recognized. The correlation between managerial or coworker ratings of someone's teamwork performance and that person's monetary rewards was close to zero.

3. Most people are not very good team players. Part of the reason they aren't is a function of our society's romance with in-

dividualism, but there is an educational component as well. Few schools teach teamwork skills. So while we throw our students and workers onto teams, we fail to equip them with the skills necessary to succeed.

But despite all these problems, you still will have to master teamwork. Most of us are going to be on teams—more teams than we would really like. Company managers are convinced that teams provide the productivity boost that individual work methods do not. So you will be ordered to be on teams, like it or not.

But star performers also recognize that teams are necessary for complex brainpowered work and that the work is getting too big for any one person, even a star. They also know that although their piece of the team project may be brilliant, it is meaningless if the overall team project flops. The star performers we've studied understand that great team players can make the difference between team success and team disaster. So although there may not be monetary rewards for great teamwork, the work itself and colleagues often require it. That's why star performers have identified it as an essential work strategy for high productivity.

THE CULTURE OF TEAMWORK

As a brainpowered worker, you will need to figure out where your company stands relative to teamwork, and to do this, you will need to utilize the star work strategies of perspective and organizational savvy.

First, see if the people at the top act as a team. Are they team players who also create positive environments for teams? Are they "walking the talk"?

Next, look at middle managers. Are they supporting teams just within individual departments, or are they building teams that cross departmental boundaries?

Then take it one step down to the team status of your own department. Does your boss expect team playing? Are the departmental stars team players or solo performers? Do your colleagues work together, sharing tasks and information? Do they trust and look out for one another? Are there cliques and infighting?

Finally, what is the level of teamwork skills throughout the organization? Even if people's hearts are in the right place regarding teams, are they capable of working together successfully? Can they plan and achieve group efforts? Do they have the necessary people skills to build trust, address conflicts, make sure that all team members are involved, and get the job done under pressure?

If your analysis leads you to the conclusion that teamwork is neither valued nor essential for star status in your organization, then you can make your team commitments accordingly. You should consider only those teams that are absolutely required for you to complete your work at a high level of productivity, that are necessary to build goodwill with your work colleagues, or that you want to join for personal reasons. But don't expect kudos from managers. You'll do it mainly because you think you'll get some intrinsic value from it. Meanwhile, avoid low-value team activities that sap your attention from more productive endeavors.

If, on the other hand, you learn that teamwork is valued in your company, then you will be hard-pressed to avoid teams and you will need to develop the necessary skills.

Jay, a forty-year-old specialist in taxable bonds, had just joined one of the country's largest pension fund firms, wooed away from a large New York investment bank where he had been a star in the bond department. He was trying to adjust to life in his new environment. At the bank, the corporate culture had been extremely individualistic, which suited him fine. His compensation had been directly tied to the revenue he generated for the firm.

Sporadically, over the years, the bank's top management had made noises about greater teamwork but had never seriously pushed it. Most of the top managers viewed one another as rivals and were fiercely protective of their territory. Against this backdrop stood Jay, who was doing his best to avoid being assigned to any task force charged with finding ways to promote greater teamwork. He liked doing *his* work *his* way to ensure that nothing interfered with *his* pay.

This mammoth pension fund firm, he began to realize, operated very differently. Although there were no formal dictates about teamwork, signs of a team culture were everywhere. Carolyn, the head of the bond department, encouraged everyone to share information and assist one another in crunch periods. On a daily basis, staffers would interrupt their own work to answer a coworker's phone because it benefited the whole department to have a customer reputation for answering phones promptly before the third ring. When a member of the bond department came across important financial news, the information would be shared immediately with others.

Jay quickly recognized the teamwork policy in the bond department, but he knew that the policy wasn't the same in every section of the pension fund firm. "Where I came from, it was sink or swim on your own," he told Carolyn. "For fifteen years I've operated that way. But I see you run a different shop. Is there room for someone like me, who prefers to do things on his own?"

Carolyn reminded Jay that his direct base compensation was still tied to his efforts and financial results, while she had control over merit bonuses. But she also pointed out that much of the work in her department required teams to keep pace with fast-changing and complex markets. The team approach had proved to bring the best financial returns for customers. Even traditionally individual tasks went faster and smoother when people helped one another out. The bottom line, however, was that the department was more productive with teamwork, bringing in more money for everyone.

"I don't consider it a small thing that it's just a more decent way to spend the workday," said Carolyn. "So I expect you to give it a try. Whether you work on teams outside our group will generally be up to you."

Although Jay still harbored a few reservations, he had followed classic star performer behavior. He had paid attention to his work environment. And he had sought out his boss's view, a critical guide to his team behavior. To further allay his concerns, he next talked to star performers in the group. Based on their input and his positive daily experiences with his work group, Jay concluded that he could not be a star in his new company on the basis of his individual actions, as he was in the bank. He needed to have basic teamwork skills to maintain star productivity.

Choose Teams Wisely

Jay, like many brainpowered workers, discovered he could no longer be just a solo contributor in his new environment. Still, he was justifiably concerned about being detoured off the critical path by teammates who would share the driving or by top managers who were mesmerized by a trendy work-psychology gimmick. Based on his prior experience at the bank, he still felt stirrings to protect his high income from team road hazards. Even in the pension fund, outside events could conspire to turn the positive team environment into a productivity nightmare.

For example, downsizing has contributed greatly to the overemphasis on teams. Where accepted management practices once dictated one manager for every five to seven workers, the short-term financial benefits of cutting out multiple layers of managers resulted in one supervisor's having responsibility for a staff of forty or more. Since effective management is impossible with that ratio, the teamwork concept has been twisted and pulled to fill the gap.

Star performers recognize the productivity-boosting potential of teamwork, but they're also keenly aware of the bloating that's occurred in team management in recent years as management ranks have thinned out.

From their perspective, team assignments and the unending meetings that go with them are often an inappropriate, knee-jerk response to organizational challenges. Whenever an issue arises, top officers immediately fire off a memo or pick up the phone: "Let's have a task force get on this, do some studying, and get back with a full report and some recommendations."

Most noticeably, teams have filled in the decision making vacuum created by the delayering of the management ranks. Where managers once made on-the-spot decisions, time-draining meetings are required under the team system in order to make the same decisions. The trade-off for giving people a sense of participation is higher time consumption.

Back when I was working full-time in academia, one of my duties was to serve on the library committee. The team was made up of the director of the library and a mix of ten faculty members from various departments and library staff. The question I had before sitting down for the first meeting was "What the hell do we know about libraries?" But as it turned out, knowing the intricacies of library management was not a prerequisite. This became clear at one of the more substantive meetings I attended, which involved making decisions on two earthshaking questions: How much later should the library remain open during finals? And: Should the library have a Christmas party for the staff?

I had a very difficult time taking the meeting seriously, because it was clear these were solely management decisions that had no connection to academic policy, no university-wide implications. Nonetheless, ten PhDs spent thirty hours in vigorous debate over issues such as library closing times. What I came to realize was that the director needed a committee to make decisions for him so he wouldn't have to bear all the responsibility for any hostile reaction.

There are many star performers we studied who have lived through the same time-wasting, spirit-draining team meetings, and they are very soured on the process. It's a shame, because these workers are excellent team players at heart. As I mentioned above, one of the top two reasons given for lack of productivity in interviews with star performers was "too many teams" and the excessive number of meetings as a result of teams.

To keep from becoming too jaded, stars, we discovered, are much more proactive in establishing relationships with managers and coworkers that allow them more discretion on teamwork.

Michela started her career as a chemical scientist, went back to school for an MBA degree with a marketing emphasis, and became a rising-star product manager for one of the world's largest consumer goods companies. Now in her late thirties, she recalls the ordeal of team assignments. Michela was so heavily recruited for teams, she thought she had won the Heisman Trophy. "At first, it was flattering, and my boss told me it would help my career," she remembers. Then reality set in.

Michela soon found she was overwhelmed. Her own work was suffering, even though she put in seventy-hour weeks to keep up with all her commitments. The countless team meetings and subsequent work was a hard lesson, she says, about learning to be more selective.

Now, Michela asks these questions before she joins a team:

1. How closely connected is the team assignment to the critical path? What is the likelihood that the outcome will add value?
2. Can the team's mission be explained in one or two sentences? If it can't, the problem or assignment may need to be clarified further before it reaches the team level.
3. Is the team necessary at all? Or is this assignment better suited to one or two people?

"I've often found that teams are assigned projects that could be done better and faster by one person," Michela says. "The team wallows for weeks still getting organized, while a dedicated person could have figured out the solution in the same amount of time."

If the answers to all three investigative questions are in favor of the team approach, then Michela, like other star performers in our research, goes through a second investigation—whether she's appropriate for the team. "I have to convince myself that the team really needs me—my knowledge, my experience, my point of view—to get this job done. I don't want to be just another person on the team; I want to be critical to its success."

Michela's other priority is to identify teams that add value to her standing in the company or benefit her résumé. One of these teams involved getting in at the beginning of an international products line connected to East Asian trade. But Michela distinguishes between teams she does for herself and those that keep the company on the critical path.

Once Michela convinces herself that the team is worthwhile and that she should be on it, she looks around at the rest of the team. Does this team have what it takes to succeed? Do the other team members have the needed talents and skills to complete the task? Is the mix right? Are there others who would be more appropriate for the team? Could the team function just as well with fewer members?

So what do the stars, like Michela, do when they have a problem with the team's makeup or its mission and they've been assigned to it anyway? Average performers often act as if they don't have a choice, resigning themselves to the task. They say, "What does it matter whether I think having a team work on this problem is the right approach? The boss wants me on a team; I'm on a team." But star performers exercise direct and indirect control.

First, stars go to their supervisor and explain their position, using the critical-path argument. One star R&D scientist lays out all his personal and team assignments for his boss. Then he asks the boss to prioritize the new assignment within the existing ones. Very often, this tactic keeps him free of extra assignments.

Similarly, if they think they are wrong for the job, they will try to excuse themselves. At the same time, star performers don't leave others in the lurch. They will suggest qualified candidates to take their place.

Michela's careful investigation and her ability to pick and choose which teams she joins would have saved her from the fate of some administrative staff people at an East Coast computer company. Top managers there had decided that spiraling real estate prices necessitated relocating a planned research-and-development facility to a new city with lower costs. To choose the new location, they formed a committee made up of finance and real estate staff.

These folks took their assignment seriously, checking land values, local tax incentives, transportation and educational infrastructures, and a host of other relevant factors. After nine months of almost full-time effort, they settled on Phoenix.

It wasn't until the company's e-mail files were brimming with angry reaction to the decision that the team discovered it had made a major mistake. They had focused primarily on economic considerations when making their choice. No one had thought to poll the research-and-development workforce as to whether they would actually move or whether the company could recruit experienced technical people to settle in Phoenix. The e-mail furor helped the company avoid repeating the costly error that MCI, the long-distance phone company, made when it moved its R&D facility but many staffers refused to follow.

This was an unfortunate case of mismatching a team to a project. The committee members were intelligent and well intended but were not qualified for this task. Almost four staff years were wasted collectively as a result. Fortunately, it happened before construction was to begin on the new facility.

One of the Bell Labs engineers we studied who had developed a painstaking picking-and-choosing process similar to Michela's told us he questioned what went into teams the same way Charles Lindbergh questioned what went into his plane before his transatlantic flight. The craft could only hold so much extra weight. Excess items created more drag and required more fuel than the plane could carry. "For each item he asked, 'Is this necessary to achieve the goal?' I look at my team involvements the same way. Does my presence on the team help me and the company achieve our mutual goals? If I can't answer a definite yes to both, then there's good reason to question the team assignment."

CONTRIBUTING TO TEAMS

Once star performers believe in the team effort and commit themselves to it, star players are not back-of-the-pack slackers freeloading off the hard work of others. They stand out front and hash out their problems with the team leader to try to influence the composition and direction of the team.

Michela was thrilled when asked to join a task force to recommend a new television advertising strategy. When she learned who else was being considered, however, her heart sank. Most of the others were included for political reasons, not because they had product or advertising expertise. This meant the heavy workload would fall on a small subgroup, while most of the group meetings would consist of political maneuvering.

To improve the odds of the team making a wise choice, she approached the task force leader. "From looking over the list, I gathered that you are trying to make sure all your political bases are covered," she told him. "My concern is that if we don't come up with a strategy that captures everyone's imagination, then selling it internally—let alone to customers—is a nonissue. To do that we need the best people, not the politically correct ones."

With that, Michela suggested her dream team for the project. She even offered a two-tiered committee: a larger oversight committee, consisting of the political members, that would offer overall guidance and get periodic updates and reviews, and a second working group that would consist of members who brought special expertise and points of view—people who could accomplish this creative, critical path task in the shortest time possible. She also offered to help recruit the working-group team.

Making Sure the Team Knows Its Purpose

Once the team is formed, the stars also work to ensure every team member understands what the team is getting into—that they agree on its mission and other basics. They are honest about sharing their perspective and their opinions without being disruptive, because it's likely the team will continue on, even if the star isn't on board. In most cases, the star team player tries to make a go of it, using influence and persuasion to bring other members into agreement on roles and goals.

At each team meeting, the stars monitor their progress and that of the group. If the product or service is going to be used by others in the company, the star sees to it that their interests are represented—either arranging for them to be invited to a meeting or by interviewing them and relaying the information to team members in some way. If a customer is going to be a direct beneficiary, then the customer's desires are kept at the center of the team's radar screen. The star teammate also works to keep the critical path flowing in the opposite direction—to keep customers and coworkers updated regularly on any changes.

Getting the Team's Job Done

Once on board, star performers self-manage their part of the team task just the way they do any other assignment: They complete it on time, on schedule, and within budget.

Another way in which stars make their mark on teams is by employing the other star performer work strategies, such as taking initiative, exercising perspective, and self-managing.

For example, stars make sure they produce their work on schedule and renegotiate deadlines if problems occur, with plenty of advance warning to the team coordinator and other members. Stars are also open to the perspectives of team members on their completed work, soliciting reviews before the work is turned in.

Star team players also look out beyond their assignment to the team's functioning. For example, they check for an equitable division of tasks. This does not mean that everyone does the same measure of work. A Microsoft marketing specialist may do triple duty on the team responsible for pitching Windows97 to the world but work only half as much representing her department on another team getting ready to launch the company's new on-line magazine. The key factor that the stars look for is the "fairness quotient." Is there one person on the team being saddled with all the grunt work? Are there three members who are working in concert to avoid their fair share of the drudge tasks?

One of the surprising patterns from our observations of team dynamics was that the stars were not prima donnas when it came to carrying their share of the load. In fact, it was the stars who most often could be counted on to do more—filling in when another team member was dealing with a sick child, or sensing when another member was falling behind on a task and pitching in to meet the deadline. Instead of standing on a pedestal for the rest of the team to admire, most of the stars are down in the trenches taking their turn with the shovel. That's just one of the reasons star performers often end up as general role models on teams, whether or not they have an official coordinating or small-l leadership position.

And stars are more comfortable in the face of criticism—and they are quick to make corrections based on sound critiques. They come to meetings prepared to discuss the work at hand, but they remain flexible enough to react to any sudden changes in the group dynamics.

Stars also are actively involved in detecting time nibblers—the lengthy discussions that often occur in team meetings when side issues overshadow critical path goals. The stars have the experience and interactive skill to flag these departures early and redirect the team back onto the critical path.

Paying Attention and Contributing to Group Dynamics

Teams often take on their own personalities. Just as it takes a certain amount of emotional intelligence to be in a relationship with another person, teamwork requires paying attention to group dynamics—commitment, conflicts, subgroup cliques, participation levels, body language, even the group's mood.

Too many people see groups as simply a loose collection of individual players. They don't understand that great teamwork requires practice on how to function as a team. When groups don't attend to the group dynamics, they reduce the probability that they will jell and that they will produce. Some teams, just like some people, become dysfunctional.

Star team players try to be a positive force both in their part of the work they do and in the way they behave as team members. First, they start with commitment. Nothing is more deflating for a team than to get to the deadline with a final product only to find that some team members are not on board and refuse to sign off on it. These group members effectively hold the team project hostage until they get the changes they want.

To avoid this scenario, Su-Hong, an industrial film script writer in Chicago, followed certain guidelines whenever she was involved in a new script project. At the start, she raised the issue of team commitment to the final product and asked how the team wanted to handle it. If she felt it was needed, she would raise examples of problems in the past and ask other team members for their own experiences. Then she solicited their suggestions on how to deal with this issue and offered her view.

One technique that had worked well for her was to poll each person at each decision point to get their public buy-in. If they had problems at that point, they needed to raise them. What she worked hard to avoid was having a team member pipe up at the end with something like "I didn't like the direction that this was taking from the beginning."

Su-Hong also learned to use rough drafts and straw models as a concrete way to solicit reactions. Once each draft had been reviewed, she asked each team member to approve it. But she wasn't trying to ramrod the scripts through the team. She paid close attention to how people were acting and reacting. If a teammate's body language suggested discomfort or quiet hostility, she would try to pull them in by soliciting their views. "Jane, you seem to have second thoughts about this. Perhaps you could voice your concerns so that we can address them or fix the script."

Commitment is closely connected to participation levels, conflicts, and frustration levels. Stars monitor these to ensure that members are involved and not sliding into passivity.

A medical equipment supplier formed a crisis team because hospitals were furious over recent failures in the company's latest monitors. The equipment gave off emergency warnings at random, causing much distress to both patients and hospital staff, who would rush into triage alert only to find that nothing was wrong. Although no one had been hurt, the malfunctioning was an annoying nuisance. If the monitors weren't fixed soon, the hospitals would be demanding costly replacement equipment—or worse, turning to a competitor.

The team consisted of professionals from five departments, including production, research, and customer service. The monitor machine business was only a small portion of the company's manufacturing base. And in fact, most efforts were being directed at launching a new product. So the team had to be staffed with workers who already had full plates. Of seven members, the only star performer was Aiden, a former mechanical engineer who had moved into customer service as a way to learn more about the customer side of the business. Now in his late thirties, Aiden had emigrated to the United States from Ireland to attend graduate school and had worked at the company for eight years.

During the third hour of the first team meeting, a heated argument erupted over what action should be taken now. One side, led by Ewing, a fifty-three-year-old production engineer with twenty-five years' experience in the company, argued to continue sending repair people to the hospitals that complained and fix the machines on site. Julie, a recent hire in the research department, argued to emulate Johnson & Johnson's example during the Tylenol disaster—recall all the machines.

EWING: This is not a life-or-death problem; it's a customer nuisance. We should give it our best lowest-cost response. Given the company's weakening financial picture—which, I shouldn't have to remind you, affects all of our profit-sharing bonuses—I can't see how we can justify any other recommendation to management.

JULIE: But that is shortsighted. The ethical thing to do is get all the machines out of the hospitals and upgrade them with our more expensive models that we've had no problems with.

EWING: Are you crazy? The recall itself is too expensive, but then you're going to throw in a higher-priced replacement for free?

JULIE: It will be a customer service gesture to keep them on our side.

The discussion continued in this mode for another fifteen minutes, with Ewing and Julie getting more heated and less civil. At that point, Aiden noticed that he and other group members were getting frustrated and fidgety. Rather than let it go on unchecked, he mentioned his observation. "I'm starting to feel frustrated because we seem to be going around and around. Does anyone else feel this way?"

When he got nods of agreement from many of the others, he suggested, "Why don't we call a ten-minute break so that we can all take a breather and maybe find a way around this."

With that, the group took a break. During the break, Aiden chatted privately with a few other group members to learn their reaction to the scene. No one was happy, but there were no concrete ideas from any of them either.

When the meeting resumed, Aiden suggested an unorthodox approach he had seen work in a different group to help break an impasse and to get the group back on track. To avoid digging themselves deeper into their own positions, Ewing and Julie would switch sides. To better understand the other side's position, Julie would present and argue for Ewing's approach, and Ewing would argue hers.

Both Julie and Ewing were wary. But when the rest of the group supported Aiden's idea and urged them to give it a try, they reluctantly agreed to take a stab at it. At first, they didn't quite know what to do. But as they began to take the same hard line with their opponents' positions as they had previously with their own, a slight transformation occurred; their original positions softened. They better understood the alternative view.

On a team-morale level, star players are also watching for those members who are pushed to the background. Many average performers believe that group members who talk the most, the loudest, or with the most conviction get their way. Star performers know that just because a teammate is quiet, that doesn't mean she or he has nothing to say. Star players recognize that some of the most insightful comments come from those who do more listening than talking, and that groups swayed by who talks the most often don't hear these insights, because they come from quiet people.

As the group above started to move forward again because Julie and Ewing had softened their positions, they still had to come up with an action plan to avert the growing crisis. As group members started to bat ideas around, Eloise, an experienced but shy designer who sat in the corner and had not said a word all day, spoke up in a soft voice. "Since not every hospital is having problems, it seems to me that we have to first find out why these particular machines are malfunctioning. So rather than pull all the machines, maybe we should only pull those having problems."

No one in the group commented on her idea, and the discussion resumed. After a few minutes, Aiden joined in. "I'm not sure everyone heard Eloise's suggestion. I think that she might have a way out of this. Would you mind repeating it for us?"

With that Eloise made her point again and added, "The faulty machines are either broken to start with or there is something going on with the hospitals that are having problems. When we remove the faulty machines we need to gather information on each setting to see if something there is causing the problem, like a high magnetic field that is interfering with our machines."

Aiden: "Eloise's idea is a good one. It shows the customers with problems that we're responsive, it's not as expensive as a total recall, and it gets us started on finding out what the problem is. I would add that we need to sample the hospitals without problems for comparison purposes. To help justify this to management, we can raise the legal liability. If someone should die or be hurt, lawsuits are sure to follow. Once any lawyer finds out that our machines were malfunctioning, they will come after us whether we were at fault or not."

The rest of the group then supported Eloise's suggestion to get through the group impasse, and they moved on to other topics. Without Aiden's intervention, Eloise might never have been heard and the group might have continued to flounder.

Aiden demonstrated an awareness of an unfortunate dynamic that occurs in groups. Ideas from introverted people, no matter how good, seldom get heard the first time. Either the quiet person has to repeat the idea, which quiet people are reluctant to do, or someone else in the group has to pick up on it.

We have often observed louder people make the same suggestion ten minutes later as if it were their own, only to then see the idea get accepted. When confronted with this observation, the louder person will deny having even heard the earlier suggestion.

The most successful team players we studied also skillfully mix substantive comments with a sense of humor in group interactions. They are counted on to offer the fresh perspective that no one else has considered. Most important, they try not to take themselves too seriously; the best team players also try to be self-effacing.

In one group, two stars got into a dispute on how to proceed, and they were getting locked into their own positions. Because these two highly regarded workers were getting into a fight, the group started getting nervous. While Karr stressed her position, her earring fell to the ground. She didn't bother looking for it while she finished her point. As soon as she stopped, Bruce, her counterpart, launched into his point.

Shortly after Bruce started, Karr distractingly started looking for her earring. When she didn't find it immediately, she pushed her chair back and got on the floor to look for it. We weren't sure how Bruce would react to Karr's seemingly rude behavior while he was talking. Without missing a beat, Bruce pushed his chair back, got down on the floor with her, continued making his point, and found her earring. The sight of these two stars on the floor cracked the group up and relieved the tension. Bruce's willingness to be silly rather than angry saved the day.

This last quality is especially important when it comes time to share in the glory of a team success. When telling the requisite war stories, the stars seldom speak in the first person: it is usually "we." If a photographer were to take a picture of the team, the stars would make it a point to attend the session because they believe in the bonds forged by teamwork. But the final print might show them in the back row or off to the side, smiling broadly in celebration of the team experience as much as celebrating in reaching the goal.

11

ORGANIZATIONAL SAVVY
Street Smarts in the Corporate Power Zone

When Seth was in the homestretch of completing his PhD in computer science from that cathedral of high technology MIT, he began to understand what it must be like to be a star college basketball player on the "must have" lists of professional teams.

The recruitment wooing came from every quarter, but the most aggressive was from Wall Street financial firms. Their tangled web of financial services and huge volume of daily stock trading demand sophisticated computer-engineering skills. The cash-rich brokerage firms can afford to go after the cream of the hacker crop.

Seth was thrilled by the prospect of going to work for a company that wanted him for hands-on software development. Most doctoral-level graduates are recruited to do research, run teams of programmers, or become professors. But Seth also was fascinated by the enormous amounts of money in high finance. Recruiters promised him a lucrative career in which his engineering background would be a tremendous boost on a career track to top leadership positions in their firms.

Seth bought the pitch and signed on with a brokerage-financial services firm—not the largest on the block and not the one making the highest offer but the one he thought offered the best opportunity for advancement.

During his first year at the firm, Seth spent many late nights learning the basics of the finance markets. But he also managed to make several important contributions in his area, including developing a complicated computer software program that would allow customers to pay bills, prepare their tax returns, and deal in securities on their home computers.

There was a hefty year-end bonus and several personal visits from the firm's top managers to commend him on his work. Seth thought he was on the express elevator to top management.

By the end of his second year, he had moved up to the top computer-services job, one he assumed was a stepping stone to a position that would give him more experience with general financial-services management.

But then came the rude awakening in his third-year annual performance review. The vice president who had responsibility for Seth's section rated him highly for his technical ability but low on organizational culture skills. "You will always have a valuable supporting role to play with us on the technical side," the senior executive said in the evaluation's overview. "But the career goal you've written here in the evaluation—moving over into mainstream financial-products management—well, that's going to be a problem, Seth," the executive said, looking down at the desk. "How do we move you in that direction given your run-ins with some of the product-line departments?"

With the uncomfortable part now out in the open, the executive looked up at Seth. "You have great ideas that can make positive contributions to this firm. But you need to learn how to get people to buy into them. If you continue to alienate key managers, you'll never go in the direction you want to go. The firm needs generalists who have more experience dealing with the realities of organizational life and sensitive organizational boundaries. I've been trying to protect you as best I can, but you have to do your part."

Seth struggled to maintain control during the review. But when he returned to his office, he closed the door; this was the first time his staff had seen it shut in his time there. He sat back on his couch and phoned his friend Pam, a just-named vice president of financial services who had worked closely with him on one of his software projects when she was a tax attorney in the legal section.

"They're putting the brakes on my career here because they think I'm an uncooperative nerd," he shouted into the phone. "They pulled one over on me, Pam. Having an engineering degree isn't a plus around here, it's a negative, because the people running the show are all MBAs."

No stranger herself to the experience of being pigeonholed by traditionalist managers, Pam worked to calm him down. "Look, Seth, if you want to be a star in this firm, you have to rise to this challenge. That's what it is, you know, they're testing you. They've clamped the velvet handcuffs on and told you why and now it's up to you to get out of them. Otherwise, they're on for good."

"I don't understand. I've had nothing but great reviews at this firm. What is it that I'm doing wrong?"

"I don't think that's the question," said Pam. "You can keep doing what you're doing in your little corner and continue to get approval and you'll have that job for as long as we need computers to do our work. The better questions, the two I had a hard time arriving at after they told me I would never move out of tax law, are 'What should I be demonstrating to people in this firm that I'm not? What kind of image do I present to the decision makers, coworkers, and clients of this firm?' And when I really examined the answer to those two questions I realized those people were getting a very restricted view of my abilities."

"So they're right. I am a nerd."

"Well, I think you're exaggerating their impressions. But if by that you're saying that they only see the technical side of who you are, then that's all they have to go on. You have to go way out of your area to match the experience that some of the MBA managers have in knowing how to maneuver around an organization the size of this firm. They know who the players are, they have some valuable interpersonal skills, and they know how to forge consensus from a very diverse group of professionals."

"Okay, Pam, I'm glad I picked you to yell at. You've raised some good points. So while I was writing computer programs to help speed up the firm's trading processes, these MBA folks were on Or-ganizational Maneuvers 101. I need to play catch-up here. I want to get out of these velvet handcuffs."

Our research experience in companies from industrial manufactur-ing to investment banking to high-tech tells us there are thousands of brainpowered workers like Seth in dozens of occupations, not just computer engineering, who have found the doors to top pro-fessional jobs flung wide open on the basis of their excellent techni-cal abilities. But after two or three years on the job, many of these same workers are shocked to discover what I refer to as the "tech-spec wreck"—a built-in bias against workers who are seen to be too locked in to their technical specialization and do not operate well in the larger organizational context. These workers are passed over because they lack an essential ability to maneuver effectively in a workplace fraught with competing interests and demanding clients and sensitive deals. Many companies have their own names for this ability but I call it by the name our star performers have labeled it—organizational savvy.

Once again, many people—managers and brainpowered workers alike—operate under the assumption that organizational savvy is on the order of charisma—innate, elusive, mysterious. They conclude that the only meaningful training helps those with the organiza-tional savvy gift to use it more effectively. Some of it is offered in MBA programs or in the backgrounds of those who have had a broad liberal arts education and exposure to popular culture. The assumption follows that since most technical-specialist workers don't have an innate sense of organizational savvy, and since they lack the broad educational background, they should serve in sup-port roles to the savvy set.

Once again, our research directly refutes those assumptions. When organizational savvy is broken down into its various compo-nents, the magic and mystery disappears and any reader will realize this is a learnable skill.

You'll find organizational savvy, like show-and-tell, at the outer-most rung of our star performer-skills model because it needs to be demonstrated later in the workplace than the preceding work strategies. To be an organizational-savvy star, you need to develop several of the basic behavioral work strategies introduced in earlier chapters.

And yet, when mixed with many of the other star performer behaviors, organizational savvy becomes its own distinct skill—*the ability to manage competing workplace interests to promote an idea, resolve conflicts, and most important, to achieve a goal.*

Brainpowered workers who don't understand how to take initiative, or who can't handle critical perspectives, or who wouldn't know how to begin fashioning a network, will also come up short on organizational savvy. But those who have demonstrated competence with the core skills are likely to have gained the trust and confidence of organization leaders so that they have wide latitude in maneuvering around the workplace.

Many brainpowered workers taking our star performers program complain about coworkers who are very slick and savvy dealing with supervisors in the workplace. They get ahead through star performances in brown-nosing rather than by demonstrated competence in the substance skills in our model.

So I ask the question: How many of you know an average performer who has won a promotion primarily because of organizational politicking and brownnosing? Almost everyone raises a hand. Then I ask: Of all the average coworkers you know who have tried to jump ahead based only on sycophantic attention to the boss, how many have succeeded? It turns out to be very few. And of those few who do, even fewer rise to a top job and stay there.

The group comes to realize that getting ahead that way is a very risky strategy for two reasons. First, the Peter Principle kicks in. As they rise to their level of incompetence, they get found out because they can't perform the work. Second, even if top managers are fooled by slickness over substance, star performers and experts are not. They typically will freeze these people out of important knowledge networks, and this makes it nearly impossible for them to do productive work. Increasingly, managers discover that even if they don't want to admit a mistake in judgment on an employee's abilities, the cream of the workplace will do it for them.

So what follows is the star performers' blueprint for developing organizational savvy after a thorough grounding in the other star-model work skills.

The Savvy Surveyor: Getting the Lay of the Land

Every organization, no matter how much it pretends to have revolutionized the way managers and workers relate to each other, has its own organizational chart. The formal chart divides responsibilities and often assigns job titles. But the star performers we studied drew upon both their perspective and networking to be keenly aware of the other organizational chart, the one that is underground and mostly developed by brainpowered workers themselves.

It is this second organizational chart that has more importance, of course, because it details the topography of the organization closer to reality—where the real power centers are as opposed to those on the formal chart, which are often exaggerated.

Reporters who worked at a large metropolitan newspaper in the late 1970s would chuckle at the formal organizational chart that listed the editor at the top of the heap with the highest authority over those in the newsroom. On the underground chart, he was relegated to his proper ranking of about fourth. The person holding the most power was his secretary, Eileen, in whom he had delegated so much power that she recommended reporters for annual raises, reviewed news desk operations, and made recommendations for assignment changes. She even ran daily news meetings when the editor was out of town. While the chain that owned the paper assumed the formal organizational chart was the accurate one, the sharp, experienced brainpowered workers on staff knew better and made sure they were on her good side.

Michela, the marketing whiz at the consumer products company described in the previous chapter, had been asked to join the team to develop the new TV ad strategy. She believed the team leader was placing more emphasis on internal politics than on the actual work that needed to be done. Instead of publicly complaining to the leader or dismissing the leader's work altogether, Michela demonstrated good organizational savvy and followership. She acknowledged the leader's efforts while at the same time drawing upon her own organizational chart to recruit a dream team to do the actual work. She even offered the leader a two-tiered committee structure that would enable both the organizational politics to get tended to and the work to get done properly.

The Savvy Insider

Just as every organization has its own underground flow chart, it also has an institutional personality. The day-to-day quirks range from dress codes to the places workers choose to mingle for office gossip. Character definers include workplace rules like privacy of employee e-mail and cultural etiquette like whether employees refer to managers by their first names.

In the movie *Jerry McGuire*, Tom Cruise plays a glib, fast-talking, but shallow sports agent. At a company retreat, he stays up late writing a brutally honest critique of his profession, "The Things We Think and Do Not Say: The Future of Our Business," which he distributes to coworkers. His assertion of principle—that the sports agency should consider human values as well as financial goals—earns him a round of applause, and then gets him fired.

Although we in the audience may cheer McGuire's first step toward connecting big business with human decency, we also understand that he didn't exercise good organizational savvy in choosing the timing or location of his sermon. It is less the subject than his breaking of unwritten company taboos that causes his downfall. What would surprise organizational savvy superstars watching this film is not that he gets sacked for his transgression but that he is shocked that it has happened.

Remember Don, the regional telephone company engineer who went outside his company's perspective to find out the truth about top management's boastful campaign slogan touting the company's position on "the leading edge of technology"? Not only was Don a star performer when it came to making effective use of perspective, but also he had developed a sharp sense of organizational savvy in learning that managers were extremely defensive about the campaign and weren't tolerating any criticism.

So Don bypassed the company entirely, going to customers and outside experts to learn that his phone company was closer to being "on the leading edge of obsolete technology." By taking stock of the inside attitudes, Don realized the problem couldn't be addressed directly, that he would have to work slowly and carefully on the side to push for an honest evaluation of the company's technology ranking. By tapping into his company's personality quirks, Don was able to avoid a confrontation with managers that could have cost him his job. In the end, Don succeeded in taking the topic from taboo status to open, freewheeling discussion at every level.

Because of his organizational savvy, Don was chosen to lead the effort in bringing the company's technology quotient into line with its lofty slogan.

In addition to internal attitudes as clues to the organizational personality, star performers also pay attention to the symbols that managers embrace—both overtly and covertly. What those symbols reveal about the organization's internal identity is invaluable to star performers who are trying to figure out the best way to advance their goals.

A very overt corporate symbol, for instance, is the famous pink Cadillac tied to the Mary Kay Cosmetics Corporation. The decision of company officials to bestow such a premium on its top sales people speaks volumes about the corporate identity—very bold, class-conscious, but basically conservative.

When Paul O'Neill moved from board member to CEO of the venerable Alcoa Corporation in 1988, industry analysts and savvy insiders watched to see, under his aggressive, no-nonsense leadership, which symbols would be retained and which would go. Within a year of his appointment, top company executives had lost many of their favorite perks. There were no more freebie country club memberships; expense account allowances were cut sharply; a posh corporate retreat in Tennessee was put up for sale; and the company's fleet of airplanes was pared down.

While the savings from these decisions was dwarfed by a massive downsizing campaign and technology improvements in the plants, the symbolism was very important. The new Alcoa was going to be completely focused on the critical path in its lines of business. Perks didn't send that message. Neither, apparently, did the company's huge aluminum office tower in the heart of downtown Pittsburgh. After cutting or transferring 75 percent of headquarters personnel, O'Neill decided to build a tighter, sleeker building on the city's North Side and directed that there be as few walls as possible between offices. Among the items not making the transition from old building to new was the company's critically acclaimed collection of modern art. O'Neill ordered much of it donated to museums and the rest auctioned off, with Pittsburgh residents getting first crack.

Sharp observers noted these changes in symbols as harbingers of more significant paring down to come and the need to put every idea or petition under the critical path microscope. Unlike the average performers who grumbled and trotted out traditional, time-worn arguments to protect what resources they had, the stars made value-added plans or developed better critical path arguments for being granted more.

The Savvy Apprentice: Finding a Mentor

When pop singer Natalie Cole met with high school students at the Interlochen Center for the Arts in Interlochen, Michigan, the first thing she told those aspiring to careers in entertainment and the arts was to find a mentor—someone who had proved himself or herself on a similar career path, who had a lot of experience and stability, who knew the key players and who could teach the aspiring entertainer or artist the language of the industry.

Her message to the students was that it is never too soon to begin building a mentoring relationship. "You need to surround yourself with people . . . who are going to be really direct with you," she said, not fawning "yes people."

Ms. Cole's advice would be just as on target to a room full of brainpowered workers in the business arena trying to understand organizational savvy.

One of the most effective ways to get access to detailed knowledge of the company personality—attitudes, symbols, quirks—is to find a mentor, a wise and trusted counselor willing to share these insights. Of course, nearly every professional in a new workplace environment would appreciate a mentoring opportunity. But the reality is that mentor-worthy colleagues are rare, and those who are qualified often don't have the time or the inclination to take someone under their wing.

Many companies have recognized the enormous value of mentoring and have attempted to institutionalize the process. Almost always, their programs are a poor second to mentoring relationships that happen independently.

The philosophy department at a large university in the South once had a policy of matching up newly hired instructors to tenured professors on the assumption that having a guide would bring them up to speed more quickly with the department's distinct ways and make the rough road to tenure a little smoother. But realities of academic life interfered. The department was split into two factions vying for control of the curriculum and influence with the university's top administrators. The new hires became cannon fodder in the struggle, and most of the mentors became manipulators instead of guides.

Even when the workplace is free of such political strife, company-sponsored mentoring isn't as rewarding for the participants because it's an arranged marriage. Many brainpowered workers in such programs report that they only get to scratch the surface of the company personality. Mentors may be willing to give these workers basic "getting along" information such as how to behave when traveling on a company expense account, but the deeper insights—how much stock company officials put in annual performance reviews, how to avoid bureaucratic pitfalls and self-serving managers on your first project—aren't offered. Personal chemistry is the fuel that gives an independent mentoring relationship its power and prompts people to share their intimate knowledge of the organization.

Harvard Business School professor Abraham Zaleznik, an expert on the mentoring process, writes about President Dwight Eisenhower, who had a mediocre record when he graduated from West Point. He seemed headed for a lackluster career as a lower-level army officer when, during World War I, he was assigned to support duty at a desk job. Meanwhile, his classmates were on the front lines of the French-German border gaining valuable combat experience and winning battlefield promotions.

After the war, it was Eisenhower who realized that if he wanted a distinguished career in the army, he had to find someone to show him how to understand the institution in ways he couldn't learn at West Point. So he sought out a highly respected commander, General Fox Connor, and requested a transfer to serve with him.

Eisenhower was fortunate that Connor warmed up to the mentoring prospect. The two men, Zaleznik notes, bonded like father and son—it was Connor who showed him the lay of the land in the army and challenged him to live up to the high expectations a mentor places in a follower.

Eisenhower later wrote that what he learned under Connor was "... sort of like a graduate school in military affairs and the humanities, leavened by a man who was experienced in his knowledge of men and their conduct." Eisenhower later won an appointment to the prestigious Command and General Staff School, where he graduated first in his class and launched his brilliant career. He owed it all, he wrote years later, to his mentor.

Star performers understand that successful mentoring relationships depend on personal chemistry and often occur serendipitously. A new law professor first met an important mentor when a downpour after a conference forced them to share a taxicab to the airport. During the hour-long ride, they hit it off personally, discovered common academic interests, and began an exchange that helped the "mentee" to make her own star mark in the legal profession.

Stars also know that by drawing upon their initiative, perspective, and networking skills, they can bring about the right conditions for serendipity. By putting themselves in the shoes of a mentor, they recognize that mentoring requires an investment of the mentor into the mentee. Mentors do this because they get some return on this investment. For some, it is the psychological gratification of helping another succeed; for others, the mentee becomes a surrogate son or daughter. In many professional firms, such as accounting or architecture firms, mentors look for protégés who will become fiercely loyal and competent and will work like hell for the mentor in return for being taken under the mentor's wing. Understanding the mentor's perspective is an important first step to finding one.

Just the way stars identify technical gurus to include in their networks, they identify those individuals whom they might like to have as mentors. From that group, they try to spot those who seem disposed to invest in a mentee and what their motivations might be. The stars may then approach these potential mentors directly for guidance. Or they may seek out assignments where they can work closely with the potential mentor. Likewise, they might first volunteer to work on committees and teams with the mentor as a way to establish a working relationship. Then, if things work out, they might approach the person for mentoring help.

Once a mentoring relationship has been established, the stars make a point of not abusing it. They modulate their needs to fit the mentor's willingness to be helpful. They don't want to overstay their welcome, but they also want to get the most benefit from the experience.

The Savvy Explorer: Experiencing the Land You've Mapped

Let's return to Seth, the PhD computer science engineer, who has taken his friend Pam's advice about showing top managers that his experience is not limited to computer codes and hard drives.

Seth wants to have a deep understanding of the stock and bond markets. He also wants to demonstrate the organizational savvy and interpersonal skills required to maneuver successfully through workers with conflicting agendas, clients with high investment expectations, and competitors with big appetites.

Short of corralling a stable of mentors representing every area, Seth's best solution may be to find ways to get experience in different parts of the company, seeing his workplace from the perspectives of several departments. Some star performers we studied were so constrained by their organizations that they could manage only brief expeditions out of their rigidly marked areas, mostly to work on a project or represent their section on a committee. Even within these constraints, when these opportunities were put on the docket, the stars lobbied to get the assignment. When they moved into an unfamiliar arena, the stars grounded themselves thoroughly in the work being done there and identified knowledgeable colleagues who would respond well to questions.

Sarah, the software-developing star introduced in the chapter on perspective skills, Chapter 7, was thought to be crazy by her coworkers when she volunteered for a stint in the testing section. Testers were necessary to catch flaws in the creative work done by others, but the jobs were viewed as drudge work, like working as a fact checker at a magazine instead of writing the story.

Sarah saw it as an exploring opportunity, realizing that since it was an integral part of the company's production process, she would gain valuable insights about how to do her creative work if she understood better how the testers did theirs. She also identified people with whom she would interact in the future and began building working relationships. These organizational bonds not only upped her standing in their eyes, they also helped smooth the way in future interactions.

THE HEART OF ORGANIZATIONAL SAVVY: RELATIONSHIP BUILDING

Many of the average performers we studied appreciated the value of understanding their organization's unique personality. Some even made attempts to use the skills detailed here. But where they came up short was in using organizational, relationship-building skills to open the channels of inside information and keep them open.

Could an average performer faced with a problem requiring help from other departments organize a work session, making sure to include the "right" people, even if those people appear in the "opposition" camp? Would they be able to navigate the dynamics of such a meeting? Could an average performer identify one or two knowledgeable employees in that session and move comfortably to either a roll-up-the-sleeves, late-night work session or a more social work session at a local restaurant? In many cases, creative brainpowered workers are likely to be incapable of identifying the need for such moves. By temperament and by training, these workers are often more comfortable working out problems alone or within the comfort zone of coworkers like themselves.

When Keith Lockhart, the youngest conductor in the history of the Boston Pops, was an accompanist during his student years at Carnegie Mellon University, he mostly hung around with other musicians. As his career progressed, however, he learned that he needed to reach out to other parts of the music community—the singers, stage workers, directors, patrons, subscribers, and administrators. Lockhart realized that being a technically brilliant musician or director was not enough if he aspired to wave a baton in front of a major symphony. His organizational savvy, combined with his other star-performer skills, helped propel his career first to the Cincinnati Symphony and ultimately to the Boston Pops.

Organizational Etiquette

In an interview in the January 1996 edition of *Technology Review*, Robert K. Weatherall, MIT's director of career services, recounted a phone call from two recently graduated students who were part of a training class of twenty-three new hires at a major Wall Street firm.

They were upset that the training class included eleven Harvard graduates, having viewed Harvard as an academic archrival during their college years. It was clear to the MIT students that their Harvard-educated coworkers were significantly better at making an impression, and they wanted Weatherall, in his position as a job placement officer, to set up a session to smooth out the MIT students' rough edges.

What the students were asking for could never be provided in a single workshop, said Weatherall, who knew well that there was a serious interpersonal etiquette problem at the school. "The idea that there could be a charming or graceful way of saying something is not part of the MIT culture," he said.

If students are going to have an opportunity to develop these skills, there must be drastic changes in the educational process—more of a balance between go-it-alone engineering classes and more humanistic, group-centered courses.

What the two MIT students had discovered on Wall Street was that every firm has an etiquette code, just as every organization has its own important symbols and mission statements. Star performers master the etiquette of their workplace as soon as possible. They observe carefully, for instance, to see whether "open-door policy" really means there is a workplace culture that encourages people to drop in on one another unannounced.

Even when the official policy is borne out in the workplace, the stars use basic personal etiquette to keep channels of communication flowing smoothly—"Do you have a minute?" Or, "Is this a good time for you?"—are typical etiquette openings that allow colleagues to opt out of an unscheduled meeting. There were scores of average performers we interviewed who had reputations as technical wizards but who were severely etiquette-challenged; many were chronic bargers, like Claude, the ill-mannered insurance manager in the networking chapter, Chapter 5, who assumed that coworkers and managers should put aside current business to tend to their needs.

On a more sophisticated level, stellar workplace etiquette involves more groundwork and careful planning. Star performers do not ask for the valuable time of coworkers and managers until they've familiarized themselves with the issue to be discussed. If they're hoping for a solution to a problem, they make all reasonable efforts to find an answer before asking for an expert's time. Our etiquette-savvy stars realize that there is a proper level of rapport among players in the workplace, just as there is in relationships forged through networking.

In a large New York advertising firm, Yuji and Ken head teams that handle the needs of the largest accounts. Both are equally adept at developing winning ideas and sharp formats for clients. But at contract-renewal time, Yuji is sitting pretty and Ken is doing a lot of late-night worrying that one of his clients intends to dump him for another agency. In addition to doing great technical work, Yuji has spent a great deal of extra time establishing a personal relationship with the decisionmakers. He sits on the American Diabetes Association planning committee with one of the company vice presidents; trades teenage-rearing horror stories over lunch with another executive in the client company before they settle into business. Yuji has also encouraged members of his team to do the same but only where there are mutual interests. There is nothing that falls flatter, he tells them, than feigning a mutual interest.

Ken has kept his relationships with company officials tied strictly to business. He is not comfortable dealing with others on a social level, and this limitation shows in his work. He has no sense of who his clients are outside of the office framework and they do not know him. He has removed his own team members from contact with the client.

Ken is similarly ill at ease in forging broader relationships with his own coworkers and managers. He doesn't see the need to include them in what he terms "his business." Agency workers often have trouble feeling that they are in the loop when they talk to Ken. When the ad agency's top officials want insights from their two managers on whether any surprises await them on contract renewal, Yuji can confidently run through a summary of the vibes he's getting from his social conversations, while Ken has little to offer except that he believes the customer is pleased with his work. Ken doesn't understand the importance of getting his colleagues' involvement and cooperation.

What the stars we studied grasp early on in their brainpowered careers is that high-quality technical work often is not enough on its own to ensure superior productivity. Workplace etiquette, both internal and external, is the lubrication that allows good work to make its way through the system.

Managing Conflict

There is no organization I know of that can produce high-quality work from a diverse group of brainpowered people without some conflict. How individuals manage that conflict as it relates to their role in the workplace is a key indicator of superior productivity.

A lot of average performers get it wrong. They assume their coworkers reach star status by not giving an inch in a conflict situation, that true stars mark their territory and fight to the death to keep it.

Reality is not nearly so macho. In our observations, the stars consider conflict resolution much more productive than duking it out in a public fight. Indeed, in an era of cut-to-the-bone staffing, a protracted internal conflict can deflect scarce resources and freeze productivity, leaving the winner a pyrrhic victory with a department or even a company in ruins.

Alfred Sloan was the legendary General Motors CEO who developed the first multiple product line for cars. It was an innovation that won great competitive advantage over the one-car-one-color production system at the Ford Motor Company.

Sloan succeeded in the more complicated assembly line and other innovations because he knew the automobile manufacturing business inside and out, but he also knew how to manage conflict. He demonstrated this skill in dealing with his star inventor and engineer, Charles Kettering. Sloan believed that continuing to develop cars with the conventional water-cooled engine was essential for selling cars to a mass market. Kettering was opposed to the idea and argued for the development of an air-cooled engine. When GM management scrapped Kettering's project, he threatened to quit if it was not reinstated. Sloan could not afford to lose Kettering's innovative ideas, his engineering skills, or his abilities as a motivator of the other engineers who looked to him for leadership.

So instead of forcing Kettering's hand in a showdown of wills, Sloan offered a compromise: Kettering could head a new division that would design, produce, and market a new car. If Kettering wanted to use his air-cooled engine in the new car, he could. Meanwhile, the other GM divisions would produce cars with water-cooled engines for the mass market. When Kettering realized the technical difficulties of making an entire car built around his engine, he abandoned the idea. Instead, he came to see the virtues of the conventional, water-cooled engine for himself. He then directed his energies into the company's mainstream products. By concentrating on the conflict-management side of organizational savvy, Sloan averted a potential disaster for GM's engineering department.

Compare Sloan's skills with those of Dick Lord and Martin Sorrell. Lord founded the advertising agency bearing his name, Lord Geller; Sorrell is CEO of WPP Group, which took over the J. Walter Thompson agency in a hostile battle. It happened that Thompson owned Lord Geller but had let it run as a very profitable autonomous unit for fourteen years. Then, as Lord recounts, "One day a perfect stranger walks in and says in effect, 'Hi, I own you.' I felt like an indentured servant. Nobody owns me."

Lord is a creative ad legend, counting the Little Tramp ads for IBM PCs among his firm's achievements; Sorrell is a custom-tailored financial executive, educated at Harvard. They could have been a perfect team; instead they became bitter adversaries. Lord didn't comprehend the realities of hardball business; Sorrell didn't pay attention to the human needs of brainpowered workers.

After a series of meetings on how to work together, the antagonism and mutual distrust only grew. Sorrell failed to address a set of five issues important to the Lord Geller partners. These ranged from the right to operate Lord Geller autonomously to employment contracts. To get Sorrell's attention, the partners decided to withhold the detailed financial reports that WPP required twice a week.

Within eight months, Lord and five other partners had quit to form a new firm. Within days, fifty Lord Geller employees had defected to the new firm. In the ensuing six months, Lord Geller's billings dropped 80 percent, from $166 million to $35 million, as clients defected to other agencies or to the new upstart firm.

To save his investment from becoming an empty shell, Sorrell filed suit and won an injunction prohibiting additional Lord Geller clients or employees from joining the new firm, although they could leave to work with other agencies.

After a protracted legal battle, both sides lost—Sorrell's Lord Geller Agency lost all its major accounts and was folded into another small Sorrell-owned agency; Dick Lord's new agency and its major financial backer, the ad giant Young and Rubicam, paid WPP $7 million. The conflict cost both sides dearly—all because they let their egos and financial agendas get in the way.

As much as stars may be adept at resolving conflicts when they occur, the best among those we studied had a talent for troubleshooting—creating an environment of conflict prevention.

Let's return to Claire, the engineer who wrote software code, in the perspective chapter, Chapter 7, who was able to visualize where potential conflicts might arise in the course of getting her work through the system. One area that seemed a likely trouble spot was the design-review session, where coworkers would have the opportunity to examine her work under a microscope and pick it apart.

Instead of sitting on the sidelines biting her nails and waiting for the inevitable conflicts, Claire decided to be proactive and try to smooth the path long before her work was due to travel on it. She summoned up her courage, promised to keep an open mind, and went to her toughest potential critics to get their opinions of her work. If she agreed with an assessment, there was time to make changes. If she did not agree, there was an opportunity to explain why and to leave the impression that she valued them enough to approach them ahead of time.

While perhaps not eliminating all potential for conflict at her design-review session, Claire succeeded in preventing the most damaging hot spots. And what conflict did emerge was cooled considerably because of her proactive work.

In addition to conflict prevention, star performers have also learned the value of what one of my former teachers, famous University of Texas professor Francis Fuller, called "disagreeing agreeably." Recall when Aiden, the engineer who became a customer service representative, helped negotiate the peace on the crisis team assigned to fix failing hospital machines. He resisted taking sides in the dispute and acted as a mediator to coax understanding from each side on the other's legitimate grievances. He then supported a compromise plan by offering the organizational rationale that would ensure its acceptance by top management.

CREATING A NICHE

Star producers who bring strong interpersonal skills to the workplace—who forge good relationships with coworkers, managers, and clients—almost always display another important aspect of organizational savvy: They create a niche that distinguishes them from the rest of the pack and market that niche successfully within the organization.

The fortunate stars are those who can find their niche—an area of expertise that interests them and one that also adds value to the organization.

In the pack of gung-ho engineers and their managers working for Bell Labs, Janet Nordin was able to stake out a niche that gave her a unique identity, one well beyond her designation as Lab Director No. 5555.

Nordin had added an MBA to her engineering expertise and had become the person who could balance and blend the technical side and the business side. But over a period of years, she also found another niche, one that she is considerably more passionate about and one that paid surprising dividends in research direction.

Nordin developed a reputation as a futurist in her organization, one of the few people who could be counted on to be projecting years ahead in terms of what the public would demand, what should be produced, and what employees needed to be productive. She was well known for off-the-beaten-path creative thinking, for being well read in areas far removed from the rigid engineering world—New Age physics and psychology among them.

But she turned her reputation into a niche of expertise by pushing ideas that were ahead of the existing technology or managerial approaches, exploring the unconventional to come up with creative solutions to problems.

In brainpowered work, many average performing workers eventually find an expertise niche that adds value to the organization. But where they fail to reach star status is in connecting themselves to that expertise in the rest of the workplace. Stars take advantage of the dozens of daily opportunities to publicize their niche area, not in an egotistical way but adhering to the thought: This is the best possible way for me to make a significant contribution to this organization.

Elena, the star performer from the initiative chapter, Chapter 4, who worked for the advanced-materials ceramics company, tutored herself to expert status on European market quality standards. She then trained others in her company so that they would be able to bid for European customers. Now Europe is the company's largest market.

As she was developing her expertise, she didn't go around bragging about it. Instead, she advertised in more subtle ways. First, she held a brown-bag lunch for her colleagues to inform them of what she had learned at a professional conference. When she became more adept, she offered detailed tutorials.

Meanwhile, she sat down with her boss to explain the benefits to the company of getting behind the special standards. Elena also quietly lobbied upper management by sending them relevant articles and short memos showing the sales-and-profit potential. She also sought her boss's blessing before she contacted top executives. So while advertising her expertise, she was tying it to the company's critical path and paying attention to organizational protocol.

Other stars advertise in different ways. Some write articles in relevant publications and then forward reprints to appropriate colleagues. Or they might give a talk to a professional conference or at a local university, and then allow it to be cited in the intracompany newspaper. If possible, they might arrange to be interviewed for the in-house publication or submit an article for it.

In the process of publicly tying themselves to an area of expertise, star performers also respect the niche-area boundaries of colleagues. They affirm their territory by consulting with them on projects and assignments where areas tend to overlap.

Katy, our star attorney who used her network (see Chapter 5) to establish herself as an expert on copyright law and the Internet, realizes the importance of respecting boundaries.

Katy sets up lunch meetings with several partners in the firm who have established niches that might overlap into her area and seeks their advice in setting up her area. Not only does she get the benefit of their experience, she also reassures them that she will not be poaching on their territory. When a legal problem arises involving an important client—such as the time a national newspaper sued for material printed on its on-line web page—Katy recognizes her own niche in the case but also is aware of others' niches. Before beginning any work, she informs the other niche holders, including the firm's expert in First Amendment law.

The advance notice is more than just a courtesy. It represents public acknowledgment that Katy is respecting niche boundaries. Later, when she consults with these colleagues, she vests them in the case and decreases chances of conflict or resentment.

DEVELOPING CREDIBILITY

So you've succeeded in creating a niche for yourself in a brainpowered work area that adds value to the organization. You've convinced others in the workplace that you deserve to rule this area of expertise. Then you've gone on to pass the tests in relationship building and respecting the niche areas of others.

So now you can collect your decoder ring and learn the secret handshake of the organizational savvy stars—right? Well, not quite.

The stars we studied had a critically important finishing trait that cemented the others into a smooth, solid base. They developed an organizational reputation for integrity and credibility.

While some operators are able to gain a reputation for a schmoozy version of organizational savvy, their success is often short-lived. Their rapid rise through the ranks is often confounding to coworkers who make credibility judgments earlier and more accurately than most managers. But just as often, these "incredible" stars prove to have no staying power. They flame out in a crisis; their lack of substance and character is found out and they are removed from the heavens. Usually, the process is carefully choreographed to deflect embarrassment on managers who fell for a worker who had superior organizational savvy skills but no credibility. Occasionally, the fall can be as spectacular as the rise.

Michael Ovitz, the former Hollywood superagent and cofounder of the dominant Creative Artists Agency, was routinely described as "the most powerful man in Hollywood." Known as shrewd and tough, he represented Hollywood's top talent—Robert Redford, Steven Spielberg, Martin Scorsese, and Dustin Hoffman were among his clients—but he also carved out a new role brokering the sale and acquisition of entire studios, such as Sony's purchase of Columbia Pictures.

When Ovitz took the number-two job at Disney to work with his pal Michael Eisner, many observers saw it as a natural extension of his visionary leadership. But what they and Ovitz himself didn't comprehend is that no one can flout the rules of organizational savvy. When you enter a new organization, even if you were a star in your previous one, you must prove yourself all over again—even Michael Ovitz.

Although viewed as the ultimate Hollywood insider, Ovitz was an outsider to Disney and its culture. Neal Gabler, a biographer of Walt Disney, summed it up: "He apparently assumed that the techniques he had used as an agent and a mediator could simply be redeployed in the corporate setting, that the entertainment business was still a people business where swagger and sass were more important than politesse and where a dream was worth more than a thousand MBAs. He was wrong. Hollywood is not exactly Wall Street, but the mergers have understandably brought a more . . . corporate style. There are more toes to step on, more variables to weigh, more limitations to operate within."

Despite these differences, according to Disney executives, "Ovitz came in like, 'I know everything.' " His big spending (he had six secretaries, while Eisner only had two) and heavy-handed approach (his clumsy wooing of NBC executive Jamie Tarses to Disney-owned ABC with full media coverage) didn't sit well at buttoned-down Disney. According to former CFO Stephen Bollenbach, "Michael Ovitz didn't understand the duties of an executive at a public company and he didn't want to learn."

At a top company like Disney, you find strong operating executives who both know and defend their turf zealously. If an outsider tries to move in without acknowledging their power, they will effectively lock out the usurper. It reached the point, according to one executive, that at top management meetings, "He was like the crazy uncle at a family reunion, and nobody ever talks to him." Within a year, Ovitz and Disney parted company, with Disney giving Ovitz a severance package worth an estimated $70 million.

So what do star producers and their star-wanna-be coworkers agree are the key elements of credibility in organizational savvy?

The most credible players, it turns out, are seldom caught unprepared. They do their homework, just as so many of the stars we profiled in the initiative chapter, Chapter 4, did thorough research before making a formal proposal.

Credibility stars also follow the initiative process by working to develop a reputation for doing work that adds value to the organization. They follow the perspective process by developing a track record for keeping an open mind on aspects of their work and seeking the opinions of others. They follow good self-management practice when they develop a reputation for dependability. The credibility stars are those whom managers can count on to deliver a piece of work of superior quality in timely fashion once they've been convinced of the worthiness of the effort. Coworkers attach the credibility label to those who accurately judge their ability to commit to a project or task. If they do commit, the stars become full partners in the effort, owning their share of the work and the responsibility for failures along the way. If they can't commit, the stars deliver that answer quickly and suggest others who can deliver.

Credibility comes from the same stew of basic work skill behaviors that create organizational savvy. The credibility trait can be traced to that pot with all those strong, productivity-rich skills from previous chapters blended together and given a long simmering— sometimes years of actual work experience with your colleagues. The skills of initiative taking, perspective, self-management, and all the others transformed into a distinct dish: organizational savvy with a rich base of credibility.

12

SHOW-AND-TELL
Persuading the Right Audience
with the Right Message

During a series of productivity presentations I gave to Bellcore, formerly the research-and-development company for the seven regional Bell operating companies, a top manager told me about a brilliant software design engineer named Luis who had achieved one of the highest IQ and Graduate Record Exam (GRE) scores ever obtained by a Bellcore employee. He was known for an ingenious ability to develop efficient and accurate computer programs that turned pipe dreams like VoiceMail and caller ID into huge money-makers for the regional phone companies.

Luis also had an instinctual grasp of the star-producer work skills laid out in this book. Coworkers regularly sought him out for advice. Managers, amazed at his skill and high productivity, fought with one another for his services.

Given all that attention, Luis should have been the most confident worker in the room at large software-design meetings. Instead, he was giving the potted plants tough competition in fading into the background. Luis was terrified of giving stand-up presentations to a group.

He was convinced he was a flop in the critical area of communicating his ideas to a wider audience—showing his work to others and telling them about it. And according to his coworkers' reviews, his low opinions were self-fulfilling.

While staff and management always prefaced their negative reviews with a refrain on his technical talent, the underlying message was the same: Their talented colleague *was* a communications disaster. His presentations at meetings were disorganized and boring. Once, an entire row in the audience had nodded off. Managers noted that in one-on-one or small team meetings, he had no problem. But once the meeting scaled up past four or five people to any considerable size, their genius software designer could not be counted on to persuade others on his approaches.

"It's really a shame," said the manager. "This guy has a technical ability that others can only dream about, but he can't communicate it to others." In large interteam meetings, lesser-quality ideas would carry the day because Luis couldn't articulate his viewpoint persuasively. More than once after these meetings, Luis privately developed the software he couldn't persuade the group to adopt. Invariably, his designs were more elegant and effective. By that time, however, the other team members had invested too much time in the previously selected design to turn back.

Although Luis's lack of show-and-tell ability hadn't hurt his personal technical productivity, it did threaten to limit his effectiveness within the larger organization, especially with managers outside his department. His poor performance on show-and-tell compromised his opportunities to become a major player who could represent high-visibility projects or influence the company's direction.

While show-and-tell is ranked at the outer edge of our star producer model as a finishing skill, this brainpowered workplace example makes clear its critical role in establishing a star performer reputation in the larger workplace. As our research uncovered time and again in the course of developing a work skills model, technical ability alone does not determine your productivity. Mastering the show-and-tell skill allows you to convince an audience to trust your expertise and your message—whether to sell your initiatives, to explain your perspective, or to accept your leadership.

Yet no amount of skill in written and oral communications can make up for your lack of basic ability in the other work skills or in the proficiency required in your job. It is the icing on the cake of star productivity. Although it doesn't make or break your productivity on a local level, it does determine your effectiveness at the higher corporate level. It solidifies your star producer reputation, enabling you to gain greater influence or get promoted into management.

SHOW-AND-TELL: THE MECHANICS OF PERSUASION

There is no getting around it. The brainpowered economy of the 1990s is a tough place for professionals who have trouble presenting their ideas to groups, especially in personal presentations. For most brainpowered workers, we're not talking about big productions, like Bill Gates or Billy Graham addressing thousands in cavernous convention halls with all the benefits of modern multimedia tools and computer-generated special effects. Nor is it mastering cocktail party chitchat or dinner party joke telling. Instead, show-and-tell refers to small end-of-the-hall conference room presentations to groups ranging from five to twenty, with an occasional auditorium presentation thrown in. The audience is either coworkers, upper-level managers, or customers. The content is usually technical and product-related. As in small-l leadership from Chapter 9, most brainpowered workers do small show-and-tell, rising to the platform only when their particular technical expertise is needed.

But even in big show-and-tell, like the splashy corporate affairs, take away all the technological wizardry—the "surround sound" speaker systems, the multicolored, graphics-stuffed handouts, the glitzy video production—and what remains is one person's ability to take information, select key points, and organize them so that they can be shared with others.

In the realm of the star producer, though, the process is more sophisticated. From our research, we observed a fine tuning of show-and-tell—from mere transmittal of information points to message sculpting. The stars we observed had mastered the ability to deliver a message to a targeted audience, to persuade listeners to accept the message, and to be proactive in deflecting criticism.

Where average performers fail most often is in making the leap from basic-level dispensing of information to higher-level influencing through the message. Their style and framework of delivery does not change from audience to audience, even though the makeup of these groups can be very different.

A labor-relations manager for a Fortune 500 corporation was given the task of reducing health care costs in a new contract to be negotiated with the company's unions. The plan he developed had to be acceptable to both the top officers of the company and the unions.

His successful approach was to fashion the same information in dramatically different ways. He presented the plan to a small group of lower-ranking union officials in bite-sized chunks over a week of meetings on their home turf. He provided them with clear, easy-to-read handouts that could be duplicated and handed out to rank-and-file members with reasonable expectations of being understood. The high point of the presentation was the message that the union's agreement to switch over to a managed-care program would be offset by the company's promise to turn the cost savings into a fund that would modernize outdated plants, making them competitive and reducing chances of closings and job losses.

His earlier presentation to the company's CEO and top vice presidents contained the same basic information but was packaged much differently. The time window for his presentation was much smaller than that allowed by the unions. The bulk of his message was delivered in a no-nonsense, well-documented, and detailed report with a persuasive section on recommendations for acceptance. He was able to reinforce his basic message in person in a one-hour meeting on the company plane with the CEO and the company president. His position was that if management demanded changes in health care benefits without any creative incentives, the unions would balk and make negotiating a new contract nearly impossible. The company was just coming into a period of impressive growth, and stockholders wouldn't take kindly to a protracted strike.

While there was internal criticism of his plan from both camps, the star labor negotiator had laid his groundwork well, visiting the company's business unit presidents individually and making personal pitches for their approval, organizing a teleconference with national union officials and local leaders from each plant. In the end, both the company and the rank and file approved the health care benefits proposal with only minor changes.

Of the many star show-and-tell lessons from this example the most important is the one that determines the difference between show-and-tell stars and average presenters: **Know your audience and shape your message to it.**

In many cases, understanding the audience framework can bring huge benefits, in terms of moving an audience not just to accept your point of view but to take concrete action as a result of it. In addition, those who are adept at this skill get noticed more quickly—their star performer status is publicly affirmed.

And there are scores of examples where the opposite holds true, where misjudging the nature of an audience can lead to spectacular show-and-tell failures.

Take note of the unfortunate prop choice of a rising young star in Rupert Murdoch's Fox Television camp, Stephen Chao, a thirty-ish brainpowered executive who had risen meteorically to become station president and head of the news division. In a daylong seminar for TV industry executives at Snowmass, Colorado, on the issue of a government-imposed ratings system for programs, Chao's presentation began with what he thought would be a real rib-tickler for the audience—a male stripper who ended up gyrating at the podium wearing only a ponytail. If Chao had carefully reviewed who was going to be in the audience, he might have opted for a tamer opener. Sitting in on the session was Lynn Cheney, the Republican head of the National Endowment for the Humanities, and her husband, Defense Secretary Dick Cheney, along with a coterie of think-tank conservatives.

Not only was the presentation coldly received, but within an hour after the event, Murdoch had called Chao in person to fire him.

Contrast Chao's fatal lack of knowledge about his audience with that of Colin Powell, who as head of the Joint Chiefs of Staff during the Persian Gulf War, deftly handled classified briefings to members of Congress and the president on the plan to remove Iraq's armed forces from Kuwait, and also managed to satisfy members of a hungry press corps in news conferences.

The public briefings contained little in the way of hard news, but they were chock-full of TV-friendly charts and other graphics.

There was nothing in Powell's job description that required he be adept at sound bites and imagery in responding to reporters' questions, but over the course of his career, Powell had taken the time to learn the techniques that would help him influence this peculiar and potentially deadly audience—the press corps.

Asked about his strategy for winning the war (as if he were a pro football coach nabbed for an interview just before the coin toss), Powell responded, "It's really very, very simple. First, we're going to cut [the Iraqi Army in and near Kuwait] it off, and then we're going to kill it." He had pegged his audience perfectly. Pens were flying across notepads and TV cameras zoomed in for close-ups. It turned out to be one of the most frequently shown clips in TV news coverage of the war, and it had a second life accompanying news stories when Powell was deliberating whether to run for president.

In many cases, star performers we studied made the effort to contact audience members ahead of time to get a sense of what their expectations were in attending a presentation. While it would have been odd and inappropriate for Powell to approach reporters about their needs ahead of his press conference, he had a department full of experienced news media advisers in daily contact with reporters. He also drew on his own personal contacts with reporters to fashion a press conference that delivered the message he wanted to get out and still satisfy reporters' expectations of getting new information on war strategy.

Show-and-Tell Tips: Delivering a Message That Sticks

The second most common mistake made by average show-and-tellers is that they become obsessed with organizing the material. The presentation is built around the delivery needs of the speaker instead of the information needs of the audience.

Most brainpowered workers have had the unfortunate college rite-of-passage experience of a boring professor teaching an introductory course who begins at the beginning, works toward the middle, and finishes at the end. The chronological approach is convenient for the purpose of dispensing information; the professor delivers his lectures from prepared notes that have all the flavor of a calculus textbook. Students are left wondering why they bother to meet in a classroom for such recitations when a textbook has the same format.

You may remember successfully memorizing the material from a course like this, even managing to spit back correct answers on examinations. But two years later, you remember very little of the material. Worse yet, you have no feel for the subject. The chronological approach and the droning delivery have killed the incorporation process of learning. Passion for the subject has not been transferred from teacher to student.

In the brainpowered workplace, star performers use show-and-tell skills to ensure that there is no corruption of the learning process, no misreading of the audience's information needs.

The stars we studied saw themselves as telling a story, not transmitting facts. A good story engages the listener with something worth listening to: an intriguing plot, a human drama with twists and turns, fascinating characters, tension and conflict that get resolved, humor, and crisp visual images that capture the imagination. They tended to stay away from a chronological approach, because it is almost always boring and it delays the recognition of the relevance of the material—the payoff for an audience's devotion of time and energy to the presentation.

Josiah is one of the world's premiere grass seed researchers, with several grass seed patents to his name. Most of us only think about grass when it is time to plant, weed, or cut it. For Josiah, it has been his life's work—more than twenty years at a state-of-the-art research farm in Oregon's lush Willamette Valley. Most of us would have to be paid to listen to someone lecture on grass-breeding techniques, but when Josiah holds court on the subject, it becomes Standing Room Only.

The reason is that he talks about the sex lives of grass and compares them to those of humans. He talks about the emotional state of various strains: their temerity, their fickleness, how the timing has to be right, how once they say "no," they mean "no" and no amount of coaxing will change their minds.

In the midst of this "seedy" domestic scene steps our hapless researcher Josiah trying to do his experiments. He recounts setting his alarm clock for 2:00 A.M.—their prime mating time—to brush the male and female plants against each other, only to find later that they have rejected his sex therapy and failed to reproduce.

After weeks of this and with mounting sleep deprivation, Josiah pulls them out by their roots and delivers a firm lecture. Within a few days, they are cooperating. Only later did he realize his mistake and, in retrospect, his foolishness—that he had jumped the gun on his experimental procedure a month ahead of the grass's botanical schedule. He had been trying in vain during a time when they could have sex and not worry about producing offspring.

Josiah grabs his audiences and bonds with them by using such self-deprecating humor. They are captivated by the vividly drawn human personalities of the various grass strains. They also learn about what they previously thought of as one of the world's most boring topics: grass breeding.

Josiah and other brainpowered stars have answered the question that should be asked before every presentation: "What is the most creative way (within the confines of the law) to lock in the audience I want to reach?"

The imaginative process kicks in—but always carefully measured for suitability with the audience.

Meara, a twenty-eight-year-old, designs software for the transmission of images—X rays, EKG readings, and live closed-circuit TV shots—over phone lines to and from hospital emergency operating rooms. She began a presentation of her team's latest software design with a short video clip of a car slamming on screeching brakes, the whine of the ambulance siren, a small child being rushed into the emergency room, and a doctor flicking on her company's equipment saying they had only minutes to save a young life.

"Our work can make the difference in saving this child's or *your* child's life," Meara told her audience. "Throughout our project, we played this video clip to remind ourselves of the importance of giving it the best we could. Now let me share it with you."

Meara then compared the effectiveness of her software to previous versions by using an electronic timeline accompanied by the thump of a heartbeat as heard in emergency rooms. First she ran the old software. As the audience waited for the images to come up on the screen, the timeline reached its end, the heart stopped beating, and the emergency room alarms went off. With the new software, the images arrived faster and beat the timeline.

Meara then explained to the audience the ups and downs of the project as they tried different solutions to shaving time off the process—what worked, what didn't, and why. She wove technical points into the human drama of health professionals working to save people's lives.

The lesson from stars like Josiah and Meara is to make your message relevant and interesting to your audience. When I was an undergraduate in college, my friends and I groaned about having to take a required philosophy course. But the professor understood that we couldn't identify with the ancient Greek philosophers. So in the first class she played snippets of the rock music that most of us were listening to at the time. She then asked us to comment on the lyrics. What was the music saying to us? What values did it advocate? Could the message provide any guidance for our chaotic world? Then she segued from the lyrics to different philosophers whose ideas were reflected in our music, showing the timelessness of their ideas.

Notice that both Meara and my philosophy professor used props to help get the audience's attention. As in a stage play, props can help your story. But they should never overshadow you or your message.

A common mistake of average show-and-tell performers is to let the props or fancy technology take center stage. I often must remind my students at Carnegie Mellon to think twice about using laptop computer projectors during their presentations. First, the technology requires that they dim the lights—a naptime invitation for the audience. Second, unless you are an expert in the equipment, the technology often does not work the way it is supposed to, marring the impact of your presentation. So the presenters have to take time away from their message to troubleshoot the technology glitches. Once lost, an audience's attention is difficult to recover.

The same attention-getting techniques apply to written materials circulated in the brainpowered workplace and beyond. Writers must have the same focus on audience type, the same proactive stance in targeting a specific group to ensure the message gets through.

Richard, an attorney in a large law firm, wanted to file a pro bono class-action suit against a large regional bank over its practice of blackballing several primarily African-American communities from its home mortgages—a practice known as redlining. He was asked to prepare a proposal for the consideration of the firm's top partners.

Richard, whose father had been a federal judge who protected hard-won civil rights legislation, was excited about the case but realized the firm had a small budget for pro bono work and that he was competing against other projects.

In order to win over his audience, Richard had to understand who its members were—highly specialized and successful attorneys who lived and socialized in communities far removed from those at issue in the redlining case.

So Richard began his memo with short profiles of residents in the affected communities who had attempted to get mortgages and were turned down—the young man on one street who had worked his way through the local community college and landed a job as a food service manager at the area's largest university; the older woman who had raised eight children with her steelworker husband until his death in a car accident and who wanted to use part of his insurance settlement to buy the home they had rented.

Five of these powerful stories were illustrated with color portraits of the people involved. A packet to each partner also contained a video that offered a tour through the neighborhoods of modest, wood-framed homes with flower-filled front yards overlaid with excerpts of interviews from residents who had been turned down for mortgages by the banks.

Richard knew that in order to win over the audience of decision makers to his project, he had to make them care about the people involved, to give them assurance the firm would be righting a terrible wrong. Of course, he also had to be on track with the legal footing for the case—the technical aspects of mounting a redlining challenge. But without the sense of concern instilled in his audience, the more technical information wouldn't have an anchor and the partners would be prone to float toward another, less complicated project.

MAKING SHOW-AND-TELL WORK FOR YOU

Show-and-tell is part of your brainpowered job. It doesn't mean that you have to become a stand-up comedian or a raconteur, however. Instead, you need to develop the specific communication skills outlined in this chapter:

- know your audience
- craft your message to that audience
- make your message relevant and interesting to the audience
- if possible, put it in human terms, not purely technical ones
- use props to enhance your story, not to steal the show

"But," you might ask, "what if I'm really no good at show-and-tell? Like Luis, the technical star at Bellcore who was a communications disaster, is there any hope? Should I take time away from my value-added technical work to learn how to do slick presentations?"

Once again, show-and-tell has to be done. But how it gets done is often up to you. Some people like being center-stage and do a good job of it. Others don't. There are a few stars who do not see it as a very good use of their time, even though they are good at it and know that it must be done.

During our research, we discovered that star performers who didn't value show-and-tell often teamed up with a buddy who would take over that part of the job—an office mate, a fellow team member, or the direct supervisor. Rather than shore up this deficit through personal mastery, they compensated by turning it over to someone who had a talent for the work.

These buddies often did it to ensure the stars' good ideas were adopted rather than losing out to inferior ones because of the stars' inability to persuade large groups. Or the star helped them so much in their technical work that they were glad to return the favor through this division of labor. When buddies stepped in for the star, they always let the audience know that they were representing the stars' ideas. The synergy of these two-person teams often yielded greater productivity for both members.

After talking to Luis and his manager, I suggested the buddy system as an interim measure until Luis decided whether he wanted to develop his own show-and-tell expertise. He has never done another presentation, but his technical influence has grown steadily to where he now leads major R&D efforts.

13

BECOME A STAR PERFORMER
Making the Program Work for You

If you have learned only one thing from this book, it should be this: Star producers aren't rare and exotic life forms, even though so much of American business culture perpetuates that myth. While some top managers and coworkers in your organization want to believe that stars are born and not made, you now know otherwise.

You're poised to become one of your organization's most valued assets as it makes its mark in the global economy. Superior productivity is your ticket to more fulfilling work, an enhanced reputation among colleagues, greater rewards and job options, and the best protection you can have from the downsizing ax. You will do justice to your job, but you will also have a life.

At the same time, your organization desperately needs employees motivated to be superproductive workers—employees like you. Only through the one-to-ten or one-to-twenty productivity boost—your work output equal to the output of ten average workers—can a company hope to outpace its competitors. Boosting worker productivity, not booting workers out on the street, is the key to an organization's long-term financial health.

The preceding nine chapters provide you with the basic tools you need to become a star performer. As our research at Bell Labs demonstrated, being supersmart or supersuave doesn't guarantee high productivity. Average workers retool themselves into stars by employing the everyday work strategies of the star performers.

Just as you can improve your tennis or golf game by doing what the stars do, so can you improve your work productivity—with one big exception. There is no one way to achieve it, nor should you become someone's clone. Instead you must filter what the stars do through your own personality and work style to develop what works for you.

While doing so, keep in mind the following:

REACH FOR THE STARS WITH BOTH FEET ON THE GROUND

When we asked people in our follow-up focus groups what essential advice we should pass on to people before they begin to improve their productivity, the advice centered on having realistic expectations. The first is that star performance isn't a cure-all for a miserable work situation. Through no fault of their own, even star performers occasionally end up in the wrong job, get the wrong boss for them, or are in the wrong company. This makes for a difficult situation, because even though you are producing at a high level, your work goes unrecognized or unrewarded. In the worst case, obstacles are put in your way, making high productivity almost unsustainable.

In these unfortunate cases, star performers recognize three separate courses of action that put to the test everything that you have learned in this book. You can try to change jobs or bosses within the company until you find a better fit. Or you can attempt to change your boss's mind or to change the dysfunctional organizational culture for the better. Or you can cut your losses and go to work for a different company that better recognizes your mastery of productivity skills.

Although I know star performers who have succeeded in each option, their overall advice is that finding a different job or boss within the company or moving to a new company is usually the more prudent way to go. Unless you have a lot personally invested in staying put, the time and energy investment required to change your boss's mind or your company's culture may not be worth it.

The important lesson is not to stay in a bad situation where your star cannot shine. Even if you can blame your lower productivity on others, your reputation suffers more in the long run—something that you can ill afford.

Star Productivity Requires Work

Fortunately, many of us work in good jobs with decent, well-meaning bosses, and in companies that value the best we can give. In these situations, the second important piece of advice is that the star-performer program described in this book is no magic pill. Even the most well-developed productivity-improvement program can't turn every average performer into a star. There are differences among brainpowered workers, just as there are differences among athletes who share the same training regimen. People not only learn differently, they have different motivational levels to change their work strategies to become star performers.

Figuring out how to propel your productivity from average to star performance requires much thought, much analysis, and all the faltering and stumbling that comes with practice. To double your productivity, you need to make the ideas in this book your own. The more you use them, the more "naturally like you" they will become, helping you to "work smart" rather than just work longer and harder.

Keep in mind, though, that the increased productivity "bang" doesn't come all at once; it grows over time. Participants in our productivity-improvement programs report that the benefits accumulate, much like a snowball growing as it rolls down a hill. As you incorporate the star work strategies into your everyday work routine, bits and pieces of new skills accumulate. The more you roll, the more you pick up. As you put all of them together over time, your productivity will grow exponentially.

Most people begin to see incremental benefits of 10 percent immediately. Significant productivity changes take about six months, however, because it takes that long to make the star model part of your daily routine. By the end of the first year, you should have internalized the model to such an extent that you move into a highly advanced level of productivity.

Several years' worth of evaluations from participants who reach that level in our productivity improvement program show that the personal payoff is well worth all those hours of self-training.

The Nine Individual Work Strategies in the Star Performer Model Are Closely Interrelated

Each chapter highlighted one star performer work strategy, but none of them exists independent of the others. The model functions like a spiderweb—when you use one work strategy, you often must use the others.

For example, initiative requires that you have good enough perspective to know which initiatives are worth taking. How is the initiative that you are considering tied to the critical path and the bottom line? How will it affect your customers, your company, and your competitors? Have you gotten input or feedback from others' perspective to improve your idea? What is the probability of payoff to you or the organization?

A good initiative also requires good self-management. You must judge whether you can realistically take on anything else or whether this initiative will interfere with you completing your core assigned duties. You also need to manage the risk of the initiative and the possible negative effects on your career.

Finally, initiative often involves organizational savvy and show-and-tell. To get them to buy in, you must persuade others that your initiative is worthwhile. Or if you bootlegged the initiative on your own time, scrounging up your own resources, you will still need to convince others of its value before it can be widely implemented. You must maneuver around potential organizational land mines, while touching base with key players who can bolster your case.

What's true for initiative is true for the other eight star work strategies. For instance, to become a great networker, you must take the initiative to figure out who you need in your network and then get off your duff to make contact with them. You must orchestrate the entire model for it to yield its most powerful synergy. This will come with practice.

Keep in mind, however, that different professions or companies may rank these nine work strategies differently. A newspaper journalist whose investigative stories depended on cultivating sources of information, for instance, may find networking a work stratagem for critical star performance that belongs in the core with initiative. Although we have increasing data that the star performer model works across different jobs and industries, you may need to discover which strategies are at the core for your situation

Whenever You Change Jobs, Departments, or Companies, You Must Start All Over Again

Over the years, I've noticed two common mistakes made by star performers when they enter a new work environment. The first is believing that their star status travels with them. The second is trying to short-circuit the star performer model by inverting it the same way average performers do—that is, starting with show-and-tell rather than at the core. Consequently, they leave an early impression that they are more interested in style than substance, glitz over adding value.

Star performer status is neither a sinecure nor a career-length guarantee. Although as a top executive told us during our research, "Once star status is attained, it takes a long time to fall from grace," you must still work at it. Should you move to a part of the company that has had little direct experience with you, however, or if you move to a new company altogether, your star status has little carry-over to the new environment. To avoid the fate of Michael Ovitz at Disney, you must demonstrate your mastery of the star performer model all over again.

Upon arriving at your new position, your colleagues and manager, much like sports fans judging a recently signed free agent, expect you to prove your productivity worth. As with any new hire, they will want to see evidence of the core work strategies in the model: that you have the requisite cognitive abilities and technical mastery and that you take initiative. Do you catch on quickly, can you do a bang-up job, and do you go above and beyond your job, pitching in to fill in any cracks? In other words, are you going to be an asset to or a drag on the work group?

After proving yourself in the core, you will need to work your way through the other layers of the model: create a star network; self-manage your life at work; apply your perspective to the challenges and opportunities facing you; exercise followership, leadership, and teamwork; develop good organizational savvy in your new work environment; and do show-and-tell when necessary.

As a result, your new colleagues will have firsthand knowledge of your value-adding productivity and can reconfer your star status themselves. This rite of passage is important both to them and to you.

The Goal Is Value-Added Productivity

Average performers often get confused between effort and results. They will say that they are working just as hard as the star performers or that they take as many initiatives. They miss the point.

The work strategies in the model represent ten years of research, collecting all the ways that star performers use to achieve their superior productivity. The star performers' goal is not to take initiative for initiative's sake. Instead, they only take initiatives that have a high probability of adding value to the critical path.

This focus on the bottom line is why our evaluations of our productivity-improvement programs (discussed in Appendix I) do not focus primarily on the work strategies. Rather, we focus on those work outcomes that colleagues and bosses use to conclude that someone is productive or not.

The important point is to keep a steady eye on the following to gauge whether you are being productive:

- Do you add value to your colleagues, the critical path that leads to the organization's goals, and the company's bottom line?
- Do you consistently spot issues and problems and make sure that something gets done about them?
- Do you always get work done on time and with high quality?
- Do you consistently delight external and internal customers?
- Do you understand how and why external competitive pressures change everyday work routines and respond positively to the challenge?
- Do you succeed at working across organizational boundaries and building bridges so that all the organization's resources can be applied to customers or problems effectively?

- Do you keep your manager informed about work progress and how it will impact other people/projects?
- Do you not get overly frustrated by politics but strive to understand the rationale behind certain decisions?

To achieve these eight work outcomes requires the underlying star-performer work strategies. For example, to consistently spot problems and make sure that something gets done about them would be impossible if you had not mastered taking initiative. Similarly, networking, organizational savvy, and teamwork are the building blocks necessary to work effectively across organizational boundaries.

Do not lose sight that the goal is higher productivity, however. Most brainpowered jobs do not lend themselves to the quantitative measurement of productivity. For researchers, it might be years before their discoveries make it to the marketplace. How do you measure the productivity of a newspaper editor, a graphic artist in a large aluminum company, or a software developer in a bank, for instance?

In the absence of these quantitative measures, your colleagues will make qualitative judgments about your contributions to decide whether you are average or a star. They will use work-outcome criteria similar to the ones listed above. You need to find out what those criteria are and then use your star performer work strategies to achieve them.

Seek Additional Resources but Be Wary of False Prophets

If you found this book helpful but need additional help in integrating the star performer work strategies into your work routine, you may want to attend one of our productivity-improvement programs, provided by Development Dimensions International (DDI) and listed in Appendix II. The program consists of six half-day sessions spread out over a six-week period. Each session focuses in depth on selected work strategies, using case studies, role plays, and class discussion. The program provides you with much feedback regarding your productivity, as well as a personalized developmental plan.

You should also make full use of star performers inside and outside of your organization. Watch what they do and how they do it.

Work your way into their networks. Talk to as many as you can. Ask them for tips. Try out their ideas to see what works for you.

At the same time, pay little attention to the latest fad of the day. There are many people hawking the equivalent of productivity "snake oil." As we found in our years of research, people have an endless supply of naïve productivity myths that they want to foist on you. Avoid them, if possible, especially if they offer a quick fix. Ask to see their underlying research, any long-term evaluations that support their program, and whether it has been published in a reputable publication. After reviewing all this, then ask yourself whether it makes sense to you.

You Can Be A Star Performer

You have the potential—the fundamental talents—to be a star performer. I have supplied the productivity secrets—the everyday work strategies that star performers use. Now you must turn your dream into a reality. Hundreds before you have done it and given us their candid anonymous evaluation.

It is never too late to improve your productivity. If you have been an average performer for more years than you care to remember, you can still become a star. Dick Hayes, one of the original members of our research team, has done considerable work on what he calls "late bloomers"—those people whose value-added contributions come later in life. He has found strong evidence that star performance is not the exclusive domain of the young. You can make it happen at any time in your career. Dick's only rule is "If you want to be a late bloomer, then you must make sure that you don't die young."

Whether you are just starting out or you are a grizzled veteran, with the requisite core cognitive abilities and technical competence for the job, the only thing standing between you and star performance is your applying what is contained in this book—nothing more, nothing less.

Imagine what your life at work and home would be like if you were a star performer. How would it feel to be highly admired and sought after by your colleagues, other managers in your company, or executive recruiters? Would you like to get your pick of the best projects? How about having more time to devote to the creative parts of your job rather than being dragged down by routine work? Finally, wouldn't you rather spend more time with your family, friends, and projects of purely personal interest? Wouldn't you rather be a star?

You can do it!

THREE

SOME PRODUCTIVE
LAST WORDS

14

A MESSAGE FOR MANAGERS
Productivity in the Brainpowered Economy

No matter how early Erin starts the day, she always ends up rushing out the door for the morning commute to her management job at Hewlett-Packard Corporation.

The routine is always the same—a quick glance in the full-length hallway mirror to adjust the outfit, the *Wall Street Journal* and the *New York Times* plucked off the front porch and stuffed into her briefcase, and the half-walk-half-run to the garage that her teenage son loves to imitate.

As Erin maneuvers her Toyota Land Cruiser into an opening in Silicon Valley's Highway 101 traffic jam, she wonders why the hectic pace of her work life hasn't let up. After ten years rising through the ranks in H-P's product development unit, life has only become more harried and complicated.

Breaking out of the traffic bottleneck, Erin relaxes her grip on the steering wheel. She is a constant complainer about the morning commute, but it is during these daily drives that she comes up with some of her most creative ideas.

On this trip, she is mulling over the elusive definition of productivity at work among her brainpowered staff. If only Erin could find a method of some sort, a field guide to the global workplace that would help people perform faster and smarter in the thousand small ways each day that add up to a huge boost in productivity over the year.

As manager of a hundred-member staff responsible for developing the company's next generation of printers, Erin is directing research teams critical to the company's success. She is a gifted manager with a rare ability to inspire confidence at both ends of the spectrum—from senior vice presidents down the line to the special kind of worker she supervises, the technical professional whose brainpower determines the company's fortunes.

In her office, she flips on her computer and dumps the newspapers on her desk, even though it is likely they will be back in her briefcase unread at day's end.

Erin is about to push the papers aside in favor of the stacked up e-mail messages blinking on her computer screen but a front-page headline catches her eye: ONCE HIGH-TECH TRAILBLAZER, APPLE COMPUTER LOSES ITS WAY; FIRST QUARTER LOSS STUNS INDUSTRY; 1,800 JOBS SLASHED.

She is shocked—not by the downsizing but by the flameout of this quirky, pioneering leader of the pack. The connections between Apple's personal computers and H-P's office printers are more than just plugs and ports. They are both hip-deep in the brainpowered worker business—the technical wizardry of their employees is the chief asset. Apple cofounder Steve Wozniak was one of those brainpowered wizards at H-P when he tried to sell the company on his idea of personal computers in every office. The bosses didn't agree, and he reluctantly went off to start his own company.

Erin pushes aside her scheduling book and a folder full of product-improvement reports, then pores over the newspaper stories of Apple's financial woes. She had heard rumblings of cash troubles at the company, but nothing about the possibility of a sale. How could this be? How could a company that spawned the personal computer revolution now be the carrion for Silicon Valley vultures?

Leaning back in her chair and staring up at the ceiling, a ritual that signaled staffers to pull out notebooks and pens at meetings, Erin poses another question that Hewlett-Packard had made famous in its television ads: "What if?" "What if what happened to Apple happened to Hewlett-Packard?"

Erin doesn't know all the future implications but she knows what will not happen on her watch. There will be no slacking off in her unit. Even in a company like H-P, with its long history of a no-layoff policy, the situation could change overnight as it did at IBM, Digital Equipment (now called DEC), and countless other companies. She has to find a way to increase the productivity of her already highly productive staff, because their productivity and innovation is what will make them bulletproof in a shoot-first-ask-questions-later business environment.

Apple's slide was like a bankruptcy estate auction in an upscale, exclusive neighborhood. She knows it can happen to anyone, but the reality of the event was so much at odds with the surroundings—prosperous, cutting-edge, well insulated. Erin takes Apple's stumble as a call to action; she knows her bosses will as well.

She schedules a meeting with three other lab managers, the unit's director, and two senior vice presidents. They all agree that even Hewlett-Packard, stunningly successful in high-tech, computer-related office products, can't afford to stop and catch its breath in an economy capable of beating up a company like Apple.

Even in the afterglow of one of the most profitable quarters in the history of the company, Erin realizes top managers are as uncertain about its future as some of her workers are about the security of their jobs. Apple is only the most dramatic casualty in an unforgiving economy. Others are bound to follow.

" 'What have you done for us lately?' means today, even if we broke production records last week," one of the vice presidents tells Erin. "Our company learns to produce something each day for the bottom line or we get booted to the sidelines. I don't like it, but that's the way it is in the 1990s, and we have to face it if we're going to stay on top."

THE PRODUCTIVITY DILEMMA OF THE CURRENT ECONOMY

Erin and top managers in this Hewlett-Packard scenario are in their best financial times and yet they fear the worst.

There is more than a touch of irony in that the very conditions that make managers like Erin and brainpowered workers she supervises feel so insecure—the need to grow revenues and market share in the face of increased competition in world markets, the demand to produce more with less, and the inevitable wave after wave of downsizing for those who miss the mark—are all embraced by their shareholders to make them feel more economically secure.

But why are companies so worried in the midst of an economy that is, by all the accepted yardsticks, booming? The country is experiencing the lowest inflation rate in twenty years; a net increase of 27 million jobs since 1979; eighty-one record stock market highs in 1995 alone and robust consumer spending. In his 1996 State of the Union Address, President Clinton tied all those numbers together in describing the economy simply as "the healthiest it has been in three decades."

And if that isn't enough, many corporations, reaping the benefits of a healthy economy, are breaking profit records at the same time they are taking a scythe to their work forces. Why?

The stresses fueling companies' drastic measures stem from frazzled nerves over trying to solve the productivity puzzle: how to increase performance in a chaotic, techno-information-driven, global economy.

Without rising productivity, many economists argue, an economy cannot raise real income levels across the board. By productivity's traditional definition—the amount valued in dollars that a worker produces in a given hour, using machines, traditional tools, or pure brainpower minues the costs of production—the American economy saw healthy productivity gains from the late nineteenth century until the early 1970s.

But since then, till the mid-1990s, the improvements had been minuscule—1 percent annually, compared with 2 percent or more in many earlier years. Individual and corporate income growth had stagnated and companies were flailing around for the Big Boost.

Enter downsizing and the high-tech retrofitting of the American workplace. Why were these embraced?

"Stunning technological progress that lets machines replace hands and minds; efficient and wily competitors here and abroad; the ease of contracting out work and the stern insistence of Wall Street on elevating profits, even if it means casting off people," Louis Luchitelle and N. R. Kleinfield wrote in the first of a seven-part *New York Times* series: "The Downsizing of America."

"Cutting the payroll has appeal for the sick and the healthy—for gasping companies that resort to it as triage and to the soundly profitable that try it as preventative medicine against a complicated future."

As the world economy has rocketed out of the industrial revolution and into the information age, companies are struggling to keep pace—to understand emerging new technologies and to figure out where they are headed.

"We live in an age of possibility," the president tells Congress. "A hundred years ago, we moved from farm to factory. Now we move to an age of technology, information, and global competition. These changes have opened vast new opportunities, but they also present stiff challenges. More Americans are living better lives, but too many of our fellow citizens are working harder to keep ahead, in search of greater security for their families."

For years, Americans have been told that a better standard of living awaits those who ride through the upheavals caused by high-tech innovations and layoffs. But now there is a rising sense among business experts that the promised productivity boost hasn't been realized from this bitter therapy and probably never will be.

While the CEOs of scores of Fortune 500 companies can claim productivity gains, especially in manufacturing, which has enjoyed an annual 3 percent growth rate on average in the 1990s, those successes have not boosted the national rate and are not viewed by economists as long-running.

Where, then, will corporate America turn for a long-term solution to the productivity puzzle? It will go back to where Hewlett-Packard managers like Erin already are: coaxing small, everyday productivity increases out of the employees who carry the company's intellectual capital; turning the so-so performers into star producers; turning the increased number of stars into a unitwide productivity boost; turning several unit boosts into a company's bottom-line production increase.

THE SHIFT TO INTELLECTUAL CAPITAL

But to better understand the reasons for investing in individual workers instead of quick-fix, system-wrenching solutions, it is important to understand the development of intellectual capital in the American economy.

The old drill, with roots in the dawn of the industrial revolution, involved setting up a system for attracting financial capital, largely from the merchant classes that had replaced the elite of the agricultural age—the rich landowners, at the top rung of the wealth-production ladder. The capital was used to acquire machines and raw materials to build the product. Last on the wealth-production ladder came the hiring of a largely blue-collar workforce, for as cheap a wage as possible, to operate the machines, bundle up the finished product, and get it to the customer.

In the information age, the new factor that has turned the traditional wealth-production system on its head is intellectual capital. Intellectual capital is all about a workforce valued for brain over brawn. If blue-collar workers are extensions of factory machines from the industrial age, these "gold-collar workers" are knowledge-centered employees who use machines or systems as extensions of themselves.

The gold-collar worker is separate from all the traditional categories, even the white-collar workforce—bank tellers, word-processing operators, restaurant servers, department store salespeople—who are often less technically skilled and less in control of their workplace. Brainpowered workers are creative and independent and usually know more about their jobs than their managers.

What distinguishes brainpowered companies like a computer software firm or a giant New York City law firm from a janitorial service or franchise is the critical intellectual capital held by the employees. At the software company and the law firm, the assets of their businesses are the brains of their professional workers.

If alien spaceships hovered above Microsoft's sprawling campus-style headquarters in Bellevue, Washington, and fired rays that pickled the brains of all its brainpowered workers, the company would be out of business in short order. Sales would dry up almost immediately, since customers would know that current products could not receive technical support and that no new products would be forthcoming. Microsoft could not recover, even with massive hiring, since new employees couldn't rise to the expert levels of the competition quickly enough to keep pace.

If the same pickling rays let loose at a fast-food hamburger chain's headquarters, the negative impact would neither be as sudden nor as serious. The company's long-term planning and marketing might be in jeopardy but the retail end of the business would go on undisturbed. Hamburgers would still be sold briskly by the counter workers who punch the pictures of fast-food items on computer cash registers. Few customers would worry about new-product development, while new marketing hires eventually would fill in the breach at headquarters.

Managers of intellectual capital find themselves in an uncomfortable position because they are increasingly dependent on brainpowered employees whose work process they do not understand and whose productivity they cannot control. In most traditional businesses, the manager knows how to do the subordinate's job. An executive at McDonalds knows how to serve up hamburgers at the counter and can step in if the worker quits. This isn't true in most brainpowered jobs. Microsoft's top executive in charge of Windows NT would be hard-pressed to take over the lead software developer's job, even after months of training.

Other businesses are even more technically complex. For example, in the telephone-switching business, most of the top executives began their careers in the 1950s and early 1960s, when mechanical switching to handle phone-call traffic was the dominant technology. Today, those top executives raised on mechanical switches are familiar with 1990s digital switching technology only in general terms. Yet they are responsible for how well the brainpowered engineers and scientists beneath them deal with this complex technology that they themselves do not fully understand.

When I talk to executives at intellectual capital companies, they worry about how dependent their fortunes are on these brainpowered workers and how quickly today's top-level technical proficiency can become yesterday's outmoded skill. For example, some telephone-switch executives think the next breakthrough will come from bio-electronic computers, which will simulate the brain by combining biological and chemical interactions with electrical impulses. But how many workers are out there who have an education in biology, electrical engineering, and computer science? Executives have to think far enough ahead to grab the available workers who have the skills to work with the emerging technology. If they don't, they risk their companies' being left behind during the next technology revolution.

In the 1980s, company profit margins were enhanced or diminished by how well the intellectual capital of their best brainpowered workers—the stars—transferred into consumer products and services. In the 1990s and into the next century, how well companies do in getting maximum brainpower from all their employees, not just the stars, will determine their very survival. Boosting the productivity of the entire brainpowered workforce is the key to success.

Increasingly, companies are also discovering that the quality of their teams of managers and brainpowered workers can have a better long-term effect on stock price and investor interest than a heavy-handed downsizing program.

On the day in August 1996 when Alex Mandl, then the second-highest-ranking executive at AT&T, left to join a relatively unknown, productless, profitless, start-up company, AT&T lost over a billion dollars of stock market value, while the Associated Group, his new employer, gained $43 million. Nothing changed except a shift of intellectual capital.

While anecdotal studies showing the value of upsizing—adding brainpowered workers to increase productivity—abound, there is also hard, empirical evidence.

An exhaustive 1994 study of a group of manufacturing industries that were reaping that 3 percent-plus productivity gain through downsizing and high-tech enhancements sent shock waves through Wall Street. Published by the National Bureau of Economic Research, the study found that while small businesses that added employees were disproportionately likely to suffer a productivity dip, large corporations increasing their workforces were disproportionately likely to increase productivity.

University of Maryland economist John Haltiwanger, who conducted the study along with Maryland's Martin Neil Baily and the Federal Reserve's J. Bartelsman, says their research rejects downsizing as a surefire productivity booster. In fact, says Haltiwanger, "there are many firms that are not going to see the returns on downsizing that they expect. And the real productivity gains are going to come from firms that are adding highly educated, technically proficient workers."

IMPROVING BRAINPOWERED PRODUCTIVITY

"Silicon Valley companies' most important assets have legs and leave every night. Management's most important job is to make sure that these assets walk into your company the next day and not a competitor's." That statement, made by me in an interview with the *San Jose Mercury News*, the paper of record for Silicon Valley industries, holds true today for brainpowered companies across the country.

In an information age economy, most of the intellectual capital is locked up in employee heads. Sure, a 3M, Microsoft Corporation, or Merck Pharmaceutical does have a substantial amount of company wealth tied up in patents and machinery. But these tools and ideas are mere extensions of the intellectual capital that created them. When the people who do the creating lose contact with the customer or when managers lose contact with these creators, financial disaster looms.

Research involving successful companies like Nordstrom and Hewlett-Packard shows that when the quality of employee work life is strong, customers are more likely to be satisfied. The most productive flow, then, is from managers to employees to customers and back again.

In the shift to a brainpowered economy, more and more top managers are also coming to realize that their key employees are considering options that workers of twenty years ago never would have dreamed of exercising. Since the first casualty of the downsizing era has been company loyalty to its workers, employees no longer have that much loyalty for their companies. These workers know their value in the job marketplace and will probably change companies several times during their careers.

One way managers contain the transfer problem is to keep brainpowered employees happy where they are—generous salaries and benefits, flexible working conditions. As extra insurance, com-

panies are requiring their brainpowered workers to sign nondisclosure agreements and employment contracts with restrictions on
how much intellectual property can leave with the worker. But the
law has yet to effectively sort out all the complications that come
from the growth of a brainpowered economy, especially in balancing the intellectual property rights of workers against the companies that employ them.

The effort to keep hold of the reins on intellectual capital by
both positive and negative reinforcement is understandable given
the fate awaiting those companies that fall behind on it in a brainpowered economy.

But the issue isn't just the amount of intellectual capital. The
more pressing challenge is its productivity. The more star workers
turn their ideas into sought-after products and services, the more
cushion managers have in determining new directions for the business.

Competitive cushions are critical in the globally competitive
business environment of the 1990s, where most high-tech products
have a limited shelf life. If workers aren't motivated to produce, the
business can quickly be overtaken by competitors.

15

CONCLUSION:
The Rewards of Star Productivity

There are two file folders that I keep on my desk. One is stuffed with news and magazine story clippings that offer tips for future projects related to my work in the field of intellectual capital productivity. The other file folder is filled with evaluations and personal letters from those who have benefited from past projects—like the productivity-improvement program based on this book.

Taken together, the files are brimming with good news about the future for brainpowered workers who are committed to becoming more productive.

Indeed, in my news clipping folder there are several stories reporting that the downsizing era has almost run its course. Top corporate executives are finally realizing that the key to achieving long-term sales and profit growth is highly productive employees, not cutting and slashing the workforce. There are heartening disclosures from top executives like General Electric's Donald Borwhat, admitting that rather than downsizing, his corporation added 3 percent more workers and had a revenue jump of 18 percent.

Even the reengineering guru Michael Hammer has joined in. "The real point . . . is longer-term growth on the revenue side. It's not so much getting rid of people. It's getting more out of people," says Hammer in a *Wall Street Journal* article. It turns out that he and all the others on the $4.7 billion reengineering bandwagon underestimated the value of people in the new profitability equations. "I wasn't smart enough about that," Hammer now admits. "I was reflecting my engineering background and was insufficiently appreciative of the human dimension. I've learned that's critical."

In the downsizing frenzy, companies suffered major unintended personnel casualties; they lost an inordinate number of star performers to their competitors. Certainly, top managers expected the stars to stay, but what they didn't count on was that the best employees have options, and they don't have to put up with a company going through downsizing hell. The stars left for companies that were on the growth curve and hadn't resorted to slash-and-burn remodeling.

Managers in these companies have told me that although they lost the top 10 percent of their workforce, they also ridded themselves of the bottom 10 percent. They comfort themselves by insisting that when all the dust settled, the workforce evened out.

It's such a silly, inaccurate, unfortunate rationalization. When your stars outproduce your average workers ten to twenty times over, the balancing assertion is quickly skewed against productivity. The company's overall performance drops sharply.

As these companies try to get back on the growth curve, they now face another obstacle. Brainpowered workers are not easily replaced. Hewlett-Packard estimates that it takes about twenty-five months and $150,000 before a newly hired engineer becomes productive. For every ten new employees you hire, you're talking about a $1.5 million investment and almost two years before these new hires are fully producing the work they were hired to do. And if you do not intervene to help them become highly productive, only one (or if you are lucky, two) of these will become star performers. So companies that have been reckless in their downsizing campaigns face a daunting uphill climb before they can even begin to compete against companies that avoided such upheaval and whose star performers are still on board.

So the good news from my clip file is that companies all across America are waking up to their dependence on you for their futures. Your organization needs a workforce layered with superproductive workers. Only through the one-to-ten or one-to-twenty productivity boost—your work output equal to the output of ten average workers—can a company hope to outpace its competitors. Boosting worker productivity, not booting workers out on the street, is the key to an organization's long-term financial health.

But how does this new corporate appreciation of workers and workplace stability affect you? The basic emphasis hasn't changed. More will be expected of you, and you will be expected to accomplish it with fewer resources. And that's where your commitment to improving personal productivity puts you at the head of the pack. By becoming a productivity asset, you also make it more worthwhile for your company to invest more in you—they now have a higher stake in your appreciating in value.

There are also signs that star performers are finally reaping the economic rewards they deserve. Our earlier research showed that the compensation difference between star performers and their coworkers was only 5 percent on average, even though their productivity was ten to twenty times higher. That is now changing. As their counterparts in sports have done, star performers are getting a bigger share of the wealth they create.

For several years out of art school, animator Andrew Stanton made about $20,000 a year doing animation jobs for commercials, cartoons, and movie producers. Then his computer animation work on the hit movie *Toy Story*, which generated over $400 million in profits, propelled him to the top ranks in the suddenly sizzling field of animation. He now collects a six-figure salary and lives in affluent Marin County north of San Francisco. The very top animation directors now make more than $1 million a year, unimaginable a decade ago.

Stanton's reversal of fortune is being played out across the country—from New York investment banks to New Jersey pharmaceutical companies to Chicago law firms to Houston-based oil companies to Silicon Valley high-tech start-ups. Companies have finally realized that star performers are not substitutable commodities but instead are wealth-creating assets. And they are paying up to attract and keep their star performers. It is not unusual for stars to get a higher starting salary and a bigger piece of the profit action, including stock options worth many times more than their take-home pay.

Steve Brody, a Silicon Valley headhunter, spends much of his time just crafting the message that he will leave on a potential recruit's VoiceMail because he knows that he is likely to be competing with other recruiters for that person. Many other headhunters are working for companies and investors, like Ann Winblad of Hunter, Winblad Venture Partners, who realize that the talent *is* the company. "The P&E is just people. . . . Without intellectual capital, you're nothing," she says.

So although star performers primarily perform for the satisfaction that comes from doing a great job and for the respect of their peers, it is comforting to know that you will now get the economic rewards—perhaps beyond your dreams—that you deserve.

STAR PERFORMANCE IS YOUR KEY TO A BETTER WORK LIFE

My second file—the one with evaluation comments from the productivity-improvement program and personal letters recounting the many positive benefits that come from a more productive work life—validates your efforts. And the benefits don't just occur on the job, they show up in every other aspect of your life.

This file takes me back to the years of follow-up focus groups that we had with participants—six months, one year, and two years after they went through the program—probing for what aspects of the training had stayed with them, what worked and what did not.

In particular, I remember a crisp October day in Chicago in 1991. I was sitting in a windowless Bell Labs conference room for hours interviewing twenty people who had gone through the program during the past two years. I was there to get answers to one simple question: What did they learn from the program that made the most difference in their daily lives?

As I went around the room, people mentioned how the nine star performer work strategies had enabled them to make quantum leaps in their productivity. And their performance had not gone unnoticed. Most in the roundtable session reported significant recognition in the workplace and the precious reward of extra time outside the office.

"I learned that initiative means going above and beyond your job and helping out others. I didn't know that," confided Tess, a thirty-six-year-old product manager who had emigrated from Vietnam. "All this time I was on the same field, but playing from a different playbook. No wonder I often felt like I just didn't get it. Now that I know what the company means by initiative and what really counts, I can do that."

Before the program, Tess didn't understand the importance of identifying critical path opportunities and volunteering where her participation could make a big difference. After learning the necessity of such initiatives, she volunteered to take on a new high-risk, high-payoff product development, which turned around the market share of an ailing telephone software product.

For Christie, a Bell employee for five years who attained star status in her first year on the job, the followership skill has had the most impact. "I was more of a leader type and tended to be much less involved. I'd kind of drop out in activities I wasn't leading. I now try much harder to be a strong, supportive follower when I'm not in the leadership role. I try to help out when the leader gets busy or is unavailable, to be proactive in suggesting ways to do things, while trying not to usurp leadership."

Sanjay, a first-level supervisor who took the course and then offered it to his staff, became a true believer because of the course's unique ability "to be different things to different people. The variety of topics covered and the way in which they're covered enables people to take out of it what they need most, while still getting value from those topics that may already be areas of strength."

Sanjay's team decided to take the program together after they were assigned a red-hot development project for a telephone credit card feature with an overly aggressive schedule. To win the Baby Bell's business, management had promised delivery in fifteen months rather than the customary twenty. Now Sanjay's team had to deliver on the promise, even though they openly wondered whether they could.

Our productivity-improvement program allowed them to jump-start their project. The teamwork-followership-leadership sections helped them come together quickly as a highly functioning team as they worked out the roles each would play. The perspective section gave the team the tools to nail down the customer's and their company's expectations. During the self-management section, they outlined a total project plan and individualized ones, while the networking part allowed them to build the knowledge networks and organizational supports that were necessary for project completion. As a result, they beat the project schedule by two months and delighted their customer and bosses alike.

These workers who went through our program were now more highly valued by their colleagues and other managers in the company than they were before. They were getting their pick of the best projects and had more time to devote to the creative parts of their jobs rather than being dragged down by routine work. Work was more fun. Many reported a flattering side benefit: unsolicited calls from recruiters.

Professionals and managers who have used the star performer materials have also gone public with their praise. Steve Miranda, who went through the program and who volunteered to become a program facilitator, told *Machine Design*, a national trade publication, "The program was a rare life-changing event. . . . It showed me that being smart and assertive and knowing how to solve the technical aspects of a problem aren't enough. To really be top-notch . . . you also have to be able to communicate your ideas, to enroll others to believe in them, and to be able to lead your team through difficult times . . . and personal challenges." Steve continues to use the star-performer material, which he calls "absolute gold mines of information."

Likewise, Marge Hillis, a star promoted to management, told *Working Woman* that she "found the course so useful that she sent six people from her department. 'I saw a real improvement in five of them,' she said. The sixth, a man who went grudgingly, is 'still a fine performer,' but in some areas has not progressed as much as the others."

STAR PERFORMANCE ALLOWS YOU TO GET A LIFE

An invaluable and heartwarming benefit of the newfound productivity in our trainee's lives shows up outside of the office, in all the aspects of living that working is supposed to enhance. Too often, workers struggling in highly demanding, brainpowered jobs with average productivity end up sacrificing their "off-duty" time to meet work obligations.

No longer is that the case with the expert practitioners of our nine work strategies. Although this was not part of our original purpose, we couldn't ignore it.

Wayne, a star product manager, used the work strategies to help make the board of his church more productive. "We used to spin our wheels in endless meetings and go nowhere. It frustrated the hell out of many of us, because we were devoting precious free time to the board and we wanted something good to come out of it. Then I introduced the other board members to the sections on teamwork, followership, and leadership. Now we actually get things done that need to be done."

For Brendan, a thirty-two-year-old father of two, the impact was closer to home. "Once I established myself as someone who could contribute to the bottom line, I felt more in control of my life and less paranoid about downsizings. I used to think that I had to say yes to every extra work request, especially if it came from a manager. I now pick and choose more carefully. Rather than working sixty to seventy hours each week to try to please everyone and never seeing my kids, I now keep it between forty and fifty." Brendan used his recaptured time to design a new house for his growing family so that they could move out of their two-bedroom starter home.

For Mei, it transformed how she felt about herself. Like John Jacobs, our downsizing poster boy in Chapter 3, she finished school believing that she had what it took to be a star. But after six years of mediocre performance evaluations, she had lost confidence in herself. She started to believe that she didn't have it—whatever "it" was. She became depressed, started to gain excess weight, and did not take much care with her physical appearance.

"The program showed me it wasn't some defect in me. Instead, I just didn't know how to work productively. Once I learned the secrets of the star performers, I just started to use them, and it changed everything. I'm now the person I always thought I could be. And my coworkers and boss look at me differently, too."

Mei's performance lifted her annual evaluations and her spirits. She started working out at the health club and took charge of her life at work and at home.

- Tim, our star design engineer from the perspective chapter, Chapter 7, who looks at God's design of nature for inspiration, is also a champion skier, making his own skis in his basement.
- Lai, our software whiz from the initiative chapter, Chapter 4, designs jewelry in her off-work time, selling it at craft shows around the Midwest.
- Chuck-Lum, a star with a taste for black leather jackets and motorcycles, fixes up broken pinball machines and resells them.

Being a star performer is not just about avoiding downsizings or adding value to the critical path. It is not just about working smarter, rather than longer. It is about you—the kind of person you want to be and the kind of life you want to lead.

Imagine what your life would be like if you became a star performer rather than staying stuck in the middle of the pack. Would you spend more time with your loved ones or volunteer in your community? Would you take up that dream project or hobby that you never seem to have time for? Would you finally learn that foreign language or take that overseas trip? Might you train for the triathlon or sail across the country in a hot-air balloon? Might you simply feel better about yourself? After ten years of working with star performers, my guess is that you would finally be the person that you know you can be.

Only you can make it happen.

APPENDIX I

The Research Story Behind the Book: The Hunt for Higher Productivity

NOTE TO THE READER: This chapter provides a fuller discussion of the methods and results used in our research on star performers. As such, it recaps some of the findings that were highlighted in Part One of the book. It is included here for those readers who want to understand our research better.

A PROBLEM AT BELL LABS: COMPETITION

Back in 1985, at the beginning of our study of star performers, Janet Nordin was director of a 250-member lab in the brainpowered workplace of world-famous Bell Labs, a division of AT&T. When I met Janet in November 1985, she was one of the managers in charge of the effort to develop a reliable cellular phone. She took it upon herself to lug around the first prototype, a clunky, walkie-talkie apparatus that was connected to a heavy battery pack, a lot like the field phones used in World War II.

At one Pittsburgh meeting early on in our project, she was stuck in one of the infamous traffic backups that plague the tunnels around the city. Janet tried to phone me at the office with her not-so-portable phone but the signal was captive in the tunnel as well. Later, at the meeting, while we were all chuckling about the idea of lugging around a phone the size of a briefcase that didn't work very well, she was promising us that someday soon, "everyone is going to be carrying one of these around and it will be small enough to fit in their pockets."

Janet seemed to have a knack, not just for thinking ahead but for developing better ways to think ahead. Given AT&T's post-breakup foray into the competitive waters, Janet's talents would soon be tested.

Indeed, the competition was already in full swing by the time our study began in 1986. An upstart competitor, Northern Telecom, was running to market with its own switching device, a scaled-down, digital version of what Bell had been producing. No longer did a spin-off company like Pacific Bell or a small phone company in Asia have to buy the Rolls Royce of switches in order to enjoy a huge improvement in its phone system, especially in its ability to catch all those long-distance calls that had been slipping out of its billing net.

While Northern Telecom was doing very well with its sleeker model, Bell Labs was saddled with a workforce geared to attending to all the extra bells and whistles on its state-of-the-art 5ESS model. Switches of that magnitude require rooms full of computer hardware and millions of lines of software code. Much of the work of Bell switching engineers involved merely maintaining the software code so the switch would function properly, but there were also other outlets for creativity. Engineers would often be assigned to write new computer code to respond to phone company requests for new services like caller ID and call forwarding.

Since there are so many facets to a switching device, and since the scale of work is beyond any one person's ability, Bell engineers almost always worked on problems and projects in teams. A software application program can require as few as five engineers or as many as three hundred, and a time frame of from six months to two years.

While searching for ideas to help improve the productivity of her lab, Janet came across my book *The Gold-Collar Worker*, where I first described how to manage workers whose value to the company is their brainpower. Janet highlighted passages that impressed her, later foisting twenty single-spaced pages of them on her staff. One concept that especially caught her interest when we talked about the book was the 100th-monkey phenomenon, which I had shared with her.

Scientists studying communities of monkeys on a group of South Sea islands repeatedly noticed a peculiar behavior among the animals. Any change or innovation introduced by one monkey—a new way to get bananas off tree branches, for instance—did not spread very fast or far until about a hundred monkeys had mastered the technique. At that point, the new learning would take place almost overnight among the thousands of monkeys in a community spread out over several islands. The point of the hundredth monkey learning the new skill was known as the critical mass that set off the chain reaction.

Janet saw this as the perfect metaphor for her productivity improvement campaign at Bell Labs. Using the brainpower of the few to improve the productivity of the group was exactly what was needed in her section. She wanted to find a system to do that, and she recognized my willingness to break new ground in the hunt for one.

Few had ever tried, in a systematic way, to determine the productivity boosts required for Bell Labs to be comfortable competing in the global marketplace. And only a few managers had ever attempted to climb the stairs of the labs housing their intellectual capital to measure brainpowered workers' productivity and how it compared with others'.

The traditional hands-off attitude has much to do with the nature of the workforce. Managers have been uncomfortable poking around in the warrens of brainpowered workers who often know their jobs better than the manager. Also, managers are reluctant to tinker with professionals known for a work ethic that often borders on the obsessive—sixty-hour weeks are common. They are defined, too, by the degree to which they tie their reputation in the workplace to the success of their piece of the project.

Many managers wrongly believe an increase in productivity can only happen with a corresponding increase in the workday. To demand too much from this group is counterproductive, they argue, because brainpowered workers have options. They can put their best ideas on hold and land a job with a more supportive company.

Janet and her boss, Don Leonard, Bell's vice president for switching systems, had rejected the temptation, common in brainpowered workplaces, to dispatch a consultant to find a formulaic silver bullet that would solve their productivity problem.

In the science world, the assumption is that if you work in the lab smart enough and long enough, you find that bullet—a cure for polio, for instance. Much the same holds in the engineering research lab. If you're experiencing a drag on production schedules, you don't examine personnel, you buy faster computer systems. Although Bell Labs managers were investing in technical productivity tools, Janet and Don believed that human brainpower, not technological wonders, would provide the longest-lasting productivity advantage.

Janet was struck by the sharp differences between her best workers and others in the pack. There had to be some way to learn what factors separate them and then find a way to clone "the ten-to-oners," the star engineers who did the work of ten average coworkers. If not that, then at least a method could be devised to test job candidates for the magic combination of star traits that would allow them to hire smarter for the challenging road ahead.

Charting a Course on Uncharted Ground

The team I put together for this expedition consisted of Janet Caplan, who had researched the causes of intellectual curiosity, and Dick Hayes, who had done groundbreaking work on creativity and problem solving. Caplan was thirty-six then, fashionably dressed and neatly organized—a perfect counterpoint to Hayes, in his mid-fifties, who shared the same physical traits as many of the Bell Labs engineers: beard, wrinkled shirts, and jeans.

Most important, however, both were enthusiastic about joining the hunt—particularly fascinated by the question of what makes one star shine brighter than another. So my expert team was assembled and ready when the Bell Labs executives came to call.

After carefully listening to the productivity problems and analyzing the goals of the study, we developed an initial plan, one that would later take several dramatic twists and turns before we saw it through.

To start, we scoured the historical research and modern behavioral studies. We also branched off from the Bell environment to study high performers in low-tech jobs, such as some aspects of steel production.

After our general research, we took our first steps toward bonding with the Bell Labs engineers, slowly convincing most of them over a period of months that this was not just another motivational, touchy-feely seminar. Eventually word got around that we were involved in serious, scientific work that they would play a large role in shaping.

In fact, we went out of our way to recruit the most skeptical, hard-nosed workers in the lab, figuring that if we could impress them with our work and get them excited by it, we would quickly generate the workplace credibility we needed to succeed.

Eventually, stars and average performers alike were contributing to the research base, making up lists of qualities they thought separated the best performers from the pack. The list included cognitive factors—the mental smarts to get hired and stay on the job, which include such factors as IQ, logic, inductive/deductive reasoning, and creativity. Then there were the social factors—"leadership," ". . . she's a better communicator," or "he's really good with people one-on-one." Psychological-personality factors that seemed to make a difference in long-range performance included a hyperaggressive personality, a will to win, self-confidence, risk taking, and sense of control.

A fourth area centered on organizational factors, how the organization treats people and how people react to such treatment. This included attitudes about compensation and other rewards, management structure, and the general work environment—"Does the company value my contributions?" "Do I trust my manager?" or "Do I like my job?"

We narrowed this list down to about forty-five factors in the four categories that separate average performers from stars and set about determining the best way to test for them, given the standard measurement tools available.

We knew that any of these forty-five factors might play a role in differentiating between any two specific engineers. But we were determined to see if they would hold up to objective testing when applied across large groups of brainpowered workers. It became clear as we shuffled through all the available theories, the methodologies, personality surveys, and interviews, that we were dealing with a unique category of worker. Few researchers had ventured where we wanted to go. We would have to do our own work by immersing ourselves in the insulated world of a Bell Labs switching unit.

Our original pilot group of study subjects relied on paper achievements, those who had received the highest performance ratings and merit awards. We also depended on the selections of upper and middle managers culled from such questions as "If you were starting a new company and could hire only ten brainpowered workers from your present staff, whom would you hire?" There was surprising consensus among managers about who these indispensable workers were.

We soon ran into the problem first discussed in Chapter 1, however: The brainpowered workers disagreed with their bosses as to who the stars were. We then asked the professional community to nominate those colleagues who were superproductive and whose work they truly admired. After polling the workers, we discovered that they agreed with managers only on half of the people.

This large discrepancy can occur because managers and workers look at different factors to decide if someone is highly productive. They also have different experience bases and reference points. In some instances, it may be that managers are out of touch with the actual work that is being done. In fact, it was our experience that workers in brain-powered workplaces are probably more accurate than managers (and often more perceptive) about who the stars are among them.

As we discovered from our own interviews, managers sometimes overlook important components of star performance, such as who originates ideas consistently and who regularly helps colleagues out of work jams. Engineers were able to evaluate a worker's day-in-day-out performance on the front lines when singling out their peers.

Another important factor was that most of the engineers in the unit distrusted the formal performance-evaluation system. They complained that it was like an unreliable drug test, turning out too many false negatives—people who were outstanding performers but for reasons of work style or humility received low ratings from managers. On the other side, there were plenty of false positives—engineers who didn't deserve their star billing.

For our study, the top performers who received approval from both managers and their peers became our star performers. (In our later validation work at 3M, we added customer ratings as the third hurdle to gain star status.)

In the fall of 1986, we conducted a pilot study of twenty engineers and ten managers to determine whether productivity and performance correlate with specific personal and organizational characteristics. After compiling the results of cognitive tests, attitude surveys, personality measures and interviews, we were thrilled to find measurable differences.

If the same results were duplicated in a larger study (three hundred engineers from three labs), we could be confident of predicting a person's productivity in a Bell Labs engineering environment.

During the next year, we planned the study and launched an intense recruiting campaign to attract the cross section of engineers we needed for the larger study, finally bringing them together in meeting rooms of hotels in Naperville, Illinois, and Columbus, Ohio, for two days to administer the batch of surveys and tests. Engineers and managers also supplied us with personal biographical information and personnel file material.

For the next four months, we coded, scored, and analyzed the data, sure in our assumptions that the differences in the few in our pilot study would be highlighted in the many.

Perhaps it was because we had built up expectations, both on our own and from those around us, that it was so difficult to accept the first numbers that came out from our crunching of the results of interviews, test scores, and questionnaire tallies:

No appreciable cognitive, personal-psychological, social, or environmental differences between stars and average performers.

I was stunned, even after finally accepting the evidence. I had allowed myself to slip into a silver bullet fantasy—that the three of us would uncover the key differences that distinguished star performers from their average coworkers.

So I had to drag myself to that fateful meeting (described in Chapter 1) with Janet Nordin and other members of the Bell Labs management team to admit defeat. And it seemed only appropriate that they would be angry over spending a lot of money and precious workplace time to learn, what seemed at the time, nothing.

Understanding Brainpowered Productivity

The nature of brainpowered work is not easily measured or understood with the tools most comfortable to managers—especially with evaluations. The subjective nature of the work and its complexity often puts the evaluator on shaky ground. The formal "How do you rate?" process becomes a grueling ordeal for the manager and a meaningless company policy for the brainpowered worker.

While the traditional corporate evaluation system doesn't do much for knowledge professionals, we didn't find the workers themselves to have any more enlightened a view of their own work.

In 1990, we asked forty brainpowered workers at Bell Labs and another twenty-five at Motorola to evaluate themselves by way of a quick e-mail survey conducted during each workday over a period of several weeks.

There were only four questions:

- How productive were you today?
- How did you measure your productivity?

- What caused you to be either productive or nonproductive today?
- Did you get any feedback (positive or negative) about your productivity?

Although you might expect that individual workers would rate their own productivity more positively than the bosses would, they actually turned out to be their own toughest critics.

On average, these self-doubters rated their daily productivity at a low 68 percent, given the performance needs of a technical environment like Bell Labs.

One reason for such uncertainty could be unclear performance standards. The most popular method, it turned out, for measuring personal productivity was compiling a to-do list—so stereotypically logical for engineers. In our study, progress on lists was cited 41 percent of the time as the standard of measurement. Gut feelings, not a comfortable area for technically grounded knowledge professionals, came in a distant second, at 16 percent. And measuring the amount of time spent working trailed at 14 percent.

Only one engineer on one day cited "amount of my work making a direct contribution to the company"—a focus on a bottom-line concept that I've labeled the critical path (see the chapters on initiative and self-management, Chapters 4 and 6). The critical path refers to those direct, essential activities that organizations must take on to ensure profitability and sustained success in the marketplace. As an indicator of personal productivity, workers must first get on the critical path and then take the most effective route to produce something that adds value to the organization.

Indeed, our work with experts indicates that many of the assumptions about what makes for high productivity in an organization are tacit. More often than not, such measures aren't spelled out by top managers. Although the professionals we surveyed preferred concrete accomplishments as personal gauges of productivity, they also complained about having a tough time deciding whether the tasks on their to-do lists added any value to the company. And on a day-to-day basis, managers don't seem to help with this problem. Of the sixty-five brain-powered workers, 45 percent said they received no productivity feedback from their managers during the period of the survey.

There is a simple explanation for this, based on our work. Managers, especially those in technical fields, just aren't comfortable making assessments without a lot of hard information—numbers, data, charts, graphs, and scales. The more subjective the area, the more reluctant the manager is to evaluate.

As mentioned in Chapter 3, there has yet to be a formula devised that allows managers to get inside the heads of knowledge professionals to make judgments about productivity. In particular, analyzing the process that produces high-quality results in knowledge work is very difficult. Most managers can't directly observe, let alone accurately evaluate, these mental processes or strategies.

So we decided to go directly to the source—the brainpowered workers themselves—to observe, interview, and collaborate on the clues to the productive brainpower going on inside. In particular, what kinds of behaviors do the stars employ to ensure their own productivity?

STARGAZING

I often tell brainpowered workers in my training seminars that my personal definition of hell is being forced to watch them do their jobs day-in-day-out, in minute detail, for all eternity. I base that on the nearly two years we spent up close and personal with the Bell Labs stars.

If brainpowered workers take that to mean that much of what they do on a daily basis is boring, well, that is exactly right—but only from the standpoint that the action is going on where it should, inside the worker's head. The internal activity may be showing spectacular special effects even though the outward visuals for any onlooker are low.

This is one reason we've found that managers are often so much in the dark when it comes to assessing the performance of brainpowered workers and understanding how they do their jobs.

Business expert Peter Drucker believes that no formula will ever be devised to allow managers to get inside the heads of knowledge professionals to make judgments about productivity. In particular, he has pointed to the difficulties of analyzing the process that produces high-quality results in knowledge work.

"The best we can do," says Drucker, "is ask 'What works?' "

Implicit in this question is the reality that the work of brainpowered workers is almost like that of the artist—private, vague, and internalized. And managers can't directly observe, let alone accurately evaluate, these mental processes or strategies.

So the only other logical place to go for answers was to the front lines to sift through the work behavior of the workers themselves, clues to the productive brainpower going on inside. What kinds of behaviors do the stars employ to ensure their own productivity?

Molding the Model

To find out, we spent days in detailed interviews, focus groups, and observations of high-performing Bell Labs engineers.

KELLEY: What are you looking for in that file?

STAR: I'm checking my phone list for someone I can call to help me out of the jam with this piece of code.

(Early evening)

KELLEY: Now who are you dialing?

STAR: I'm calling to order a pizza.

KELLEY: Why now?

STAR: Because it's going to be a long evening and I'm hungry.

KELLEY: What made you decide that it's going to be a long night, and why work on it tonight rather than put it off?

The hundreds of behavioral details on scores of engineers required more than sketchy notes on paper. We compiled checklists, a catalogue of regular work routines, and compared them at various points along the way.

Observing an engineer who takes an entire day to write four lines of computer code can be maddening. But revealed in the observation notes and daily logs was a valuable nugget. Because she made two phone calls to other experts, her four lines accomplished the same function as the hundred lines of computer code written over a week's time by a coworker down the hall.

In another situation, a lab engineer known for star ability would be interrupted a dozen or more times during a typical day by needy coworkers. Our notes on networking informed us that some visitors would get valuable time from the star, while others were politely fluffed off.

"Why did you spend time with Charles and not Cynthia?" I would ask.

"Oh, I just didn't have any more time left." This was what we referred to as the Motherhood-and-Apple-Pie-non-response response. It was, in effect, a way for the engineer to placate me as the nosy researcher and not admit to having an informal network of preferred coworkers.

By confronting the apple-pie attitude—"Hey, it looked like more than that to me. It looked like you deliberately blew her off, and if I'm correct, then I'm curious to know why"—we were able to peel through the surface layers to find truer motivations behind behaviors.

Our analysis of the daily checklists, another part of the peeling process, was so productive that we expanded the sessions to include feedback from the workers we were following. We strongly encouraged them to challenge some of our conclusions and add their own insights from our observations.

We wanted to avoid the trap of falling into nonsensical productivity recipes, because a lot was at stake. The new goal of our research was to develop a master model of behaviors on the job—or as we later defined them, work strategies. The next step would be to build a productivity improvement program that would allow workers to tailor these skills to their own individual work styles.

In order to accept the program, stars and average performers had to trust the research. We wanted them to find parts of their own personalized behaviors embedded in the findings.

Certainly the Dumpsters of behavioral psychology are filled with training programs rejected by trainees as less than relevant to their work lives.

Remember the "peak performance" athletic-training craze of the 1980s? That was based on researchers' intense interviews with athletic champions who dutifully recounted a typical daily regimen that might include stretching at dawn after waking up, eating their Wheaties, and spending an hour or so visualizing their success. Then they practiced their sport intensely for three hours. The same testimony from dozens of champions led to a truckload of bestsellers and videos on how to reach peak performance in sports, sales, or management.

What was missing from the basic research was the most basic insight into the training regimens of those athletes who fell short of bringing home a medal when all the traditional predictors had them as strong contenders. Chances are these also-rans followed the exact same regimen—waking up at dawn, stretching, eating Wheaties, visualizing winning, and intense practice of their sport under expert coaching.

It's not nearly enough to ask the stars what works; honest research demands that star regimens be compared to the medal-less pack to identify differences. It was this standard to which we held ourselves and which resulted in the star performer model in this book. By comparing and validating separate models of the star and the average performers, we were able to both pinpoint the differences and determine whether those differences led to higher productivity.

Using the Stars to Create the Productivity-Improvement Program

In the Bell Labs program, the model proved itself with dramatic increases in productivity from middle-of-the-pack workers who began using the work strategies that we culled from the stars.

One reason for the effectiveness of the program was that we worked with the stars to understand how adults learn best and to design a program that eliminated their major complaints with traditional training programs. They then helped us design a program that had as its foundation action learning combined with self-discovery rather than the more typical passive classroom format, where quick-fix formulas are dispensed.

In this spirit, we asked the stars to rank the work strategies in order of importance. For example, initiative is the core strategy in this expert model. Yet initiative is one of the most misunderstood strategies and therefore one of the most difficult to put into practice successfully without outside help.

"I go into my supervisor's office for a performance evaluation, and she tells me I need to take more initiative," said one Bell Labs engineer. "I say to myself that I'm already taking initiative, so what exactly is it that she wants me to do?"

Given all the anecdotal evidence, any program for improving the productivity of professionals must first target taking initiative. During our discussions with experts, one expert proposed creating a practical checklist to detail the specific steps that the stars take in each work strategy. As a result, checklists were developed and validated as a sampling of specific actions and behaviors that define each work strategy.

If you're like most of the knowledge workers we studied, you have a low tolerance for off-the-shelf productivity programs—either as a manager who solicits a course or as a worker assigned to attend one. Our discussions with professionals at Bell Labs and elsewhere show that these people like to make their own choices. These professionals readily admit they could do their jobs better, but they're also wary, as at least many knowledge workers put it, of "becoming a clone."

Most knowledge professionals are very adept in scoping out the stars in their workplaces. Many have even made the effort to seek out informal training or advice from them in the course of a project. That's why respected engineers led the program we developed from the expert model. In fact, the process of using stars to develop the model became the foundation for the program itself.

The Bell Labs experts we interviewed reported increases in their own productivity because they had picked up valuable tips during our research from listening to their star colleagues.

Now, as a brainpowered worker intent on improving your productivity, mentoring may seem like the best route. But the expert model is superior in one critical respect: While many professionals are experts in their own productivity, no single star performer is adept at every skill. Instead of the one-to-one format of the mentoring method—senior professional taking promising junior staffer under wing—the expert model is a many-to-one proposition. The strategies of many stars are collected and transferred to you, on your own or in a group.

In the spring of 1989, a pilot productivity-improvement program for the Switching Systems Business Unit began with sixteen brainpowered workers chosen by management. Meeting once a week for ten weeks, the group included a mix of stars and middle performers, but the number of stars was slightly higher, since one of the goals of the course was to have them become facilitators in future courses taken by other staffers.

The goal of the first course was to make the critical work strategies concrete, accessible, and learnable. Each week of the pilot program focused on one of the nine strategies. The last week was used for a wrap-up.

But despite this carefully outlined schedule, the stars stayed true to their reputations for excellence. They revised the curriculum as they went along, testing ideas out in real time, keeping what worked and discarding what did not.

For example, in reaction to a teamwork simulation centered around the group surviving in the desert together—which they judged irrelevant—they developed a teamwork exercise based on work-related issues at the Switching Systems Business Unit. The group formed a mock task force to focus on a pressing company issue (one involved a dilemma over whether the software development process should be standardized). Participants decided to spend part of each remaining session in this mock task force. A few weeks into the exercise, however, one participant complained that while the task force exercise was more realistic than most training activities, it still had no impact on her day-to-day work or that of the company. Within a week, top managers at Bell Labs told the pilot group they would read and respond to a written report from this no longer "mock" task force. Suddenly, this particular teamwork exercise became more compelling than anything the group had done before.

By the end of the pilot program, the sixteen participants had created a detailed curriculum for each of the nine work strategies. Each piece of that curriculum included frank discussion, work-related exercises, ratings on the work strategy checklists, and homework that required participants to practice while they learned. The Bell Labs workshop sessions involved specific case studies with exercises that prompted emotional give-and-take among participants.

Eventually, the Bell Labs program was streamlined to six weeks, with the sessions led by star performers involved in the original course. Yet continually reshaping the curriculum in response to critical events on the job became the current program's most important feature.

For example, during one of the later sessions, top management issued a memo on company quality initiatives. Switching Systems engineers thought the memo was blaming them for poor quality. So participants in the training program decided to respond directly to the memo as part of that session's work.

At that time, it was highly unusual for engineers to take such a step, because most believed top managers would not appreciate, let alone respond to, a direct approach. But as it turned out, engineers got a quick and constructive response. Top managers responded, either through e-mail or in direct conversations with participants.

If professionals are going to make an effort to analyze their own productivity, they need hard information on how others, especially managers, view their performance. Program participants received feedback from peers, managers, customers, and fellow participants. They also rated themselves on the work strategy checklists and filled out other self-evaluations. With such a range of feedback, most participating engineers knew what their strengths were and where they most needed to improve by the end of the program.

THE BOTTOM LINE

Since 1989, Bell Labs and several other companies have put hundreds of their brainpowered workers through our program, now known as the Breakthrough Program. Since these engineers were scattered across many projects and departments, it's difficult to demonstrate the program's effectiveness through such traditional measurements as fewer worker hours spent on a particular project. In their self-evaluations, however, participants reported a 10 percent increase in productivity immediately after the sessions ended, which grew to 20 percent after six months and 25 percent after a full year.

This steady, upward curve is the opposite of what follows most training programs. Typically, effectiveness is greatest on the last day of the program and falls toward zero after a year.

But even if participants reported substantial productivity increases, this doesn't prove that the performance of these engineers actually changed. The corporate goal for Breakthrough was not, for example, taking initiative for initiative's sake, but adding value to the company.

Table 1
Factors That Lead to Judgment of High Productivity and Performance

- Consistently spots issues and problems and makes sure something gets done about them
- Always gets work done on time and with high quality
- Keeps manager informed about work progress and how it will impact other people/projects
- Consistently succeeds at delighting internal/external customers
- Succeeds at working across organizational boundaries
- Understands how and why external competitive pressures change everyday work routines and responds positively to the challenge
- Does not get overly frustrated by "politics" but strives to understand rationale behind certain decisions

The Work Strategies of Star Performers Pay Off in On-the-Job Productivity

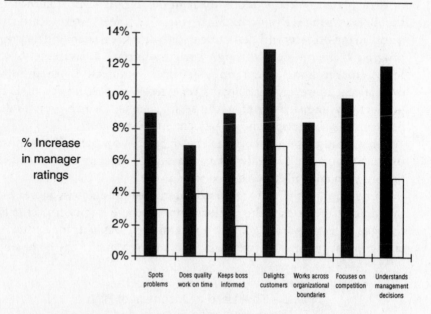

Figure A-1
Star-Performer Program Participants Increase Productivity 100%
More Than Controls on Average

Results independently validated by performance evaluation data and self-reports.

So we decided to do a long-term evaluation study using a control group that did not take our training. As the basis of our evaluation, we met with managers and star performers asking them to list the factors indicating increased productivity in a person working in their departments (see Table 1). Then we asked direct managers to rate 300 participants and 300 nonparticipants (controls) on the items listed in Table 1, both before the training sessions began and then eight months later.

Doubling the Rate of Productivity Improvement

The results from that analysis showed a 100 percent increase in the rate of productivity improvement compared with nonparticipants over an eight-month period (see Chart 1). Managers cited improvements in seven key areas, including spotting and fixing problems, getting work done on time with high quality, delighting customers, and working well with members of other departments. Average performers were not alone in these improvements; star performers improved at similar rates.

We also compared our manager surveys with the company's standard performance ratings, which are collected annually and are the basis for salary adjustments and promotions. Unlike our manager surveys, which were filled out by the participants' direct supervisor, the performance ratings are a joint effort by all the supervisors in a department. To get a higher performance rating, a participant has to demonstrate higher performance that convinces all the supervisors, not just her or his own.

We looked at these ratings before participants began our training program and then eight months to one year after they had finished. Interestingly enough, the performance ratings of our participants improved at twice the rate of nonparticipants, mirroring the results of our manager surveys.

400 Percent Improvement for Women and Minorities

In addition, our program had an especially strong impact on women, minorities, and newer workers. As Charts 2 and 3 show, their overall rate of improvement was 400 percent greater than that of comparable nonparticipants. On the individual dimensions that most directly affect managers—"Does high-quality work on time" and "Keeps boss informed"—the productivity of women and minorities who didn't participate in our training program actually decreased during the survey period.

This tremendous improvement rate for women and minorities underscores two important points. First, these groups are most likely to be excluded from the rich sources of informal knowledge that is essential for high productivity. For many, their productivity will not keep pace and they will be branded as "average performers." Traditional methods to remedy this situation, such as support groups and mentoring, while emotionally beneficial, may also contribute to the problem. They limit the contact women and minorities have to an unnecessarily narrow band of company experts. Our program gives them access to a broad cross section of stars—including both genders and all races—and the full repertoire of productivity strategies used by these experts (see Chart 4).

Second, as I pointed out in Chapter 2, when women and minorities

Figure A-2
The Star-Performer Effect for Minority Participants Is
Very Strong—400 Percent, on Average

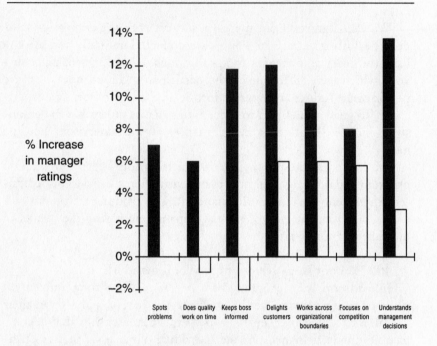

% Increase
in manager
ratings

Spots problems | Does quality work on time | Keeps boss informed | Delights customers | Works across organizational boundaries | Focuses on competition | Understands management decisions

Results independently validated by performance evaluation data and self-reports.

do have lower productivity, it is *not* because they are less capable. It is because they were never taught the work strategies that lead to high productivity. There is no magic to high productivity.

Impact on the Bottom Line

Ultimately, of course, all such productivity increases for individual professionals fall to the bottom line. If the total compensation package for a knowledge professional is about $75,500 (salary plus fringe benefits), then the investment return is $750 each year for every 1 percent increase in productivity. Thus a 10 percent increase yields $7,500 for each participant, while a 25 percent increase would return $22,500,

Figure A-3
The Star-Performer Effect for Female Participants Is
Very Strong—400 Percent, on Average

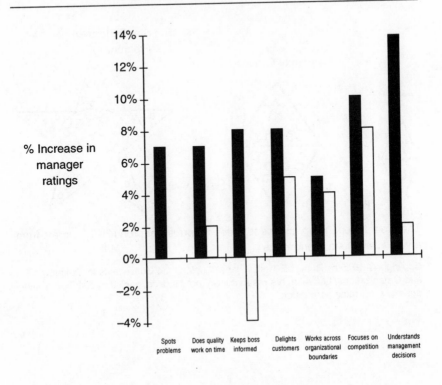

and so on. Our long-term evaluations indicate that these returns continue to accumulate each year even though the initial investment occurs only once.

But these investment return figures don't include the more indirect productivity benefits. Participants improved dramatically in the ways they assisted colleagues. These workers also built stronger ties to customers and were more attuned to competitive threats. While such positive changes are hard to measure, they are essential to a highly productive workplace.

Figure A-4
The Star-Performer Program Leads to Greater Productivity
Improvement Than Mentoring or Affinity Groups

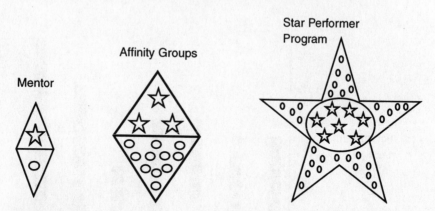

The program opens up access to a rich repertoire of productivity secrets from a vast array of star performers

APPENDIX II

Resources for More Help

If you found this book helpful but need additional help in integrating the star performer work strategies into your work routine, you may want to attend one of our productivity-improvement programs. The program consists of six half-day sessions spread out over a six-week period. Each session focuses in depth on selected work strategies using case studies, role plays, and class discussion. The program provides you with much feedback regarding your productivity, as well as a personalized developmental plan.

The program, called Breakthrough: High-Performance Strategies for Knowledge Workers, is distributed exclusively by Development Dimensions International (DDI). DDI is a Pittsburgh-based international consulting firm whose mission is to help their clients align their people strategy with their business strategy. Since 1970, DDI has helped thousands of organizations improve their results by applying sound organizational change, selection and assessment, and learning and development strategies to the way they conduct business.

For further information, contact Development Dimensions International (DDI) at 1225 Washington Pike, Bridgeville, Pennsylvania 15017-2838, USA; 412-257-0600 (phone); 412-257-0614 (fax); or on the Internet at http://ddiworld.com/bthome.htm

COMMUNICATE WITH THE AUTHOR

Let me know your experience with star performance. What makes a difference in your company? What productivity measures do they use? How should they measure your productivity?

How have the ideas in this book helped you?

Contact me at the following e-mail address: Robert@KelleyIdeas.com and visit my website: www.KelleyIdeas.com

STAR PERFORMER OF THE YEAR AWARD

Who are the star performers that you know? Nominate them for our annual Star Performer of the Year award. E-mail me the person's name, position, and company. Then tell us why this person is so great and deserves the award. We'll announce the winners each Labor Day.

NOTES

PREFACE

xvii "... it pulls together ten years ..." Robert Kelley and Janet Caplan, "How Bell Labs Creates Star Performers," *Harvard Business Review*, July–August 1993, 128.

Laurie Kretchmar, "(Work) Secrets of the Stars," *Working Woman*, November 1993, 18.

"Using New Kinds of Corporate Alchemy, Some Firms Turn Lesser Lights Into Stars," *Wall Street Journal*, May 3, 1993, B1.

Paul Ciotta, "Individual Performance Strategies Yield Impressive Productivity Gains," *Bell Labs News*, September 13, 1993, 1.

David Stamps, "Are We Smart for Our Jobs?" *Training*, April 1996, 44.

Daniel Goleman, *Emotional Intelligence* (New York: Bantam, 1995).

Alan Farnham et al., "Are You Smart Enough to Keep Your Job?" *Fortune*, January 15, 1996, 34.

20/20 (ABC News Television broadcast) October 20, 1995.

Daniel Goleman, "What's Your Emotional IQ?" *Reader's Digest*, January 1996, 49.

xviii "... productivity output is worth ten average workers." Alan W. H. Grant and Leonard A. Schlesinger, "Realize Your Customers' Full Profit Potential," *Harvard Business Review*, September–October 1995, 59.

John E. Hunter et al., "Individual Differences in Output Variability as a Function of Job Complexity," *Journal of Applied Psychology*, February 1990, 28.

CHAPTER 4: INITIATIVE: BLAZING TRAILS IN THE ORGANIZATION'S WHITE SPACES

39–42 "For ten years, Kathleen Betts ..." Peter J. Howe, "The $489 Million Heroine," *Boston Globe*, June 5, 1991, 32.

Peter J. Howe, "A Bailout Plan for a Bailout Planner," *Boston Globe*, June 6, 1991, 32.

Mary B. W. Tabor, "State Worker's Budget Coup: A Windfall for Massachusetts," *New York Times*, June 8, 1991, A1.

Bella English, "She Finds Cash, State Finds Hero," *Boston Globe*, June 10, 1991, 19.

Peter J. Howe, "For the State's Deficit Heroine, a $10,000 Happy Ending at Last," *Boston Globe*, August 8, 1991.

Robert Pear, "U.S. Moves to Curb Medicaid Payments for Many States," *New York Times*, September 11, 1991, A1.

"Byzantine Health-Care Financing," *Boston Globe*, December 2, 1991, 10.

50–51 "... referred to as 'managing the white space' ..." "Managing the White Space: The Work of Geary Rummler," *Training & Development*, August 1992, 26.

CHAPTER 5: KNOWING WHO KNOWS: PLUGGING INTO THE KNOWLEDGE NETWORK

65–66 "In his book *The Care and Feeding of Ideas* ..." Bill Backer, *The Care and Feeding of Ideas* (New York: Times Books, 1993).

66 "A recent survey of 461 ..." Joann S. Lublin, "Women at Top Still

Are Distant from CEO Jobs," *Wall Street Journal*, February 28, 1996, B1.

67 "Experts estimate that more knowledge . . ." Robert E. Kelley, *The Gold-Collar Worker* (Reading, Mass.: Addison-Wesley, 1985), 11.

72 "Hicks Muse, an extremely successful . . ." Stephanie Anderson Forest, "Where LBO Means 'Let's Be Offbeat,' " *Business Week*, July 1, 1996, 86.

CHAPTER 6: MANAGING YOUR WHOLE LIFE AT WORK: SELF-MANAGEMENT

88–89 "Jerry Meyer is CEO of Pinnacle Brands . . ." *Nightline* (ABC television broadcast), April 9, 1996.

89 ". . . crowed an analyst for Bear Stearns . . ." Ibid.

91 "As W. Brian Arthur, a dean and professor . . ." W. Brian Arthur, "Increasing Returns and the New World of Business," *Harvard Business Review*, July–August 1996, 100.

92 ". . . labeling tasks according to their importance . . ." Robert E. Kelley, *The Gold-Collar Worker* (Reading, Mass.: Addison-Wesley, 1985), 144.

98–99 "Gore was a young chemist . . ." Frank Shipper and Charles C. Manz, "Employee Self-Management Without Formally Designated Teams: An Alternative Road to Empowerment," *Organizational Dynamics*, Winter 1992, 48.

100 "This is what Mihaly Csikszentmihalyi . . ." Mihaly Csikszentmihalyi, *Flow* (New York: Harper & Row, 1990).

CHAPTER 7: GETTING THE BIG PICTURE: LEARNING HOW TO BUILD PERSPECTIVE

111–13 "When furniture designer William James . . ." Interviews by Doug Root with William James, furniture designer, Pittsburgh, Penn., October 26, 1995 and February 22, 1997.

115 "Bell Labs CEO Arno Penzias . . ." Alan Farnham et al., "Are You Smart Enough to Keep Your Job?" *Fortune*, January 15, 1996, 34.

115–16 "Dick, along with Nobel Laureate Herb Simon . . ." John R. Hayes, *The Complete Problem Solver*, 2d ed. (Hillsdale, N.J.: Lawrence Erlbaum Associates, 1989).

Herb Simon and W. G. Chase, "Skill in Chess," *American Scientist*, 61 (1973), 394.

Herb Simon and K. Gilmartin, "A Simulation of Memory for Chess Positions," *Cognitive Psychology*, 5, 1973, 29.

118   "Consider Michael Jordan ..." Jim Naughton, *Taking to the Air* (New York: Warner Books, 1992).

121–122   "... Nobel Prize–winning physicist, Richard P. Feynman." Richard Feynman, *"Surely You Are Joking, Mr. Feynman"*: *Adventures of a Curious Character* (New York: W. W. Norton, 1985).

122   "In his book, *Lateral Thinking* ..." Edward De Bono, *Lateral Thinking: Creativity Step by Step* (New York: Harper & Row, 1970).

Edward De Bono, *Lateral Thinking for Management: A Handbook of Creativity* (New York: American Management Association 1971).

128   "... Don Norman extols in his book ..." Donald A. Norman, *The Psychology of Everyday Things* (New York: Basic Books, 1988).

134–6   "On paper, fifty-seven-year-old Solomon Snyder ..." Gina Koalta, "Brain Researcher Makes It Look Easy," *New York Times*, May 25, 1993, C1.

136   " 'The picture painted of Michael Jordan' ..." John Leland, "Hoop Dreams," *Newsweek*, March 20, 1995, 48.

Mark Starr, "Raging Bulls," *Newsweek*, February 12, 1996, 63.

137–8   "Stanford University's Brian Arthur ..." W. Brian Arthur, "Increasing Returns and the New World of Business," *Harvard Business Review*, July–August, 1996, 100.

CHAPTER 8: FOLLOWERSHIP: CHECKING YOUR EGO AT THE DOOR TO LEAD IN ASSISTS

139   "... as I have in my other writings ..." Robert E. Kelley, *The Power of Followership* (New York: Doubleday, 1992).

Robert E. Kelley, "In Praise of Followers," *Harvard Business Review*, November–December 1988, 142.

143   "Can you imagine a team ..." Arnold "Red" Auerbach, "Misleading Followers," *Harvard Business Review*, January–February 1989, 152.

147   "[Frank] is a great devil's advocate ..." John Huey, "Secrets of Great Second Bananas," *Fortune*, May 6, 1991, 64.

148   "The decision as to whether ..." Chester I. Barnard, *The Func-*

tions of the Executive (Cambridge, Mass.: Harvard University Press, 1938).

154 "A study by University of Pittsburgh . . ." William Frederick and James Weber, "The Values of Corporate Managers and Their Critics: An Empirical Description and Normative Implications," in William Frederick and Lee Preston, *Business Ethics: Research Issues and Empirical Studies* (Greenwich, Conn.: JAI Press, 1990).

154 "In a survey I conducted . . ." Robert E. Kelley, *The Power of Followership* (New York: Doubleday, 1992), 171.

154 "After analyzing ten studies of ethical problems . . ." Rick Wartzman, "Nature or Nurture?: Study Blames Ethical Lapses on Corporate Goals," *Wall Street Journal*, October 9, 1987, 27.

155 "In 1989, Timothy Mock . . ." Associated Press, "Alcoa Admits Pollution Violations, Agrees to Pay $7.5 Million," July 12, 1991.

155–6 "Not so fortunate was . . ." Len Boselovic, "Alcoa Replaces Exec in Charge of Mexico Plants; Failure to Report Accidents Spurs Ouster," *Pittsburgh Post-Gazette*, July 23, 1996, B7.

159 ". . . Harvey Hornstein did a study of . . ." Harvey Hornstein, *Managerial Courage* (New York: John Wiley & Sons, 1986).

160 " 'Our first responsibility is to the doctors . . .' " Tad Tuleja, *Beyond the Bottom Line* (New York: Penguin Books, 1985).
James Keogh, *Corporate Ethics: A Prime Business Asset* (New York: The Business Roundtable, 1988).

161 "Hal Sperlich, who moved from Ford . . ." John Huey, "Nothing Is Impossible," *Fortune*, September 23, 1991, 135.

161 ". . . a public relations director for the Pittsburgh Brewing Company . . ." Len Boselovic, "Job County Story Riled Carlow Executive," *Pittsburgh Post-Gazette*, July 31, 1996, B7.

CHAPTER 9: SMALL-L LEADERSHIP IN A BIG-L WORLD

164 " 'I have attended a few leadership seminars' . . ." "All Things Considered," *NPR Transcript* #2249, June 19, 1996.

165 ". . . to paraphrase the science fiction writer Robert Heinlein . . ." Robert A. Heinlein, *Time Enough for Love: The Lives of Lazarus Long* (New York: Putnam, 1973).

CHAPTER 10: TEAMWORK: GETTING REAL ABOUT TEAMS

192 "... repeating the costly error that MCI ..." Alex Markels, "Innovative MCI Unit Finds Culture Shock in Colorado Springs," *Wall Street Journal*, June 25, 1996, A1.

CHAPTER 11: ORGANIZATIONAL SAVVY: STREET SMARTS IN THE CORPORATE POWER ZONE

213 "When Keith Lockhart ..." Elizabeth Smith Loving, "Hip Photogenic Led Zeppelin Fan Takes Over Boston Pops," *Carnegie Mellon Magazine*, Fall 1996, 12.

213 "... January 1996 edition of *Technology Review* ..." Stephen D. Solomon, "An Engineer Goes to Wall Street," *Technology Review*, January 1996, 29.

216–17 "Alfred Sloan was the legendary General Motors CEO ..." Alfred P. Sloan, *My Years with General Motors* (New York: Doubleday, 1964), 439.

217–18 "Then, as Lord recounts ..." Faye Rice, "Madison Avenue's Bloodiest Brawl," *Fortune*, September 26, 1988, 106.
Gary Levin, "Time Runs Out for Lord Geller," *Advertising Age*, July 9, 1990, 1.

221–22 "Michael Ovitz, the former Hollywood superagent ..." Kim Masters, "Ovitz and Out at Disney," *Time*, December 23, 1996, 56.
Bernard Weinraub, "Ovitz, Hollywood Power Broker, Resigns from No. 2 Job at Disney," *New York Times*, December 13, 1996, A1.
Frank Rose, "What Ever Happened to Michael Ovitz?" *Fortune*, July 7, 1997, 120.

CHAPTER 14: A MESSAGE FOR MANAGERS: PRODUCTIVITY IN THE BRAINPOWERED ECONOMY

250 "But why are companies so worried ..." Louis Uchitelle, "Not Making It: We're Leaner, Meaner and Going Nowhere Faster," *New York Times*, May 12, 1996, D-1.

250 "... improvements have been minuscule ..." Ibid.

251 " 'Stunning technological progress' . . ." Ibid.

251 " 'We live in an age of possibility' . . ." Bill Clinton, 1996 State of the Union Address.

252 "The old drill, with roots . . ." Robert E. Kelley, *The Gold-Collar Worker* (Reading, Mass.: Addison-Wesley, 1985), 6.

254 ". . . AT&T lost over a billion dollars . . ." Dennis Kneale et al., "Dialing for Dollars: AT&T's Heir Apparent Jumps to a Tiny Firm That Offers Huge Pay," *Wall Street Journal*, August 20, 1996, A1.

254 "An exhaustive 1994 study . . ." John Haltiwanger, Martin Baily, and J. Bartelsman, "Downsizing and Productivity Growth: Myth or Reality?" *NBER Working Paper* No. 4741, May 1, 1994.

255 "Research involving successful companies . . ." James L. Heskett, *Managing in the Service Economy* (Boston: Harvard Business School Press, 1986).
David E. Bowen and Benjamin Schneider, *Winning the Service Game* (Boston: Harvard Business School Press, 1995).

CONCLUSION: THE REWARDS OF STAR PRODUCTIVITY

257–8 ". . . heartening disclosures from top executives . . ." Joseph B. White, "Re-engineering Gurus Take Steps to Remodel Their Stalling Vehicles," *Wall Street Journal*, November 26, 1996, A1.

258 "Even the reengineering guru . . ." Ibid.

258 "Hewlett-Packard estimates . . ." Tom DeMarco, "Human Capital, Unmasked," *New York Times*, April 14, 1996, D13.

259 "For several years out of . . ." Steve Lohr, "Woody and Buzz: The Untold Story," *New York Times*, February 24, 1997, C1.

260 " 'The P&E is just people' . . ." "Silicon Valley's Hiring Frenzy: It's a Sellers' Market for Nerds," *Fortune*, December 9, 1996, 31.

262 " 'The program was a rare life changing' . . ." James Braham, "Star Engineers Grab the Initiative," *Machine Design*, October 24, 1994, 79.

262 ". . . Marge Hillis, a star promoted . . ." Laurie Kretchmar, "(Work) Secrets of the Stars," *Working Woman*, November 1993, 18.

REFERENCES

Backer, Bill. *The Care and Feeding of Ideas*. New York: Times Books, 1993.

Bowen, David E., and Benjamin Schneider. *Winning the Service Game*. Boston: Harvard Business School Press, 1995.

Csikszentmihalyi, Mihaly. *Flow: The Psychology of Optimal Experience*. New York: Harper & Row, 1990.

De Bono, Edward. *Lateral Thinking: Creativity Step by Step*. New York: Harper & Row, 1970.

———. *Lateral Thinking for Management: A Handbook of Creativity*. New York: American Management Association, 1971.

Feynman, Richard. *"Surely You Are Joking, Mr. Feynman": Adventures of a Curious Character*. New York: W. W. Norton, 1985.

Frederick, William, and Lee Preston. *Business Ethics: Research Issues and Empirical Studies*. Greenwich, Conn.: JAI Press, 1990.

Heinlein, Robert A. *Time Enough for Love: The Lives of Lazarus Long*. New York: Putnam, 1973.

Hesket, James L. *Managing in the Service Economy.* Boston: Harvard Business School Press, 1986.

Hornstein, Harvey. *Managerial Courage.* New York: John Wiley & Sons, 1986.

Kelley, Robert E. *The Gold-Collar Worker.* Reading, Mass.: Addison-Wesley Publishing Company, 1985.

———. *The Power of Followership.* New York: Doubleday, 1992.

Keogh, James. *Corporate Ethics: A Prime Business Asset.* New York: The Business Roundtable, 1988.

Norman, Donald A. *The Psychology of Everyday Things.* New York: Basic Books, 1988.

Sloan, Alfred P., Jr. *My Years with General Motors.* New York: Doubleday, 1964.

Tuleja, Tad. *Beyond the Bottom Line.* New York: Penguin Books, 1985.

INDEX